ACCELERATION

ACCELERATION

The Forces Driving Human Progress

RONALD G. HAVELOCK, PhD

Prometheus Books

59 John Glenn Drive
Amherst, New York 14228-2119

Published 2011 by Prometheus Books

Cover image © 2011 Media Bakery.
Author photograph by JCPenney Portraits.
Jacket design by Grace M. Conti-Zilsberger.

Inquiries should be addressed to
Prometheus Books
59 John Glenn Drive
Amherst, New York 14228–2119
VOICE: 716–691–0133
FAX: 716–691–0137
WWW.PROMETHEUSBOOKS.COM

15 14 13 12 11   5 4 3 2 1

Library of Congress Cataloging-in-Publication Data

Havelock, Ronald G.
    Acceleration : the forces driving human progress / by Ronald G. Havelock.
        p. cm.
    Includes bibliographical references and index.
    ISBN 978–1–61614–212–4 (cloth : alk. paper)
    1. Progress. 2. Social change. 3. Technological innovations—Social aspects.
4. Technological innovations—Economic aspects. I. Title.

HM891 .H38 2011
303.44—dc22

                                                                        2010044230

Printed in the United States of America on acid-free paper

CONTENTS

INTRODUCTION

And so we have gone on, and so we shall go on . . . prospering beyond example in the history of man. And I do believe we shall continue to grow, to multiply and prosper until we exhibit an association, powerful, wise and happy, beyond what has yet been seen by men.
—Thomas Jefferson, letter to John Adams, January 21, 1812

PROGRESS: IS IT GOOD OR BAD?

It is hard to believe that we have come so far in just these last five thousand years. After all, our genes go back more than three billion years! Our remotest ancestors were something like bacteria. It took millions upon millions of generations to turn them into plants and then animals, and then mammals. It is just a scant six million years since our branch of apes separated from the chimpanzees, our nearest genetic cousins. Five thousand years is but a blink on this almost unimaginable time scale. Yet in just these five thousand years the human race has made some amazing, life-transforming discoveries. We turned grass seeds into reliable food. We captured language in writing. We began to build secure, weatherproof structures for living and working. Then, astonishingly, we began to convey ourselves all over the globe, first by land and by sea, then by air at great speed. We even learned very recently how to capture words and pictures and beam them instantly to anyone, anywhere. All these feats are obvious signs that the human race is changing the way it lives on Earth. The way we experience life is now radically different from the way even our great-grandparents experienced life just three generations back.

Most notably, we live longer, and—depending on where we live—sometimes much longer. Moreover, recent advances in technology are making many millions of human lives more interesting and enjoyable even as they last longer. This is all because, in the very short span of a few hundred years, humans working together have managed to create an enormous knowledge platform. This book will try to explain how that platform came to be created in the first place, and then how it became the secure foundation for a continuous stream of remarkable life-enhancing changes.

The changes in the human condition in our times may not all have been for the better. There are many recent trends in civilization that are cause for alarm. There has been an accelerating increase in world population. There has been a proliferation of weapons of mass destruction. Accelerating increases in carbon dioxide in the atmosphere may be affecting the climate and therefore the livability of the entire planet. Some of the great intellects of our day see these trends as portents of near-future doom unless the major industrial powers are somehow able to curtail their consumptive ways.

The human future can also be viewed in a more positive light. The overall record of the nineteenth and twentieth centuries reveals some remarkably favorable trends that may ultimately far outweigh the negative trends. These include increasing rates of food production, increasing standards of living, sharply reduced rates of infant mortality, and increasing average life spans. These benefits first become evident in isolated pockets of prosperity, but over time they tend to spread outward across the globe to more and more people and, ultimately, to humanity as a whole.

The more we investigate our past, the more obvious it becomes that the benefits and pleasures of life were in short supply before 1800. The good life, such as it was in ancient times, was the reserve of a tiny minority. The lot of the common man only began to change significantly within the last two centuries with the birth of the Industrial Revolution. Then, when science merged with technology in the twentieth century, all sorts of innovations sprouted, changing the way humans lived through all succeeding generations.

Some changes were very good and some were not so good. Looking back over the twentieth century, the bad certainly stands out: the first two world wars—the largest and bloodiest in all history—topped off by the first use of the deadliest invention ever to derive from the marriage of science and human ingenuity. Yet the worst of the worst was mostly over before 1950. What has happened since then is equally remarkable and far more hopeful. We have had more bad news, of course, but the balance has shifted such that the collective, worldwide, human life experience has now been fairly steadily improving for sixty years. Current trends suggest an even brighter future for most of our children.

In this work I have three main goals. The first is to establish that progress is real and irrevocable. We humans are moving, however haltingly, toward the making of a better world. The second is to explain why this progress is happening, and why it is happening at an ever-accelerating rate. The third is to lay out the prospect of what we should do with this understanding so as to guide our future in a steadier and more fruitful way. Short of a nuclear catastrophe, which grows increasingly less likely, there will be continued progress in all areas of concern for humanity; but it will come slowly or quickly, haphazardly or smoothly, depending on what our leaders choose to do. There is much that can be done to make the process of progress work better, but first we need to understand how it has worked in the past and why it has been accelerating in recent times. With that knowledge we can project the near future, but, more important, we can guide the future to a better place.

THE ENGINE OF PROGRESS

All societies are sustained by a constant flow of information. Most of this flow is required simply to keep things going the way they are, but some special categories of information have the power to change the way things are, to make systems function better, and to provide more rewards and security. Scientific knowledge is one such information type, and technology creation is another. In the past two centuries new institutions have emerged within the larger culture to support both the generation of scientific knowledge and the development of new technologies based largely on science. These new institutions are sustained by a back-and-forth flow of highly reliable and very detailed specialized information. This flow is driving an *acceleration* of human understanding and a new mastery of Earth and its surround. It affords us the ability to change and remodel our environment in the service of the great range of humanity's self-perceived needs and desires. Furthermore, because it is embedded in a much larger flow of knowledge from innovation to production to widespread distribution and use, it has become a veritable engine of progress, advancing the well-being of the entire human population.

HOW IT ALL BEGAN

The earliest version of "civilization" followed from a convergence of four forces. The first was the capacity to *learn*. All animals have this to an extent. Plants and other forms of life seemingly do not. The second is the capacity to *store* what is learned outside the brain of the learner, what seems to be a uniquely human skill. The third is the capacity to create and expand *social connections* in the service of problem solving. Many other animal and insect species have elaborate social skills, but the human capacity trumps all other species in its pervasiveness, flexibility, and spontaneity. The fourth is the ability to store what has been learned in coherent, integrated, and widely shared *knowledge platforms*, stable caches of information that can be expanded indefinitely and passed on, intact, from one generation to the next. Only humans can do this.

The widespread adoption of the *scientific method*, which has taken place only over the last two hundred years, added yet a fifth element to humanity's progressive powers. Now, for the first time, there was a universal standard for judging and comparing truth claims regarding the natural world. The age-old search for truth was set on a new and more certain track. When the new tools of science were then applied to solving the many problems that have beset humanity through the ages, the results were amazing.

A sixth element that emerged over the last few centuries, aided and abetted by science, was an ever-increasing capacity to spread the platform's knowledge. Modern technologies of diffusion have allowed the spread of knowledge and life-enhancing artifacts over long distances, between cultures, and across generations. The numerous inventions of the last few centuries— starting with printing, then mass publication, motorized transport, telegraph, telephone, radio, television, and now the Internet—have transformed the lives of all who are connected to the worldwide network. If science is the new engine of progress, *diffusion* is the accelerator.

These six forces, the four old and the two new, act together as the drivers of continuing human progress. As they play out through time, they will lead us and our descendants to a progressively more enjoyable life. In the long run, a positive future is ensured because each of these forces is relentless. We humans never stop learning and externalizing what we learn. We never stop socializing or building on the knowledge platform of science. We will always continue the pursuit of truth and will continue to solve problems, even as the magnitude and complexity of some of these problems becomes more daunting. From our perch at the beginning of the twenty-first century, we can only dimly perceive the outlines, but we should be reassured that the human future will be guided by these six forces, what I will call in this book our *forward function*. Because of it, our great-grandchildren will know a lot more than we do, and they will have the tools to enjoy a life that is both longer and richer than most of us now living can imagine.

There is an inevitability to progress in the long run, but this truth has been obscured by many factors. We each live out our lives only within a given era, and we suffer the consequences. Our ancestors typically lived lives that were short and difficult by the standards of today, especially in the developed world. They watched helplessly as their children died of diseases that have now long since been conquered. Yet we, too, are prisoners of our own time and our own level of development, born too soon to benefit from the great advances in science and science-based technology that will surely come after we are long dead. If only our scientists had moved just a little bit faster, made their discoveries sooner, applied their new knowledge with greater urgency!

When it comes to progress, as with anything else, understanding the phenomenon should come first. Understanding how the forward function works is thus the key to improving the circumstances of living for everyone. There is no reason to fear what we can wisely and reasonably control. We can move forward faster or slower as our collective interests dictate. If we know what we are doing and where we are headed, we can move much faster while still maintaining a safe speed, preserving our heritage as we go. We can reduce, not increase, the pollution of our environment; reduce, not increase, the threat of nuclear, chemical, or biological annihilation; and increase, not reduce, the livable space for each and every human on the planet. We can do all these things and still move forward into a much richer and much longer future life if we collectively desire to do so and if we organize our collective efforts to those ends. We can achieve all this by applying and sticking to a relatively small set of principles.

If the forward function is the key to human progress, it follows that there is an *urgency* for its full application. Millions everywhere suffer and die every hour of every day for a lack of progress in one area or another. Other millions lack adequate food and shelter. Millions more on every part of Earth are crippled by grief at the suffering and dying of their loved ones. We can pile high this list of human misery. Technical progress addresses all these matters directly and provides a steadily improving base of solutions. There is no area of human concern where the application of existing science-based technical knowledge cannot make a huge difference. The sooner such knowledge is generated and the faster it can be diffused and used to help people, the more this suffering can be alleviated. That is reason enough to be in a hurry to understand and apply these principles.

STRUCTURE OF THE BOOK

Acceleration: The Forces Driving Human Progress is divided into three parts. The first part introduces the concept of the forward function and makes the case for the reality of human progress and its acceleration in modern times. It leads off with the observation that the concept of "progress" has always been controversial, there being both a "forward" and a "backward" tendency in human thought, polarities that have run against each other as persisting themes through all recorded history. Chapter 2 points out the many ways in which lives can be valued as the key criteria for measuring both progress and regress, all that should go into the making of a good life for the one and for the many. The third chapter reminds the reader of the many positive changes that have taken place just since the end of World War II. These changes demonstrate an unmistakable and dramatic trend in human affairs, giving reason to believe that genuine progress in individual lives and in humanity's collective life has been made and will continue.

Part 2 describes the six forces that drive progress, the essential ingredients of the forward function, and explains their impact on contemporary life. Chapter 4 covers the first essential ingredient, shared by all our fellow species from the lowly worm on up, *animal learning.* This is the ability to modify behavior based on particular experiences and to hold those modifications in the brain as "memories" available for future use. Chapter 5 deals with a feature more uniquely human, the ability to *store* such learning *outside the body* of the learner. Chapter 6 highlights the significance of *social connections,* a phenomenon not unique to our species but so highly developed in us that, when linked to our learning and storing capacities, greatly expands our collective problem-solving powers, allowing civilization to emerge. Chapter 7 describes the gradual building of knowledge and know-how *platforms,* continuously expanding caches of stored and widely shared information on which progressively more successful human action can be guided.

Chapters 8 and 9 add the two new forces that have accelerated the forward function in modern times, merging the essential material from the many disparate knowledge platforms into one and giving them extraordinary new power. Chapter 8 explains how problem solving has been made progressively more effective through the invention and refinement of the scientific method. Chapter 9 describes the explosive expansion of knowledge *diffusion,* the ability to transmit all kinds of information from the few to the many. Diffusion enhances information access and integration, and it equalizes knowledge possession within and across cultures so that the benefits of technology can ultimately be shared by all humanity.

Part 3 explains where the forward function is now taking us. In chapter 10 the human experience is viewed from an ethical perspective. Is there such a thing as *moral progress*? If so, is humanity now on the right track? *Yes* is our tentative answer, but moral progress has often seemed like a shaky proposition, even within living memory. The massive suffering and killing of the twentieth century cannot be ignored. Too many are still locked in by a tribal mentality that puts high value on only the lives of fellow tribesmen, the small "us." The key to increasing morality lies in the widening of everyone's definition of *us* until we are all included in each other's "us." Some people are already able to adopt such an inclusive outlook, but too many still can think only tribally, locally, ethnically, religiously, or nationally. Increasing world prosperity, supported by advances in science and technology, tends to increase the ranks of the globalists year by year. Someday it will be the prevailing view.

Chapter 11, "Fears for the Future," takes up some of the reasons why the optimistic vision of the forward function is not widely shared. It returns to many of the themes raised in chapter 2 and addresses the common tendency, especially among intellectuals, to face the future of humanity on Earth with gloom. Sometimes this attitude seems to be bolstered by "facts" loosely derived from science. In the by-products of advancing civilization some are inclined to see the seeds of decline and fall. These signs include depletion of natural resources; pollution of air, land, and water; climate change caused by human activity; and uncontrolled population growth. To each of these looming miseries there is a rational response that is both constructive and positive. We should look exclusively to science to provide clarification on the nature, extent, and seriousness of real problems, and we should then look to science-based technologies to provide the solutions and countermeasures called for by the science.

Chapter 12, "What Will the Future Bring?" considers where the forward function will take us in this new century. Two major trends of the last half of the twentieth century, one in biology and the other in physics, will transform the human condition in the first half of the twenty-first century. A new era in biology will transform medicine, prolonging lives and eliminating some of the major threats to human health. Accelerating electronic storage and transmission will transform all types of information processing, leading to a new integration of the knowledge platforms of science and technology and multi-plying our problem-solving capacity.

These changes will soon allow us to take on problems of ever-greater complexity and difficulty. The digitization of information storage and trans-mission promises to lead to the integration of *all* knowledge in the service of human progress. It is our destiny to move forward, expanding the spectrum of human needs and aspirations as science and technology show the way.

PART ONE

THE FACT OF HUMAN PROGRESS

Let me relate to you the tragedy of man
How from the miserable creature that he was
I made him conscious and intelligent.
I speak the human race not to condemn
But to explain my kindnesses in what I gave to them.
Seeing they did not see, nor hearing grasp
That which they heard, they lived like ghosts in dreams,
In lifelong anarchy and dreariness.

No houses built of brick to catch the sun
Nor carpentry they knew. Like little ants
They lived in holes and sunless cavities.
They had no signs reliable to mark
Winter and scented spring and harvest-time,
Nor conscious plan to guide them, till I showed
The variable rise and setting of the stars.

For them in triumph intellectual!
Did I devise the count numerical,
And history's instrument, skill of the bard,
The great compositor, the written word.

I was the first to yoke the animals
In service to the strap, and lay on them
Inheritance of man's excessive toil.
Between the shafts I led the obedient horse,
That ornament of luxury and wealth.
The gleaming sail that wafts across the sea
The intrepid mariner was my device.

The inventor I, who many a shape did show
Of science to mankind, now do not know
What science will my own release allow.

—Aeschylus, *Prometheus Bound*[1]

Something quite amazing was happening among the Greek city-states of the fifth century BCE.[2] There was a great flowering of art, literature, science, and technology, following on the heals of some extraordinary military victories over the giant, invading armies and navies of the Persian Empire. The Greeks of this time had deep thinkers in abundance, people they called *philosophers*. Such men were intellectually fearless, making fresh observations and expressing new ideas about all sorts of things: politics, religion, the nature of the universe and the matter in it, and the nature of man himself. For the first time in human history, they were also able to *write down* their thoughts and observations. Aeschylus, a veteran of Marathon, did his thinking and writing in the form of poetic drama, and he used the myths passed down through earlier poets, such as Homer and Hesiod, to pose important issues for his countrymen's consideration.

Prometheus, the forethinker, was the god of technology, and he stole the special technology of fire making from Zeus to give it to man.[3] Aeschylus expands on what this gift symbolizes to include the wisdom to create all manner of new technologies. Thus, he is a stand-in for *human-as-creator*, the special human capacity to fashion new artifacts and develop new skills to improve his or her lot on Earth. According to the myth, Zeus is so angered by this deceit that he punishes Prometheus, chaining him to a rock where the buzzards feed perpetually on his flesh. But why is Zeus angry and why does Prometheus need to be punished? Could it be that there is something wrong about humankind's efforts to improve itself? Are humans trying to achieve godlike status through their own clever invention? The play is a dialogue around this issue: humankind's arrogance and hubris in trying to improve itself, in reaching for godlike powers, in defiance of the power of God himself. Prometheus could be punished and restrained but not killed because he, too, was immortal—as is the capacity in humankind to improve itself, using its intellect to advance toward a more and more godlike condition. That is what the forward function is all about.

Since the time of Aeschylus, this human drama has been replayed countless times, pitting the hopeful promises of humankind's progressive drive against its fears of what punishments might have to be endured for challenging the old ways and the powerful old gods of our fathers. On the pages that follow, this battle is engaged once more as we take up the cause of human progress. This is another time of amazement, a time when science is finally cracking many of the mysteries which befuddled our ancestors and a time when wondrous new technology "fires" are transforming the very meaning of our existence.

The case for progress requires two issues to be settled. The first is to determine what *better* means, and the second is to marshal the evidence, the pros and cons, regarding any detectible advancement toward whatever that "better" is. Part 1 works on both issues.

WHAT WE HAVE COME TO KNOW IN AN AMAZING TWO HUNDRED YEARS

For some time we have known that we live on a solid, spherical mass. We also now know that our planet has been circling our sun for more than five billion years. In contrast to this multibillion-year extent, individual lives seem absurdly short, spanning at most eighty-five or ninety years. Even a long human life is just a tiny tick on the universal clock on which our "old" planet rates as just a youngster. It was not even two centuries ago that we first began to realize the vast stretch of the ages. This dawning awareness began when Scottish naturalist Charles Lyell, a founding father of geology,[4] started looking at old rock formations, many then recently revealed in clear detail by the new railway cuts tracing across the countryside of the British Isles. In some of these layers he also noted the fossil tracings of animal creatures similar but not identical to many of the sea animals living in his own (and our own) time. He correctly concluded that the only way these traces of animals could have gotten into that rock was by falling as sediment to the bottom of the oceans and lakes of a long-ago time. Yet these layers could be thousands of feet thick, as we can readily observe in such places as the Grand Canyon of the Colorado River.[5] Then the question arises, how long does it take for such layers to form, one on top of another, upper layers eventually crushing and heating lower layers with such pressure that they turn to stone? Lyell reckoned the answer in millions of years, a substantial underestimate as it turns out, bu a time span long enough to upset the authority of biblical teaching and stir the minds of his contemporaries.

We have come a very long way in the two hundred years since Lyell's insightful observations. Charles Darwin, a friend and admirer of Lyell,[6] followed with some systematic observations of animals, both living and fossilized, and put together a rather simple but highly plausible theory of animal origins and transformations. Darwin was aware that his theory made sense only because of Lyell's enormous stretching of the time line of earthly existence. The layers showed the way, and a detailed examination of what was in the layers began to provide something like proof that Darwin was essentially correct. We have also come to realize in just the last few years that all living things have a common ancestry, and this common ancestry is nearly as old as Earth itself, perhaps three billion years or more.[7] This common heritage encompasses all the life around us: plants and animals, both large and small. To this strange list of our cousins we can now add the multitude of microscopic creatures that were beyond our awareness two hundred and fifty years ago.

We now also know that we have a common chemical genesis.[8] Every living thing has a common basic structure that we call a *cell*, even though some animals and plants are single-celled while others are aggregates, sometimes of billions of cells, that operate as a single unitary system. In any case, it is an established scientific fact that all the cells in all living things today are the direct descendants of the first cells that were planted or organized themselves on this planet four to five billion years ago. We don't yet know exactly how this all started in the beginning. We don't know, for example, how single cells came into being; nor do we know how multicellular systems started; nor how animals derived from plants, or perhaps vice versa. Yet we have done one big thing just within the last fifty-five years: we have broken the chemical code that governs heredity, that special complex molecule that exists in every cell of every living thing, the code that links us to the still-mysterious billion-year-long past. We know that in a biochemical sense, at least, we are all actually billions of years old, and without those intervening billions of years there would be no humans here on this planet. It took almost all those billions of years for nature to select out all the peculiar attributes that make us human.

the very short span of a few hundred years, we have invented a
ss for continuously discovering more about who we are and what
is all about. This process is called *science*. We have also been
and more about how to take this scientific knowledge and use

it to steadily make our lives better and ourselves wiser. Those fortunate enough to be born into the most developed countries of the world will most likely also live long lives in safety and comfort, exposing themselves to an expanding array of rich experiences.

APPLYING WHAT WE KNOW
TO MAKE LIFE BETTER

Nothing in our world is expanding faster than our knowledge about it. That should be very good news. If we can only get our minds around what is really happening, surely we can use our new knowledge to make things better. A bewildering array of transformations are going on everywhere about us. New knowledge and its offspring in new technologies are probably the largest contributors to this noisy confusion. That is reason enough to take a little time to think about the nature of progress. What are likely to be the true consequences of the knowledge explosion for the human future, near term and far term? We need to take a time-out for some thoughtful analysis of all the facts at hand before we jump to any conclusions and certainly before we take any drastic actions. We should be wise, informed, careful, and cautious, but we need not shroud our thoughts of the future in gloom. Neither should we be arranging our lives to forestall any imagined but grossly improbable near-term catastrophe. The near and far prospects for humanity are not easily foreseen, but there are many reasons to believe that these prospects may be getting better, not worse.

WHAT WE ALL WANT AND
WHAT WE WILL COME TO WANT

The words proclaimed as inalienable rights in the United States Declaration of Independence, "*life, liberty* and the pursuit of *happiness*," overflow with meaning. They define in a simple but comprehensive way what we all want. There is room here for an enormous array of different lives, different forms of liberty, and many different paths to happiness. The implication is that we should be free to pursue our own paths as much as possible without coercion by others and their particular definitions of what these words might mean. Progress can be measured as the extension or expansion of a life on any of

FIGURE 0.1.
THE OVERALL DIRECTION OF HUMAN PROGRESS

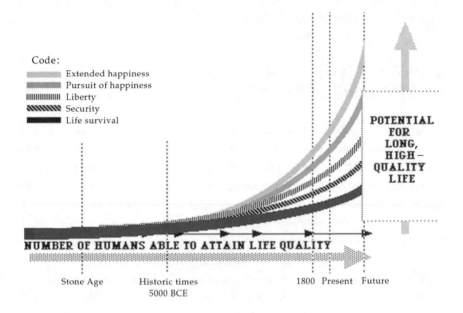

these dimensions: the life dimension, the liberty dimension, and the happiness dimension.

Progress can also be pictured on a scale of two dimensions as pictured in figure 0.1. The vertical dimension represents the summation of life, liberty, and happiness as it might be for a given people at a given time in history. The steep high curve represents the optimum life experience attainable by an individual or a group in any given epoch. The black curve at the bottom represents life itself, however long or short it might be. As we move up the scale of civilization, more attributes may be added to the potential of a given life, including liberty, leisure, luxury, artistic enjoyment, and a panoply of varied experience beyond. The vertical axis thus represents the ever-growing potential of a single life, including all the experiences that are summed up in the years of that life.

The possibilities of what can go into a full human life have expanded enormously through the five thousand years of civilization. They continue to expand into new areas, as suggested by the progressively lighter-shaded curves that keep building on top of the basics as more and more progressive steps are taken. How much of this expanse of life experience can be enjoyed by a particular individual depends on many factors, starting with the mere length of that life. A very short life barely gets out of the black. Longer lives impoverished by pain, failure, subservience, and the sheer emptiness of feeling are not much better off. A long life loaded with education, travel, and opportunities of every kind can reach way into the light. Until our own times, this sort of life was the preserve of kings and princes, but as we have advanced through the last few decades, the number of people who have access to this kind of life has been rising exponentially.

Now imagine that the horizontal axis represents all humanity of a given era. When the earliest modern humans started spreading out from Africa some one hundred thousand years ago, there were perhaps no more than a few thousands of individuals. At the end of World War II there were about two billion. Now there are closer to eight billion. So this horizontal axis is also stretching out over time with no end in sight. Millions of these lives are filled with diverse, pleasurable experiences hardly dreamed of by their ancestors. Much of humanity is still in the black but nevertheless is still lucky to be alive. Most of our earliest ancestors surely lived short lives at close to a subsistence level. Preoccupied as they must have been with food gathering and child rearing, they had little time for much else.

There is a steady trend through human prehistory and history toward both population increase and increase in the length and quality of individual lives. This is not a trend that is consistent year to year, nor is it equal among all peoples. Nevertheless, as time goes by, more and more members of the human race are living lives of higher quality and length. Moreover, such positive life experiences tend to spread out to benefit an ever-widening circle over time. The overall trend is relentlessly progressive. These first three chapters state the case.

Chapter One

THE IDEA OF PROGRESS

*The destiny of mankind
is not to turn towards Heaven,
but to progress on this earth,
by means of intelligence and reason.*

—Diderot, *Encyclopédie*, 1751

There is an inherent desire in all humans to improve their condition. This is the drive for progress. It has its origins in the drive shared by all animals to survive and thrive as long as possible and at least until progeny are secured to guarantee the survival of the species. However, as the human race has evolved over the last five thousand years, this progressive drive has been transformed into something quite different. This emerging conception is more coherent and more powerful than that primitive drive that we inherited from our distant ancestors when *Homo sapiens* first became differentiated from the other apes.

TWO PARABLES OF PROGRESS

In 1843 Charles Dickens published *A Christmas Carol,* one of the most loved stories in the English language. It is a story of redemption through transformation. The grouchy, stingy, and generally mean-spirited Scrooge becomes a kindly and generous old man. The transformation comes through an intense and dramatic learning experience comprised of three dreams. In the first, he sees his past life, the achievements of his youth, and a parade of the people who had helped him and enjoyed his company in his younger years. In the second dream he is allowed to see what is happening this Christmas Day in the life of his cheery nephew, his downtrodden but generous-hearted clerk and his family, and various others who pause from their toil on land and sea for a happy one-day respite. In the third dream he sees a prediction of all the bad things that will come, including, of course, centrally his own death along with the premature death of his clerk's son for lack of any understanding and generosity from Scrooge. When Scrooge finally awakes, he is a new man, overflowing with kindness and generosity—traits that he will presumably carry for the rest of his days.

The Scrooge story is appealing in many ways, but its force stems from the credibility that it achieves through the three dream sequences. In the course of this night, Scrooge goes through a thorough relearning of what his life has meant up to now. He is allowed to overview his past, present, and future in a way that he either had forgotten or was unable to appreciate before. These intense relearning experiences transform him, making him wiser and, inevitably by Dickens's logic, much kinder and more generous. Dickens himself was barely thirty years old when he wrote this story, but he had already lived a life rich with experience, including a childhood of poverty and its associated miseries and indignities. Now he could look back with a clear and sympathetic eye on what had happened to him and his family when he was much younger. Just as Scrooge used his dreams as a platform from which to build a new and better life, so Dickens used his own understanding of his past as well as his sharp observations of his present to make himself a better writer, all while giving both pleasure and enlightenment to his readers.

The 1993 movie *Groundhog Day*, written by Danny Rubin and Harold Ramis, has as its central character Phil Connor (expertly played by comedian Bill Murray). Phil is a big-city television weatherman, self-confident and self-centered with a disdain for his fellow workers and for the various folk of this small Pennsylvania town he is forced to visit in the dead of winter. After various things go wrong, the long day is over, but then the departing television crew is forced back into the town by a blizzard and Phil must return for the night to the same bed-and-breakfast he had previously vacated. What Phil describes as "the worst day" of his life is then repeated over and over again. When the bedside radio alarm goes off each morning, he hears the same music and the same announcer welcoming his listeners to Groundhog Day. As each repeated day unfolds, all the other characters play their parts exactly the same, unaware that they are reliving the same day many times over. Only Phil knows they're all caught up in an endless repetition of the same day.

At first Phil is horrified because he sees himself trapped in a miserable repeat of a day he didn't much enjoy in the first place. However, it gradually dawns on him that even though the other characters remain the same, he can *change*, building on his knowledge of what happened the previous "same" day. He starts out by using this advantage as a devilish prankster, being extra rude, aggressive, and exploitative of those he encounters as the day progresses. Then he becomes crazily reckless, realizing that he won't die because he will wake up the next day just as before.

As these repeated Groundhog Days roll on, however, he begins to realize that the repetitions give him the opportunity to become *a better person*, not just by learning more skills and gaining more knowledge, but by applying his newly won knowledge to helping other people, especially those in dire circumstances. He even starts to save lives. The movie ends when he finally persuades his lovely and very worthy producer, Rita (Andie MacDowell), that he has become just the kind of good man she can love. Thus, like *A Christmas Carol*, *Groundhog Day* is a story of redemption. Both men learn to be wiser and kinder through a learning experience. In *Groundhog Day* the process of learning becomes more explicit. Whereas Scrooge gains all his new insights in the course of a long, dream-filled night, Phil learns something new every day and builds on his past learning day by day for many hundreds of days.

What happens to both Scrooge and Phil can be taken as metaphors for the forward function as it might be realized in a single life. Through a learning process, both men become wiser and then, ultimately, kinder. In the process, their lives also become richer and more enjoyable. As in real life, there is a lot of luck involved, and the transformation that each of these characters experiences is not experienced by any of the others in their environment. It is only Scrooge who is allowed to view the panorama of his life and only Phil who gets this chance to improve himself in daily increments. Similarly, the great benefits of the forward function are only fully realizable by a minority of humans while the majority of humans repeat their days in endless cycles without much change. The great majority of humanity will do tomorrow what they did today and yesterday and countless yesterdays before that.

The experience of Phil in *Groundhog Day* is also an apt metaphor for what has happened to humans over the last few hundred thousand years. As their great ape relatives have repeated the same cycles of life over and over again, humans have built on their collective experience, repeating cycles with modest increments, generation after generation, ultimately transforming themselves in remarkable ways. The process accelerated with the invention of writing about three thousand years ago. It got another enormous boost with the invention of the scientific method fewer than three hundred years ago.

The pace of progress quickened still further with the digital worldwide integration of the knowledge platform beginning barely thirty years ago.

DEFINING THE FORWARD FUNCTION

The forward function is the process by which humans make progress. It started out simple, deriving from our animal nature, particularly the animal ability to learn from experience and to apply that learning for survival. As distinct from other animals, however, humans have learned how to store and build on what they have learned. This storage capacity depends largely on elaborate forms of social integration. Humans have existed in their present biological form for roughly one hundred thirty thousand years.[1] Over this span of time and through those five thousand generations of painful struggle, they have gradually improved their ability to work together for their common good. This probably began with nuclear families and then extended to larger family groupings that became clans and tribes. Tribes gradually improved their success in hunting and gathering, protecting themselves from weather hazards and predators while fending off their ever-pesky fellow tribes. Those who were less successful simply did not survive. Along the way the survivors invented lots of new tactics, artifacts, tools, weapons, hunting methods, and killing methods. Most important, once they acquired these valued items, they never forgot how to make them. They created tools and weapons from wood and stone. They built shelters and fashioned clothing from the skins of hunted animals. They learned to control and selectively breed certain animals for their own use. They eventually learned how to cultivate edible plants and replant the seeds of the most productive varieties.

One human invention stood out among all the others in both its intricacy and its usefulness. This was *language*, the ability to make special sounds to attach to objects, persons, and actions. Our distant ancestors learned to use language to make stories and to save instructions about how to make things. They used stories to remember people (living and dead) and happenings (present and past, real, dreamed, or imagined). All these things could be shared throughout the tribe. There could be a tribal oral memory, a history. It was out of these language elements that modern humanity emerged. Language was the invention that transformed our being and made us human.

As language evolved and symbolization became more differentiated, much more elaborate messages were passed on from one generation to the next. The knowledge platform for human problem solving thus expanded at a more and more rapid pace. Language development was further advanced by the development of ever larger and more complex social units and more sophisticated and effective tools and weapons for hunting, gathering, and, much later, farming.

The forward function was further advanced by the invention of systems for recording spoken language, starting about five thousand years ago with pictographic symbols and proceeding through stages to a more and more precise rendering of common speech patterns, culminating in the invention and diffusion of the alphabet some twenty-five hundred years ago. With written language, the knowledge base could be recorded and accurately repeated with ever-increasing elaboration and refinement.

The forward function was even further accelerated by the discovery and refinement of the scientific method, beginning about three hundred years ago. This was a new type of process that provided for the systematic sorting and verification of knowledge, making the knowledge platform for the first time a reliable basis for all types of problem solving. The forward function, as it has evolved only within the last three hundred years, is a form of problem solving in which solutions are recorded, replicated, stored, integrated, and then widely diffused. In its modern configuration it drives members of the human race toward ever-expanding uses of an ever-expanding scientific knowledge base, building on the past in the service of a more fulfilling present and future.

THE BACKWARD FUNCTION

The actual rate of progress is determined by a large number of forces, many of which are nonprogressive or even antiprogressive. Prominent among these forces is a phenomenon that could be called the *backward function*, an attitude of mind that puts the past before the present as the prime source of wisdom and the proper guide to human conduct. According to this view, there was a past time when we were somehow more "natural," had higher moral standards, were wiser, and lived a better life. This view is as old as history and is echoed in many ancient texts, including the Old Testament story of the Garden of Eden and the writings of the early Greek poet Hesiod, who probably lived about 800 BCE. In his epic poem, *Works and Days*, Hesiod lays out the stages of humankind in a downward spiral, starting with the "Golden Age."[2] Plato later transformed this idea into a vision of the ideal (city-) state that humans could try to approximate but never attain.

In the early fifth century CE, St. Augustine developed a Christianized version of Plato's ideal that he redefined as "the City of God."[3] Progress toward this city of God was to be sought in reflection, self-denial, and concentration on the holy texts passed down from the great prophets and evangelists of the past. A strong argument can be made that many religious movements are progressive at least in intention. Each new religion represents a new or revised way of looking at the world, the nature of life and of humankind; providing a framework for understanding the past and the future; and especially laying down the guidelines for how humans should behave to become "better" humans. The idea that we can become better by behaving differently is essentially a progressive idea. Difficulties arise when we try to figure out which directions are better.

Religions generally reach *backward*, to an authority in the past, preferably an authority for which there is some *written* residue, the holy word. For the Hebrews, this text is the first five books of what Christians refer to as the Old Testament, which dates back perhaps as far as three thousand years but is supported and supplemented by a near-endless series of follow-on books and rabbinical interpretations referred to as the Talmud, all of which have degrees of value as parts of the Holy Writ. What constitutes the Christian Holy Writ varies with the particular sect. All accept the Hebrew Bible up to the time of Jesus and add both the Gospels describing the life of Jesus and the writings of the apostle Paul, but Roman Catholics give sacred status to the many works of saints dating into the later middle ages.

Islamic religion is similarly founded on a holy scripture, the original of which is deemed to be the pure and unchanging truth about all things, rendered directly by God to Mohammed, the Prophet, in multiple episodes. As in Christianity, the original text is supported by innumerable interpretive commentaries by later wise men, but these later texts do not reach anywhere near the same level of authority as the originals transmitted orally and sometimes in written form by the Prophet himself. As noted in the *Encyclopædia Britannica* entry,

> the Qur'an is, however, left untouched by criticism; as the infallible word of God it cannot have been influenced by the circumstances under which it was revealed, it can contain no mistake, and it cannot be superseded by any new discovery.[4]

This is a classic rendering of the backward function. It allows for no path to the truth other than through documents written long ago and preserved in a fixed form, sometimes through a dubious lineage. If there is any progressive logic in such conceptions, it is a determination to re-create an imagined world of innocence and purity that predates sin.[5]

Many of the most widely respected secular thinkers of our own times are also deeply pessimistic about the future prospects of humanity[6] and routinely deplore what they see as major and perhaps unstoppable negative trends.[7] They see the modern human as in decline from an imagined better "natural" state in the remote past. They tend to belittle the achievements of modern, science-based technology while deploring its negative consequences. This view of the future as something to be feared rather than welcomed is especially character-istic of those who embrace the modern perspective of environmentalism. Many such people also view humankind's strivings, particularly in the area of tech-nical and economic advancement, as leading inevitably to global catastrophe.

This is a complicated world in which there are lots of things to worry about, some human-made, some not. There continue to be wars and still no mechanism is in place to prevent them from happening. There continues to be poverty and squalid living conditions in many parts of the world. The human environment certainly becomes more crowded by the year and more polluted in some places while less so in others. There are trends and countertrends that make the assess-ment of progress an extremely complex business. It is made even more complex because the pace of change is quickening. Accelerating change in the wrong direction is, indeed, something really to be feared and countered aggressively.

ONGOING STRUGGLE BETWEEN FORWARD AND BACKWARD WORLDVIEWS

It is probable that the great majority of humans presently living are more inclined to view the future in a negative light than in a positive light. This is a considerable paradox.[8] As scientific knowledge has transformed our under-standing of all natural phenomena, as the applications of this knowledge have flooded the world with countless life-enhancing and life-extending innova-tions, as life spans in most countries have become longer and longer, and as living standards by almost any measure have risen worldwide over the last half century, majorities even in the wealthiest countries cling to the view that the past was in most ways better. Many of our esteemed leaders in politics and the arts continuously promote ancient texts of uncertain origin as the prime sources of received wisdom.

The counterargument of the forward function does not simply discard the wisdom of our forefathers. Rather, it advances the idea that one should receive the entire body of accumulated past knowledge with a critical eye both for what it offers and for what it lacks. The knowledge of the past gives each succeeding generation a great platform on which to stand, but much of what comes down to us has been demonstrated over and over again to be in error, based on faulty premises constructed by people who did not and could not know what we have come to know in more recent times and particularly through modern science. Indeed, the older the source, the more faulty the wisdom is likely to be. We should embrace the received wisdom of the past only where it can pass contemporary standards of evidentiary observation and logical reasoning, contributing meaningfully to a sound knowledge platform for progress. There is an alternative way to view the past that is entirely consonant with the forward function. This is to take the past in its own terms for its own time. This allows us to better understand our heritage and the struggles of humanity at different times to comprehend and master the world they lived in, using the tools and ideas that were at their disposal.

WHO ARE WE AND WHERE DID WE COME FROM?

Within the last one hundred fifty years there has developed an awareness among some members of our own species that we, ourselves, are products of a biological evolutionary process three or more billion years in the making. This small, scientifically informed minority have also become aware that the emergence of our own species is an extremely recent event on this time scale, perhaps encompassing the most recent two million years, or one one-thousandth of the total evolutionary scale. On this same scale the entire Industrial Revolution from the invention of the steam engine to the present has been but an instant, one ten-thousandth of the time man has walked upon Earth. Yet in that instant we have achieved incredible advances at an ever-increasing rate.

Advance means progressive steps toward the control of the human environment and control of our own heredity, accompanied by the spread of individual prosperity and well-being. We humans are made of the same stuff as the stars and the planets and the interstellar dust, yet we are creatures who have become aware of our own existence and increasingly of our environment out to the farthest galaxies. We are strivers. We are continuously reaching out toward an uncertain future state of betterment. The striving could also be called "advancement," and this advancement could apply either to ourselves alone, as individual beings, or to ourselves and our "kin" or a much larger social entity, such as a clan, a nation, a racial entity, or a religious group. Our definitions of completion and advancement are themselves ever-expanding, so that for many they now include a *prolonged* life, increasing *varieties* of experience, and increasing individual and shared sensations of satisfaction and joy from myriad stimuli. As humanity advances on all of these fronts, we can be said to be making *progress*, moving forward toward a better world and a better awareness of our being. It is lamentable that most humans are entirely unreflective about their condition relative to any other place or time. They do not trouble themselves with thoughts about who they are and where they are headed either as individuals, as groups, or as a species.

MORAL PROGRESS

It can be argued reasonably that there is no real progress in human affairs unless we are moving forward and becoming better in a *moral* sense. All the great achievements of civilization are meaningless if civilization itself has no ultimate meaning. This is very rough intellectual terrain, but it must be crossed over in any comprehensive treatment of the concept of progress. It will be argued here that every individual human has a *moral horizon*, a perimeter of awareness and interest within which life is most valued and outside of which the lives of others are less valued or not even valued at all. Expansion of this perimeter represents moral progress. Expanded to the farthest extent, the entire human race can become "the family."

Three fundamental questions frame the topic of human morality:

[1] *Whom* do we care for?
[2] *How* do we care for them?
[3] *How much* do we care for them?

[1] Whom *do we care for?*

We all start our lives knowing or caring little about anything except the nipple. As we grow, our consciousness and our concern extend gradually outward from the nipple to the breast, to the feeder as an entity separate from ourselves, thence to a concept of mother, and then to others who help us manage our way into the world. The immediate family comes next after the mother, then the extended family, and then an assortment of "significant others." As the social horizon extends, it is the tribe or the community, and, then, the "culture," which can have various meanings from ethnic identity to sociocultural surround. As the horizon extends even further, those we care about may come to include an entire culture or a nation. As humanity has advanced through the twentieth century, this horizon has haltingly extended even further for many to include all humanity on the planet. For some it extends far beyond the human race to include animals at various levels on the phylogenetic ladder. Very rarely it also includes plants. In the future it may even come to include other living members of the universe with whom we have no present contact and of whom we have no present awareness.

One sign of moral advancement is the emergence of concern for people and animals with whom we currently have no direct personal connection and may never have. We retain this concern even though these remote people may never be in a position either to return the favor or to provide us with any personal gain whatsoever. To the extent that this is true, we can say that these concerns are "altruistic."[9] Much has been made of the moon travel of the late 1960s and early 1970s as causative factors in raising our sights to this inclusive broader horizon of all humanity, but the concern probably goes back at least to 1919 and to the arrangements that were made after what was then called "the World War" to try to end further wars by bringing into being a kind of world government.[10] The fact that this effort failed should not distract us from the importance of the attempt and the trend in world affairs that it foreshadowed. After a second more extensive and devastating world war, there was a better and more unanimous effort to put together a world organization called the United Nations. Even though this organization has always been weak and usually crippled by internal conflicts, it remains in existence sixty years later and has performed many useful functions, not the least of which is to uphold a standard of morality for humans, which we call the "United Nations Declaration of Human Rights."

[2] How *do we care for them?*

Caring for someone can mean various things in varying degrees. At a basic level it means simply "wanting to have," "to possess," or "to hold." An ethical step up from this is being concerned about others, wanting them to remain in a state of well-being and to remain in our space. Again, as the ethical horizon expands, caring comes to mean "wanting to preserve," "to help," and "to nurture." It may also mean to preserve the cared-for objects the way they are, or to improve them from their present condition to a new condition that is better than what they are, perhaps a condition such as we, ourselves, are experiencing.

We can express this caring in many ways, and sometimes even in contradictory ways. We can do so by giving, sheltering, supporting, educating, protecting, perhaps even challenging and punishing. In short, the range of caring can cover practically the full spectrum of human activity. We fall into the moral abyss, however, when we start dividing the peoples around us into "us" and "them" and deciding we will care for "us" but not "them."

[3] How much *do we care for them?*

There is a scalar dimension to ethical behavior that starts at zero for "no effort" and extends upward to full preoccupation and even to the surrender of one's life for the sake of others. It varies greatly among people and probably even within families. Generosity is likely to be at a much higher level for family members than for others, for our own group and people we know personally versus for people we know only as a class or tribe. We are more generous to members of our own tribe, but some members of the tribe are much more generous to their own tribe than others, even if they show no generosity to people outside the tribe.

As we become more aware of others outside the tribe, there is a tendency to become more generous toward them. This greater awareness comes with more education, more contact, more frequent contact, and more substantial contact and exchange. Multiple contacts tend to make people think more like each other on a whole range of issues and to make them like each other much more. Ethically advancing individuals also come to share more values and to subscribe more wholeheartedly to one common set of values such as is reflected in the UN declaration.

The twentieth century left many mixed messages regarding moral progress. The first half was witness to hate-filled, murderous wars of national identity and racial-political extremism, yet much of the second half was different. There were fewer conflicts involving race, religion, nationality, and ethnicity. There has been a noticeable *reduction in prejudice*, *increased tolerance* of other races, religions, nationalities, and cultures; *increased awareness*, *sharing*, and *mixing* across races, religions, nationalities, and cultures; and increased perception of a *common interest* across humanity. We can also note the decline of totalitarianism, the end of authoritarian Marxism/communism, and a general increase in representative democracy and personal freedom in economic and social affairs. Not all countries, peoples, tribes, and individuals have reaped the same moral benefits and experienced the same gains, but the trend is unmistakable and irreversible for the world as a whole.

IMPORTANCE OF MORAL PROGRESS

Moral-ethical progress is *a priori* a good thing, but it is also very important for other aspects of the forward function argument. First of all, moral progress is our insurance that progress in technology will be used in beneficial ways. We know that evil people like Hitler, Stalin, and (most recently) bin Laden, can use technology in brutal and virulently regressive ways for humanity. When such people gain power, their ruthlessness in maintaining and extending that power knows no bounds, and they will use any technology to these evil ends. Thus, in effect, further progress for humanity in general depends upon the depowerment of such leaders by whatever means possible. If the time should arise when the aggrandized power of a malevolent despot exceeds all the countervailing power in the world, then we may experience a real stall and a suppression of the forward function.

THIS GREAT MOMENT IN TIME: *CARPE DIEM!*

What are the defining moments of history? This book is being written just past the turn of the turbulent twentieth century. Every generation wants to take itself seriously as the defining moment, the crucial turning point in human affairs, and so forth. The fact that it is the end of a particular century or even a millennium is not very meaningful because the starting point is so arbitrary. We might better number our days from the death of Socrates or the sack of Rome, or perhaps the burning of the library at Alexandria. The French revolutionaries tried to restart the dating system with *their* revolution, but it didn't stick.

The cataclysmic twentieth century may have a greater claim to endings and beginnings. For example, there were a lot of endings and beginnings in the year 1945: the defeat of Hitler and Japan; the invention, first use, and only military use to date, of atomic bombs; and, not least, there was the UN charter. A good case could also be made for some more recent developments, such as the invention of the transistor (1952), discovery of the structure of DNA (1952), the first microprocessor (late 1960s), the first space satellite (*Sputnik*, 1957), the first man in orbit (Yuri Gagarin, 1961), the first landing on the moon (1969), or the birth of the Internet (actually hard to pin down, perhaps the mid-1970s, although it remained a kind of high-tech toy and a curiosity until the mid-1990s, nearly a generation later).

Despite the tendency for every age and every generation to claim unique status for itself, there are especially solid reasons for such a claim today. First among these is our entrance upon the age of the Internet, the transformation of humanity into a fully connected entity. All of us here on Earth will soon be electronically connected to one another. Hundreds of millions of people are already on the Internet, performing all sorts of exchange activities from just saying hello to gambling, banking, buying and selling stocks, buying groceries, getting medical advice, and soon, perhaps, drug prescription and even medical treatments. There is no limit to this interconnectivity. It already connects millions of people representing all the countries of Earth, all professions, all fields of science and engineering. Thanks also to global-positioning satellites, we are able to make instant contact with anyone anywhere in the world, even those thousands of miles out to sea. We are further able to locate their present position geographically within a few feet and to guide our ships and vehicles safely and precisely to any destination.

These extraordinary changes have been realized in only about a decade, and they parallel other changes in technology, such as the dispersion of millions of computers and electronic receivers with greater and greater power and, amazingly, at ever-diminishing cost! This has never before happened in the world, and we will never return to a time when these connections and this electronic interconnective power will not exist. What this all means is not yet clear to anyone. The only certainty is that the changes are profound. Is human nature a constant? Even the answer to that question is not at all clear. These technologies may be changing our very nature as human beings, even changing what it means to be a human being.

Science itself is changing in the digital age. Telescopes and microscopes are becoming far more powerful, and their data far more precise. At the same time, the number of scientists is multiplying into the millions. This vast, new, worldwide infrastructure of scientific expertise constitutes a veritable "discovery machine" with an ever-increasing capability of answering almost any question about our physical and social environment.

We are also close to an even more important human achievement that might be called the "universal problem solver." Science answers questions. Science and engineering together solve problems. The stronger the science and the more powerful the tools of discovery, the more problems can be solved, including many that were formerly thought to be utterly beyond our grasp. The foremost of these problems are medical, psychological, and social: How can we extend lives and stay healthy throughout life? How can we become and remain happy? How can we create and preserve the happiness of our children and loved ones? How can we carry on human affairs without resorting to wars or to other forms of brutality? How can we create new environments for ourselves and for our offspring that will continuously increase our sense of well-being? It may seem unbelievable, but we are well on our way to finding real answers to all such questions.

Neither the discovery machine nor the problem-solving machine are quite with us today even though we can see some of their elements coming into place. Nevertheless, there are steps that could be taken within the next generation to move toward a positive human future at a much more rapid pace. By better understanding our forward function, that is, by seeking out the patterns and understanding the processes by which progress is achieved, it will become more and more possible to improve the many pathways to progress, making them safer, more reliable, more efficient, and more productive. It will also become possible to apply scientific knowledge building to enhance the well-being of all lives, individually and collectively. This includes developing much better ways to understand and reorder our priorities, so we can set coherent and sensible goals. Some of these will be entirely new and more ambitious goals heretofore inconceivable.

Despite these wondrous developments, the body politic seems to be stumbling forward in the dark, looking backward for guidance and definition, and not realizing and capitalizing on the new opportunities that have been created just in the last few decades. Our purpose here is to shine a bright light on these momentous changes, showing how they derive from our past and how they will propel us toward a positive human future. This is what the forward function is all about.

Chapter Two

MEASURING PROGRESS IN HUMAN TERMS

Humans are born, they live, and then they die,
This is the order that the gods have decreed,
But until the end comes, enjoy your life,
Spend it in happiness, not despair.
Savor your food,
Make each of your days a delight.
Bathe and anoint yourself,
Wear clothes that are sparkling clean,
Let music and dancing fill your house,
Love the child, who holds you by the hand,
And give your wife pleasure in your embrace.
That is the best way for a man to live.
　　　　—Gilgamesh (oldest-surviving epic poem, ca. 2000 BCE)[1]

In these twelve lines the ancient poet explains what life should really be about, but it is not so easy for most of us. Many times we are just too busy doing whatever we do, even wallowing in misery as we wonder what will befall us next. We wolf down our food just to fill our stomachs so we can get on to the next task in an endless series of tasks. There is no time for the dancing or the music. We can't stop to admire the view, or even take the time to love the child as much as the child wants to be loved. Yet we *want* to do better, and when we then *succeed* in doing better, there is a great satisfaction. Striving for something "better" is an essential aspect of human nature even though the striving is not always successful and what exactly *better* means is not so obvious. Sometimes, ironically, striving for the "better" leaves humans worse off than they were to start with. Nevertheless, the driving desire for "betterment" sticks with us. *Humanity never gives up.*

It is the perception of this "better" end state that gives meaning to human striving and to life as a whole. People keep going and going, working and working, because there is something out there that they want, something more than what they have, something that they believe they need. At the meanest level it may be just survival. At more exalted levels it may be "salvation" or a complex mix of things that together add up to "quality of life."

This chapter summarizes what humans strive for in their lives as individuals, as families, as tribes, and as civil societies. It is a difficult story to tell because it is so large, so multifaceted, and, above all, *so completely open-ended.* There is really no limit to the scope and variety of the things human beings want, and as they continue to make progress in particular areas, the list of wanted things expands right along with that growth. The very definition of who we are as selves and as cultures also keeps changing, becoming more and more complex, more interesting, one might say, and more potentially enjoyable in many different ways.

Plato was possibly the first to envision the ideal state, governed, he imagined, by the philosopher king. St. Augustine of Hippo later sanctified Plato's conception as the "City of God." Whole nation-states have more recently been cast as ideals, but all these idealistic conceptions do not describe what most humans want in a real way. What most people want out of life is much less grand. There are day-to-day needs that must be attended to first. The very experience of just having *a good day* must be counted as one of the essentials. The number of good days one has in a life is surely a big item in the summing up of what people strive for. Therefore, a summary listing requires us to take into account the small things as well as the grand. Here is a short list of ten important items that most humans want.

To be free from hunger and thirst
To have satisfying sexual encounters
To have children to carry on one's hereditary line
To nurture and educate one's children into successful adulthood
To be free from physical trauma, pain, or mental distress
To have congenial and loving relations with others—family, friends, neighbors, and work associates
To feel useful and fulfilled in one's occupation and work
To have rich spiritual experiences through religious identification
To vicariously experience the lives, thoughts, achievements, and fantasies of others through works of fiction and nonfiction

To experience the aesthetic pleasure to be derived from humanity's cultural inheritance, including art, music, architecture, and culinary craft

Such a list is a good way to start thinking about what progress really means. If there are more of any of these experiences over a longer period of time and for more people, then each of these "mores" represents a measure of progress, small or large. If a million more people are free from hunger and thirst, then that can be counted as a big progressive step. If even just one new person experiences the beauty of a Beethoven symphony, then that is also a small item of progress. If a million people are introduced to Beethoven through the innovation of sound recordings, then that is a bigger step, though not in league with a million being saved from starvation.

WHAT DO WE ALL REALLY WANT OUT OF LIFE?

All humans have a core set of needs that is buried deep in our heredity. Understanding progress starts here with what might be called the animal basics of our existence. Thanks to the discovery of DNA, human ancestry can now be traced back millions of generations to creatures that don't at all look like or act like we do today. Nevertheless, there are commonalities and consistencies, the most prevalent of which is the determination of each species to survive and propagate its kind. Perpetuation of the genetic material of life thus appears to be a defining attribute of living things. The will to survive almost defines life. Individual creatures in all species have this same determination to survive as intact organisms as long as possible unless and until individual survival threatens species survival.

Note that in the above list of ten life values, the first five could apply in varying degrees to all our ancestors, and animal rights advocates are perfectly justified when they base their concerns on these commonalities. However, although survival and propagation of species remain fundamental goals as much for humans as for all other living beings, something strange has been happening with human goal seeking in the last few thousand years. Propagation is still high on the list, but for at least five thousand years, humans have been reaching for a whole lot more. Confronting death, they imagine gods who are immortal and human souls or spirits who likewise live on after the body has ceased.

In our own times we have turned to scientific medicine to ward off disease, mend injury, and prolong our own personal lives in various ways long after the genetic material has been passed on. We now engage in sex for pleasure without reproductive consequences. We seek and routinely achieve prolonged periods of leisure to pursue sports and entertainments that have nothing to do with survival. We want to be amazed and thrilled by sights and sounds. We strive and seek to taste ever more complex combinations of sweet and sour, spice and texture, providing an ever-widening fulfillment for all our senses. None of these wonderful things has much to do with survival of the species, but they have a lot to do with what makes us uniquely human.

War has also been a consistent theme in the human narrative. Wars are fought not only to preserve, empower, and expand ethnic groups but also to uphold abstract ideals, such as freedom or nationhood or self-determination, and to maintain diverse ethnic groupings. In all these wars humans deliberately put forward their best genetic material for sacrifice, the youngest, the strongest, the most physically able, the most skilled, the bravest, even the brightest. There is, nevertheless, a cruel Darwinian logic to warfare. The winners in wars generally have a better chance of passing on their DNA. Thus, we may have been bred not only to be the best and brightest hunters and gatherers but also to be the best warriors and killers of our "fellow" human beings. We must contend with these dark elements in our nature along with the good elements.

Philosophers, theologians, and psychologists have tried at various times to provide frameworks for understanding human motivation. There is no one system that is adequately comprehensive, but Thomas Jefferson may have made the most succinct statement when he crafted these words in the Declaration of Independence in 1776:

> We hold these truths to be self-evident,
> that all men are created equal,
> that they are endowed by their Creator
> with certain unalienable Rights,
> that among these are
> Life, Liberty and the pursuit of Happiness.

The secular "enlightenment" philosophers of the eighteenth century tried to make sense of the human condition without reference to deities, miracles, or magical thinking. In drafting the Declaration of Independence, Thomas

Jefferson drew from this body of thought and hit upon a formula for describing the range of human aspirations, which still serves us well today: life, liberty, and the pursuit of happiness. It subsumes much of what we have described above as survival instinct and libido but also offers a simple set of concepts accessible to all people. Thus it serves as a very useful framework for looking at a wide range of human aspirations, and it will be used here in this way. It is noteworthy that a decade later the French hit upon a rather different formula for human rights: *liberté, egalité,* and *fraternité.* Fraternity is a worthy addition, standing for the many types of fellowship that are also fundamentally important to humanity. The American colonists waited for twelve more years to add this concept, stating that their new constitution was to form "a more perfect union."

THE LIFE TOTALITY

Life is not just one story, one sequence, one journey, leading toward one end point. Rather, it is the sum total of thousands of stories piled one on top of another over twenty thousand to thirty thousand days. Some of these days are wasted; most are forgettable and soon forgotten. Some are good, some bad, in one sense or another. Sometimes days form a sequential pattern leading to something we care about, but often they don't. A particular sequence of many days or even hundreds of days can add up to a single coherent "experience." Some days we may feel like we have got it all. On other days it may seem as if we are hopelessly mired in the minutiae of daily living. Sometimes we may feel we have "flow," but much of the time most of us are just treading water.

A *whole life* might be thought of as a life that has some completeness about it, such as achieving the cycle of reproduction and the passing on of the genetic material. Not all lives achieve even this much. No child who dies of a fever, no soldier who dies in battle, and no mother who dies in childbirth can be said to have lived a full life, and therein lies the great pain of their ends. Fewer still are able to pass on to their offspring the full measure of their cultural inheritance. Nevertheless, *wholeness* can have many diverse meanings, and what represents a satisfactory whole life for some may not seem so for others.

A *full life* is a whole life lived to the fullest. A really full life is crammed with diverse experiences, many happy, many not. It is likely to be a life of extensive exposure to other people, other cultures, ideas, books, music, challenges, triumphs, and tragedies. It is possible to have such a full life lived in only a few years, but the fullest lives are those lived long. The very definition of *fullness* expands as human experience and human achievement expand. For example, before Mozart and Beethoven, a full life could contain much music but not their music. After their time, a full life of music could not be lived without exposure to their works. So the possibilities of fullness expand as collective human achievements expand.

THE GOOD LIFE VERSUS THE FULL LIFE

Philosophers and theologians are probably more concerned about the "good life" than the "full life," so something should be said about that distinction. In considering what it means to live a good life, we are probably crossing over into the moral or spiritual realm. Here *good* means "worthy" or "exemplary" in the eyes of others, a life that lives up to certain ethical standards. This "good" also typically is imbued with a kind of happiness, the happiness that ensues from the sense or the certitude that one is doing or has done the right thing. Thus the hunger striker suffers the pains of starvation in happy exchange for the pleasure of contributing to a good cause and the pleasurable prospect that that good cause might triumph out of this suffering. Such self-sacrificing behaviors might seem to fly in the face of Jefferson's "life, liberty, and pursuit of happiness," but they are nevertheless part of the human equation, and we must account for them in assessing the range of human goals. Whether they are derivative or sui generis, these ideals are powerful drivers in the adult lives of many humans. This kind of "good life" leads to a glowing obituary.

THE EXPANSION OF HUMAN ASPIRATION

What we humans think of as happiness is not only constantly changing but also constantly *expanding*. One of the most remarkable human attributes is the capacity to conjure up *new* images of what we want. Jesus, Buddha, Mohammed, and all the other great spiritual leaders and prophets had this ability. Their word pictures of paradise were able to move millions to suffer all manner of privations in attempts to get to these imagined but fervently believed places. This process of verbal fabrication and image conjuring goes on and on even in our own times and will continue on long after us, as long as words have the power to evoke beautiful thoughts. As we read the sayings or writings of these wise men, we are beckoned to follow, to accept the new idea of what is right and true and good. Their ideas may, indeed, represent important new contributions to an evolving conception, a kind of master synthesis of human aspiration. However, the "ultimate" goals of humanity are unknowable from the perspective of the human past and its spokespersons, however wise and holy they appeared to be in their own time or in later times.

Our advancing technology and our increased success at problem solving in every need sector add to this evolution of aspiration. We now "want" to visit other, distant places and to communicate with other peoples around the globe because *now we can*. We want to hear and rehear great music in our living rooms and in our automobiles and even on our boats because *now we can*. We want to have the full enjoyment of sexual experience with or without the necessary consequence of children because *now we can*. So many of the past "inevitables" of human existence have been tossed aside in the last few generations that none of the old formulas for human goals work very well anymore. Even the "three score and ten" of the human life span will soon be gone. We will live much longer lives because *now we can*!

As these advances become embedded in the culture, humans will change as beings. The range of experience that they deem "essential" for the good life has already expanded a great deal in the last two centuries, and the range will expand even more rapidly as humans are exposed to a larger and larger universe of possibilities. As they take on this ever more varied and richer cloak of experience, they will be transformed, becoming unrecognizable to their parents and grandparents. From the point of view of the elders, the changes will sometimes seem disagreeable, even frightening and terrible; but to those in the midst of the experience, such changes more typically will be considered thrilling, liberating, mind expanding. In any case, because of the forward function that is embedded in human culture, the die is cast. This expanded human future will come to be. Such a posthuman extension of the experience of life need not involve any mutation of our genetic material, as some welcome and others fear.[2] Nothing was added to the human genome to bring on the steam engine, the automobile, the telephone, the airplane, the television, the computer, or the Internet—all innovations that have changed and that continue to change the experience of life for humans in profound ways.

EXPERIENCES OF BELONGING AND IDENTITY WITH LARGER HUMAN ENTITIES

Humans are intensely social animals, and their associations are vital parts of themselves. To a very high degree, happiness depends on social connections. Starting with the mother in infancy, social awareness expands throughout life. As awareness expands, to a greater and greater extent so does the ability to differentiate, to relate in two-way interactions, and to control how others respond.[3] As the child grows into the adult, awareness and identity extend to schools and then to work settings of increasing complexity. The degree to which a person can form meaningful social bonds with people and institutions large and small is a major measure of success in life. Every bond enhances the experience of life and hence happiness and sense of well-being. Harmonious ties that allow high productivity through cooperative effort add special value.

THE FAMILY

There is probably no source of human happiness stronger than the family. Such family pleasure includes the sense of belonging to a family, recognizing family members, defending them, admiring them, sharing with them, and loving them. Each generation re-creates the nuclear family through marriage and transfers those familial attachments from the old nuclear family to the new nuclear family. In recent times the power of family has been attenuated by some other aspects of cultural progress. New human wants have crowded onto the stage. New technologies allow more choices, some which have never been available to anyone heretofore. This expanded choice reaches out in every direction, including a much larger range and a more rapid flow of human contacts. For just one example, it has moved the dating and courting game all the way from the girl or boy next door to the girl or boy who displays her or his picture and miscellaneous attributes on the Internet. Nevertheless, any developments that lead to better marriage choices, happier families, stronger family ties, and more rewarding contacts with the extended family can also be counted as progress.

CULTURAL IDENTITY AND THE DIVERSIFICATION OF HUMAN EXPERIENCE

It is now generally accepted that the genetic prototype of modern man emerged in Africa about two million years ago.[4] The earliest version of large-brain humans, the Neanderthals, migrated north out of Africa about two hundred thousand years ago, and the first modern humans began their migrations about one hundred thousand years ago.[5] From that time onward, hunter-gatherers slowly spread out, reaching all the habitable continents by forty thousand years ago. In spite of almost total sharing of genetic material, each localized tribe developed its own identity, its own language, its own primitive technology, and its own mythology and folkways. These tribal differences evolved to become what we now call "cultures" and "ethnicities." Until the twentieth century, the most prized achievement of each segment of humanity was its culture, defined separately in either ethnic or national terms, and sometimes both.

The unique American culture is a relatively recent phenomenon that now has fewer ethnic overtones than many older cultures. It came into being first with thirteen separate English colonies, many supported by imported African slaves. One hundred and fifty years after the first settlements, the colonies broke off from English political rule and formed their own "United States" government, the cornerstone of which were two founding documents, the Declaration of Independence and the Constitution. In a major way, these documents came to define the new culture. Through a subsequent two hundred and thirty years that included a traumatic, bloody, and tragic civil war and several further waves of immigration, this culture has evolved into a swirling mixture of ethnicities, subcultures, and religions.

This hybrid American "culture" is referenced here because it may well be an early prototype for what most future human cultures will be like. With twentieth-century developments such as mass transit across borders and oceans, jet travel, and worldwide telecommunications (now crowned by the World Wide Web), culture separation as a satisfactory identity is slowly disappearing. It is being replaced by cultural *multiversity*, which assumes an acceptance, understanding, and appreciation of what *all* cultures bring to the human experience. This is not so much a homogenization, as many have feared, but an expansion of consciousness and experience such that non-Chinese can appreciate and even make Chinese food, non-Jews can laugh at Yiddish humor, non-Christians can experience the spiritual splendor of medieval cathedrals, and so on.

Twentieth-century technology also allowed the better recording and preservation of cultural emblems, artifacts, music, and language. It further allowed the broadcast and wide dissemination of all this cultural data to members and nonmembers alike. Modern technology also allows more members of more subcultures to find each other and to get together physically as well as electronically. The simultaneous results are accelerated cultural diversification and cultural amalgamation and synthesis. Both can be viewed as progressive trends that lead to an expanded human consciousness.

As people travel more, as they read more, and as they connect themselves more to various media, including television and now the Internet, they inevitably are exposed to more and more diverse cultures. They then mix their experiences with these other cultures. They expand, diversify, and mingle their experience in ways our ancestors could not imagine. It is important to realize that this is a process that *never stops* until death. As increased access expands human horizons, lives become more interesting and more pleasurable.

This opportunity to absorb diverse cultures was at one time a rare privilege. The great place-bound and illiterate majority got a taste of this rich diversity only when adventurers came home to tell their often-embellished stories. Increased trade, travel, and literacy, and the publication of more stories, have now exposed hundreds of millions to these multicultural experiences. For Americans, the Civil War was the first such awakening, when millions of men were marched into different regions of their own country for the first time. In fact, it was only after the Civil War that American people started to refer to their land as a singular entity ("the United States *is* . . ." versus "the United States *are* . . .").[6] In the twentieth century, no events were more important in opening up cultural horizons than the world wars, especially World War II, when millions of North American men were sent overseas to Europe and Asia and came back with an entirely new and expanded view of what the world was and who was in it. This expansion of multicultural consciousness continued in the postwar years with the Peace Corps and with the expansion of worldwide travel, which was made possible by the safe commercial airliner.

UNIFICATION OF HUMAN EXPERIENCE

As the human race diversifies, it also becomes more interconnected and hence, essentially, more united. Through the Internet as well as the United Nations, world trade, and world transport, earthlings are coming to be some kind of organic whole. We know we are now something together—even though we are not sure what we are, how we got here, or where we are going.

DIVERSIFICATION AND EXPANSION OF HUMAN NEEDS, WANTS, AND GOALS

As our awareness horizons expand, our wants and needs expand as well. This makes the task of explaining what it means to be human a lot more difficult because what we want out of life today is a lot more than what our parents wanted or "had a right to expect." The mental framework we use to identify and order our needs and goals inevitably advances in step with our expanding scientific understanding of our environment and ourselves and with the advancing technology that allows for the expansion and diversification of our experience.

GENERATIVITY

All living things are driven to create copies of themselves. It is therefore understandable that humans, the thinking members of the great life family, often busy themselves by creating things. All our "needs" are probably manifestations of that same basic procreative instinct, but after six thousand years of city life they are on display in ever more elaborate disguises.[7] Human creativity extends far beyond the reproduction of ourselves in our children to creating families, homes, and life spaces with unique and infinitely varied attributes.

A flood of twentieth-century innovations vastly extended the bounds of human creativity. As a result, we can now do more, see more, experience more, and create more. We can also more easily share what we create with others if we wish to do so. There is no real limit to this kind of generativity. Any full life can now generate a rich stream of original output that would baffle our ancestors. The well-lived life of today overflows with possibilities. The typical well-lived life of tomorrow will be an even more complex and more interesting bundle of creation.

SORTING OUT THE MEANINGS OF
LIFE, LIBERTY, AND *HAPPINESS*

In order to understand something about the totality of human experience, we need to think about categories. Jefferson and his eighteenth-century colleagues made a good start with the Declaration of Independence. Most of the ideas in that document were already floating around in the European intellectual circles of that time, and quite a number could be traced to the late seventeenth-century English philosopher John Locke, but they have stood the test of time remarkably well. Furthermore, the fact that they got to be included in such an illustrious consensual proclamation lends them a kind of authority as a list that they would not otherwise have had. An analysis of the many meanings inherent in these few revered words is a good starting place for a twenty-first-century reformulation of what is desired not only by Americans but also by all the people of the world, regardless of ethnic origin, religion, or national identity.

Life

Life itself is the number one human right, and with it, by logical necessity, comes the ability to sustain life through the basic provision of adequate food, shelter, safety, and health. Modern first-world governments have only recently come to accept the responsibility of providing minimal life sustenance for all persons within their borders. The only exceptions are those who are killed in accidents, by murder, in war, by illnesses, and by other "natural" causes. In rare instances, some modern states also allow publicly sanctioned executions. This guarantee of a safety net was much more difficult to provide in former times and remains unattainable today in the third world. When many of the people in less-fortunate places sustain injuries or contract diseases that are technically reversible or curable with the application of modern medical knowledge, they nevertheless are allowed to die because such services are not made available to them.

Beyond such a safety net is there more to say about life? Yes! We now are more likely to ask, "*How much* of a life?" or "*How long* a life?" The modern, technologically sophisticated society answers the long-life question thus: "Life should be extended to whatever the current level of medical science will allow." Thanks partly to medical science and partly to reliably good nutrition, the number of longtime survivors is gradually inching its way upward. As the capabilities of sustaining life increase, *expectations* also rise. There is no obvious end in sight: there is no age at which anyone is willing or desiring to say: "That's enough, good-bye; you can be dead now; we will no longer feed you or provide you with medicine." In some instances, so-called living wills may provide for voluntary removal of life support, but in almost all cases such wills are only effective when the quality of life by various measures has descended below the level of what a consensus of observers would call "human existence."

We humans are profoundly ambivalent about the end of life. We do not really accept it, even though we know that for any of us living at this time, the end is inevitable. Thus it was also for those who lived in all earlier times. There is a large school of thought that holds that life *should be* limited, that the medical devices used to extend life at the end are somehow inhumane. When it comes down to specific cases and specific loved ones, however, the choices are much tougher than they seem to be in abstract contemplation. If it is *my* mother and there is an outside chance that she will come through this crisis and then live perhaps another six months, experiencing at some level some of the modest pleasures of life, then I say, "let us try to keep her alive." So it is with every son and daughter and every husband and wife the world over.

Life Extent

It is generally recognized that the worst thing that can happen to anyone is life termination, death, even though it comes to everyone sooner or later. The death of a very old person is seen as a sad event. The death of a child, in contrast, is a horror that we turn from in agony, as do the figures in the famous Edvard Munch paintings. The death of a young adult person is also a terrible tragedy, as are deaths at succeeding ages on a vaguely defined declining scale as the years roll on. Nevertheless, we all want our loved ones to live on, even our grandparents and the grandparents of our friends. We regret all these life endings as they occur to such an extent that this life wish must be counted as perhaps *our strongest drive*, extending from ourselves to all those we know. Probably for this reason we have established the great edifice of modern scientific medicine that pursues all life-threatening conditions with a steady competence, intensity, and avowed intent to someday conquer.

Life Quality

Durability or a simple count of years of life is no longer a satisfactory definition of what life is for most of us. We more and more are asking, "What *kind* of life?" Thus the term *quality of life* has taken hold in the latter half of the twentieth century and promises to be even more of a preoccupation in the twenty-first century. In essence, *quality* means "happiness, richness and fullness of experience." The quality of a life is a kind of grand mathematical proportion, the positives above the line, the negatives below. Thus it can be viewed as the ratio of happiness to misery, day to day, through all the stages of life as well as for the life as a whole. There are all kinds of such ratios, and they will not be the same from one person to the next. Nevertheless, when we say "quality of life," we have definite things in mind, a summing up, and a set of values that get placed on an imaginary scale that says, "this is more, that is less." In a way, this entire chapter is more about quality of life than about life itself. Our argument is that life's quality is the sum of a whole lot of things, and because all these things are important for human motivation, there should be some sort of "quality list" in every thinking person's head so that everyone can understand both what it is that most humans want and why humanity is forever moving forward toward that attainment. This is the essence of the drive to "progress."

Lives Other Than Our Own

We can't really think about the quality of single lives without also considering the quality of life of the many. The great English economist Jeremy Bentham coined the expression "the greatest good to the greatest number" as the fundamental principle on which all social policy should be based. It still works as a vector, even if the "good" and the "number" keep requiring updated definitions. More basic, perhaps, is the categorical imperative proposed by the great philosopher Immanuel Kant: if we value our own life, we must also value all other lives.[8]

Yet to what extent do we really value other lives? It seems to depend mostly on how close these others are to us as individual selves. Our own kin we value most, and we like to think that we value all our children equally, but do we extend this to the unborn? To the just conceived? Some do, some apparently do not. Beyond the unborn there are the limitless numbers of the yet-to-be-conceived. Do we value these also, and, if so, how much? Many intelligent people shrink with horror from the idea of making deliberate selections among these yet-to-be-conceived individuals, as if the quasi randomness of future generational genetics is somehow sacred. Many other intelligent people are horrified by the prospect of uncontrolled population growth. Philosophically and ethically, it is a very squishy area. Everyone is "pro-life," but there is consensus neither on when life begins nor on how the creation of lives should be regulated, if at all. The forward function ensures that prospective parents will be continuously provided with new choices at every stage, from conception to birth. There has been more technological progress in this one sphere than perhaps in any other in the last two decades, yet this is an area where progress may bring more conflict than less because there is no consensus about what is good in a moral sense and therefore what represents progress.[9]

Human Life versus Lives of Other Species

Does the right to life extend beyond our species? In recent years there has been a growing view that humans have a responsibility as caretakers to guarantee the survival of nearly all other species. With some (e.g., various vegetarians) this is taken to include all creatures above a certain level of complexity who are alive. More broadly accepted is the notion that the species (as distinct from individuals) needs to be preserved. Along with this comes the idea that natural selection, as a principle, should not apply to human beings vis-à-vis other species. In other words, animals can kill each other for food, territory, or sport, but humans cannot. It is important to note these distinctions among human beliefs, but there is no need here to take sides in the debates that rage among factions. What is especially important to note is that humans have arrived at a state of evolution where they have within their power the ability to make such decisions regarding the survival, growth, shrinkage, perpetuation, and evolution (via selective breeding) of virtually any other species, from single-celled organisms to primates.

It is reasonable to propose that preservation of species is a priori a worthy goal. In addition, however, other animals of all kinds have enormous value as resources for present and future human use. As "resources" they serve many purposes, including food sources, medical models, medicine factories, fabric and leather suppliers, companions, and even entertainments. In the near future, many mammals will also become suppliers of substitute organs to sustain and extend human lives. Not the least of their admirable attributes is that of companionship. Dog, cat, and horse are all "man's best friend" some of the time, and for some almost all the time. This is wonderful, but the fact remains that these lives have meaning only within a human context.[10] When the lives of both animals and humans are at stake, the humans come first, and the animals' lives are first to be expended. When starvation is the issue, the other animals turn soon from being friends to being food. As a mere dietary preference if not a nutritional necessity, most humans continue to eat meat and fish, though certain species—like dogs, horses, cats, and now whales, monkeys, and a long list of other mammals—are off the table for a variety of reasons.

As we progress into the future, our ability to manipulate the human diet for both taste and nutrition will expand enormously, possibly leading to the demise of meat eating for both ethical *and* practical reasons. Until that time arrives, there will continue to be an unresolved ethical conflict concerning the status and right-to-life of other species.

Liberty

The idea of liberty probably first arose as a contrast with something else, slavery. The first conquerors may have merely slaughtered the vanquished, but at sometime at least four thousand years ago, it must have occurred to some victors that their vanquished could be more useful alive than dead. Thus was born the idea and the practice of slavery. Nobody ever volunteered to be a slave and wanted to be cast as such, but it was a whole lot better than being dead, many must have thought. Indeed, the role of the slave and the role of the child are very similar with the exception that the child is expected to grow out of this dependent and powerless situation and the slave is not.

It seems reasonable to suppose that early humans knew no condition such as slavery but for the fact that they were all slaves to nature. They had liberty in a sense, the liberty to track the animal herds and to scramble for edible roots and berries to feed themselves and their offspring. But survival was often a chancy thing, and life almost always trumps liberty despite what Patrick Henry so boldly stated. We do not think of the invention of slavery as a stage in human progress, but it was probably just that. It was the situation in which one adult person's life could be controlled in major aspects by another person who had more power. Humans are makers and users of tools, and what better tool could you have than another person to do things for you that you didn't care to do for yourself? As civilization evolved, slavery was probably the first division of labor.

"Slavery" can also be seen in relative terms. All ordered groupings seem to depend on a hierarchy in which the lower orders are subservient to the higher orders. In medieval Europe, feudalism was an ordering in which, starting at the bottom, each social layer was subservient to a smaller layer above, up to the king. In theory, feudalism involved *reciprocal* rights and obligations and, as such, represented a kind of social progress, but the rights resided more strongly in the upper layers and the obligations lay more heavily on the lower layers. It was to moderate this system of dependency that the English lords of the thirteenth century forced King John to sign the Magna Carta. They did not want liberty in the fullest sense but only to establish a counterbalance to the power of the king.

As English history evolved over subsequent centuries, more and more lower layers obtained rights and powers, even up to the present time. In England, Scotland, and Wales, it was a gradual stepwise process. In the American colonies, in France, in Ireland, and in many other places, the surge toward equality took a more dramatic and sudden turn through "revolution," leading supposedly to liberty or freedom. But this liberty was by no means absolute. It had nothing to do with the mundane business of earning a livelihood. For that one had to surrender at least eight or ten hours a day to the lord and master on the plantation, in the industrial shop, or in the business office—except for the lucky few or the exceptionally skilled who could make it to the other side. What freedom and liberty really meant to the nineteenth-century American (and Englishman) was freedom from arbitrary and unfair treatment by others and freedom from political coercion by people not elected to serve as representative leaders.

As social progress has been made through the twentieth century in many parts of the world, one of the important things that has changed fundamentally is the concept of liberty. Like so many other old ideas, it has expanded beyond all recognition from the original concept. As this expansion has taken place, the word *liberty* has tended to be displaced by its near synonym, *freedom*. A dictionary definition of *freedom* is: "the widest term, suggesting complete absence of restraint." In the first world's advanced democracies, one can now expect to be able to say practically anything in public, as long as it is not specifically injurious to another. Likewise, one expects and gets freedom to travel and to relocate anywhere in one's own country or in some other. One expects and often gets freedom of choice in everything purchased, as long as there is money to buy. All manner of clothing can be worn within very broad limits, and almost anything edible is available to eat and can be eaten at the place and in the manner chosen by the eater. In such advanced countries and within their expanding networks, there is now freedom to send and receive messages to and from practically anyone at any time. As technology and industry have expanded, this array of options and the *desire* for freedom to choose among them have also expanded. Clearly, expanding freedom for humanity is related to the forward function as both cause and result.

There is a connection between freedom and *creativity*. We all require a large measure of freedom to create our own unique lives, to fulfill ourselves, to create our own autobiographies, to define and then to live the good life. We want to be able to express ourselves with fewer and fewer limitations. We want to associate with more and different people, to experience our own culture and to share with other cultures without fear of censure or punishment.

There is also a connection between freedom and *wealth*, or what the economists call "disposable income." In democracies people want to preserve the fiction that they are all equally free, even while they implicitly recognize that this is not literally true, nor could it be. Those with wealth and power are much freer to do more things and to make more choices than those without either. Property rights, for example, conflict head-on with the freedom of others, namely, with freedom of movement. Consider the contrast between Miami Beach, where almost all beachfront is privately owned, and the Hawaiian beaches, which are all publicly accessible. The poorest person in Hawaii can walk along the beach and swim anywhere; this is a dimension of freedom that is clearly stronger in Hawaii than in Florida.

Even in so-called free societies, the workplace (where most people spend about one-quarter to one-third of their waking lives) is manifestly unfree. Very few persons are free to choose what they will do on a given day, and fewer still are free to work or not work on any given day. Here again, the wealthier we are, the more freedom we have; but the wage earners on the bottom, those who are utterly dependent on the given job to feed and house themselves and their children, are not free at all. These people, constituting the majority in all societies, are really wage slaves until the workday is over.

In the third world and the authoritarian remnants of the communist world, even such conditional freedom as discussed above is still largely a reserve of the elite. There is no freedom with poverty, no respite after eight hours of work and, depending of the level of oppression, there is little freedom for most in an authoritarian regime on or off the job. Nevertheless, the vector is clear. All these peoples *aspire* to greater freedom sometime in the future. This is what they want and will inevitably strive for, given the opportunity.

Finally, there is a real connection between level of freedom and *technology*. Technology creates new things first for the restricted use of some privileged humans, but later, inevitably, both use and benefit spread to more and more humans as mass production and diffusion take effect. These new technologies then open new choices and expose new needs. This is a well-established expansive process that repeats itself over and over again as new science leads to new technology. As the technology becomes refined, its output moves toward increased efficiency and reliability of production, making mass production feasible and economically profitable. Prices fall and the refined output becomes available to more and more people until everyone within a culture who wants the item can have it virtually as a matter of free choice. Consider, for example, what proportion of the very poor in the United States, Canada, Australia, England, France, Germany, Italy, Scandinavia, the Netherlands, Japan, and a host of other advanced countries now have electricity, running water, sewage, color television, telephones, and either mass transit or an abundance of cheap automobiles. That covers about a billion people, and the number is rising. The countries named above were among the first to industrialize and to develop mass production. These are also the countries in which the notion of freedom expanded greatly in the twentieth century. The rest of the countries of the world are following, expanding the choices for *their* people along the path already followed in the advanced countries, provided that wars or other unforeseen calamities do not get in the way.

It would be very difficult to come up with definitions of *freedom* or *liberty* in the year 2010 that would satisfy humans of the later decades of the twenty-first century. The definitions will continue to expand, coming to include more self-expression by anyone in any medium. It will soon include access to multiple modes of communication, including the telephone and most particularly the Internet. It may come to include the choice among multiple modes of child rearing and schooling, job choice, and job changing. The limits are set only by the imagination.

Happiness and Its Pursuit

"The *pursuit* of happiness" is the inspired turn of phrase inserted in the Declaration of Independence to stand for all aspects of life quality that extend beyond life and liberty. Why did Jefferson decide on these particular words? Why not just "happiness"? Is happiness an illegitimate goal, whereas "pursuit" is OK? Clearly the underlying assumption is that there is such a thing as happiness, and whatever it is, it is an end state beyond life and liberty, beyond the mere existence that all humans strive to achieve, and beyond the limited array of freedoms available in Jefferson's day. Let us now look at the concept of happiness head on and try to arrive at a more fulsome idea of what *happiness* really might mean at the beginning of the twenty-first century. In so doing, let us tip our hat to Jefferson for the notion of *pursuit*, because it points to the reality that human aspirations are not fixed points but *vectors*, directions in which humanity should be going rather than fixed states of being or end places. *Pursuit* says "we want to go in this direction, chasing after something powerful yet open-ended, never fully defined."

Happiness has many meanings, and in recent years the concept has drawn the special interest of psychologists and followers of trends in popular culture. College courses on the subject now draw large audiences.[11] Some social scientists have even rated different cultures in terms of their self-perceived happiness.[12] There is obviously a hugely subjective component as well as definitional confusion regarding any such ratings. However, if we confine ourselves to specific emotional, psychological, and physiological states, it should be possible to define and even quantify this all-important human condition.

Every life contains a balance of happiness and unhappiness. On the happy side there are day-to-day items like eating, drinking, sleeping, working, playing, reading, and listening. There are caring for others, helping others, socializing with others. Each of these activities can have a happy side, ranging from mere satisfaction to euphoria. There are also longer episodes of life activities that may consume hours, days, or even years, goal-directed serial activities that are invested with energy and charged with emotion. This investment and absorption can provide great pleasure just by itself, in addition to the pleasure of anticipation and the sense of accomplishment as the serial nears its conclusion. The most common of these is child rearing, but there are many others, such as the many tiers of educational advancement, the taking and completion of a course, a journey, a book (reading one would be a short serial, writing one would be a long serial).

Set up against each of these possible pleasures of life there is the contrasting possibility of unhappiness. The possibility of disappointment and pain lurks around the corner of every promise. The pleasant anticipation of success is matched by the dread of failure. The happiness of food on the table contrasts with the misery of no food on the table. Everything that is potentially good in a life can also turn sour. We can say we have progress when the balance between the two, the amount of happiness in things large and small, shifts more to the positive side of the scale.

THE NET HAPPINESS QUOTIENT: H-U

Therefore, in measuring whether or not there is progress, we need to engage in a kind of mental calculus. People are continuously making choices throughout life, trying to maximize happiness and minimize unhappiness. It is a simple equation: sum of H (happiness) minus sum of U (unhappiness) should be greater than zero. Most of our choices are made subconsciously or semiconsciously, so we have little control over them. They are made minute-to-minute, hour-to-hour, and day-to-day, while a few are determinative of whole periods of a life. We are also always trading short-term unhappiness for long-term happiness, or visa versa. Some suffer the grinding toil of four years of medical school for the lifelong privilege and status of becoming a doctor. Others may delight in a luxury cruise to an exotic place for which they will later spend months or years in debt. It would be nice for each of us if the sum total of our lives at that most unpredictable moment of our death should end up on the positive side in a balancing of positive and negative experiences. Complicating this calculus is the fact that our notions of what should go into the equation and which experiences constitute "positives" and "negatives" change as we grow older.

Ultimately, progress has to be measured as the sum of all these individual H-U equations for however many people are living on Earth at a given time. If, of the six billion inhabitants of Earth, two billion continue to live short, miserable lives, this by itself does not say much about the overall state of humankind because one has to ask the associated question, compared to what? If these two billion live shorter and more miserable lives than their parents, then clearly humanity is moving in the wrong direction, negative progress or regress. If they are no better off than the preceding generation, then there is

FIGURE 2.1.
THE HAPPINESS QUOTIENT
IN AN INDIVIDUAL LIFE

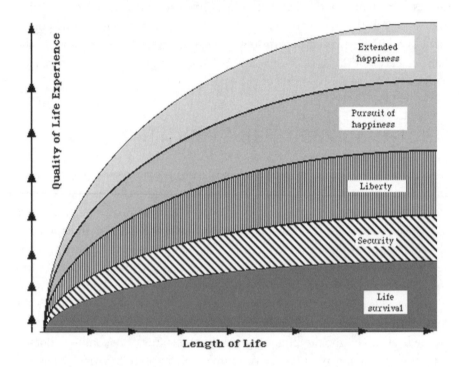

no progress. If, however, there is more net happiness, even on simple measures like food intake, then progress has been made.

Figure 2.1 shows one way of looking at the whole life of an individual person. This life begins on the left with the basic qualities that all life shares, shown as black. As the duration of this life advances, the various human qualities begin to emerge with expanding experience. At the same time, the many possibilities of achieving life fulfillment in happiness emerge. Progressively lighter shades indicate these different types of experience, culminating in the lightest layer for the indefinite but expansive future of human possibility. Lives are of varying lengths, and the length of a life is what we might think of as the quantitative dimension. If we draw a vertical line anywhere along the horizontal dimension, the area to the left represents that quantity. A life cut off when an individual is very young loses out not only on quantity but even more on quality, hence the double tragedy. The fortunate ones who live very

FIGURE 2.2.
COMPARING LIVES WHEN THEY ARE OVER

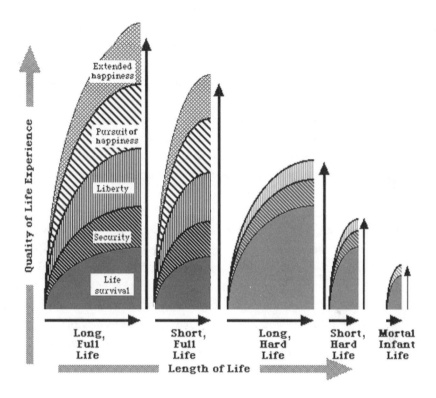

long lives have the opportunity for enormous fulfillment from multiple experiences, an opportunity that expands as civilization advances.

Figure 2.2 suggests a way of comparing individual lives employing this same scheme. The fortunate person on the left lived a long life, a life full of varied experiences, day to day, year to year. The figure is not intended to specify which way this life has been lived, which experiences were had and which paths were followed, because there are about as many paths to the good, full life as there are people on Earth. There will also be more and different paths available to our children and still more to our grandchildren. No doubt there was also a measure of unhappiness in this full life as well, although it is not possible to show it here. The net H-U was, in any case, high.

Next to this person is another who lived a life of half the length, but that life, too, was still relatively rich while it lasted. That person was also able to absorb much that the culture had to offer in that time and place, all the way up to a tragically early end. We might imagine this kind of life as something like that of a movie star who foolishly crashes his sports car while racing along the Riviera, or it could be anyone caught up in an accident or killed in a war or cut down by a deadly disease. The tragedy comes from the thought of the longer life that could have been lived but wasn't. The parent who has observed this son or daughter grow up through the various stages of development to flower as a mature young adult feels the pain of this ending most keenly.

Moving on to the right, we suggest a long life in which there was less opportunity or inclination to expand experience into the larger cultural realms of music, art, history, sport, religion, and so on. It may be a life, like so many human lives, in which the struggle for existence is paramount, where long hours of toil are required just to put bread on the table. Perhaps it is a life lived with severe handicap or illness or involuntary servitude. In ancient times, even this type of life was relatively rare just because it was long. With modern medicine and public health, it is possible to prolong life up to and beyond eighty years even when life quality leaves something to be desired.

From what can be gathered from our remote human past, most people were lucky to live even into adulthood. Childhood disease was rampant and sustaining young life was chancy. Hobbes's "nasty, brutish, and short" was a fair characterization. Even today, in much of the third world and especially in sub-Saharan Africa, these descriptors still apply.

Then, finally, at the rightmost side of figure 2.2, there is the brief life, one that is snuffed out early with no opportunity to get a taste of the good things life has to offer. We could start with the millions of lives that do not survive the womb. These lives are mourned by many millions of would-be parents and siblings, as indeed they should be. Therefore, anything that reduces infant mortality obviously deserves to be counted as progress.

SUMMING VALUE ACROSS LIVES

All the lives depicted in figure 2.2 are equally precious and have something like equal potential when they start out. That they don't all end like the first one is a continuing tragedy of our collective life. We would like it to be otherwise, and to a large extent, progress should be measured as the increase over time in the number of lives that resemble the first in this figure. Progress in

FIGURE 2.3.
SUMMING HAPPINESS QUOTIENT
FOR ANCIENT TRIBE

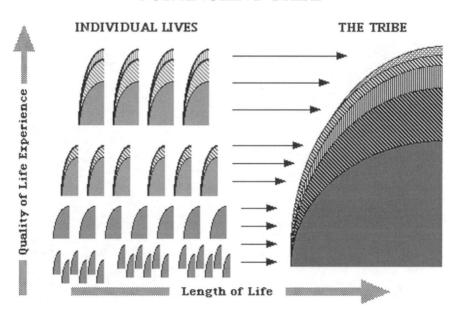

an individual life can be measured from left to right in figure 2.1. The closer one gets to the right-hand side, the more we can say that progress has been made. If the life is made just an hour or a day or a year longer by the miracles of modern medical care, that has to be rated as progress. If the life has been rendered more enjoyable or less painful on any dimension by medicine or by any other means, then that, too, must count as progress for that individual.

We also have to think of groups and whole societies when we think of progress, and there the equation becomes more complicated. Figure 2.3 shows how the life-quality level of an ancient human tribe might have been characterized using the same scheme. For most members, life is hard and short. Like the untold thousands who must have toiled to make the great pyramids of Egypt, we have scant record of what their lives were really like. We don't know who they were. What little we do know comes from the records of their lords and masters. Yet within the tribe, as civilization developed, the possibilities of liberty and a measure of happiness were available for at least a few members. Even those at the lower rungs of these primitive cultures must have received

FIGURE 2.4.
SUMMING HAPPINESS AS
CIVIL CULTURE REPLACES TRIBAL

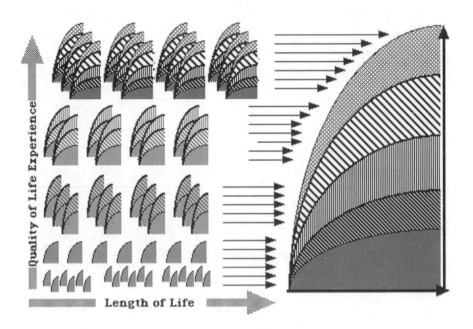

some measure of happiness through vicarious identification with their masters, through admiration of the products of their labor, performance and
observation of the same rituals, and through veneration of the same tribal
ancestors and gods. Increasingly elaborate social connections, the requirements of shared defense survival in the face of famine and both human and
animal predators, and a shared history converge over time to make the tribe
an ongoing entity that can be said to have a collective quality of life as well as
a life extent over many generations.

History is marked by the rise and fall of tribes, the advancement of successful tribes into city-states, empires, and nation-states in which the social
order becomes more complex and the lives of many individuals become richer
and richer. Even as civilizations ultimately fail, they are eventually replaced
by follow-on civilizations that provide greater levels of happiness for many of
their members, a trend that continues to the present. Historically, such
progress tended to come at irregular intervals. There was, for example, an
Egyptian "high," a Persian "high," a Greek city-state "high," an Alexandrian

"high," and a Roman "high," spread over a period of about four thousand years. Between each high, there was a tendency toward social disintegration and a return to tribalism. Through each such period of high culture, a greater and greater proportion of the population was able to enjoy the good things in life that were available to anyone at that time.

Figure 2.4 is intended to represent this advance over tribalism in terms of life quality. More and more members are now able to achieve longer lives filled with more freedom and more pleasures in greater variety. Clearly not everyone will enjoy such advantages in equal measure, but a greater and greater number are able to do so, and the extent of enrichment tends to filter down to the less-privileged members over time. Indeed, an important measure of progress in a society is the extent to which cultural riches are shared among the entire population. Figure 2.4 shows an improvement over figure 2.3, as might have been depicted for the Roman Empire or the Renaissance kingdoms and principalities of Europe, not the perfect picture of an advanced culture but significant progress nonetheless.

The twentieth century was a mixed bag as far as progress was concerned. In the wars and other man-made calamities that especially characterized the period between 1914 and 1945, there was a return to tribalism and massive killing of people at all ages. This was topped off by a trail of misery for tens of millions of the survivors. But after 1950 things got better, first gradually, then at an accelerating rate—first in North America; then in Europe and Japan; and, by the turn of the twenty-first century, in the giant population centers of China, India, Eastern Europe, and Russia. Many of these remarkable changes will be discussed as part of the case for progress in the next chapter.

What we have tried to do in this chapter is to show what progress really means in human terms. It is, first of all, the advancement of life, liberty, and the pursuit of happiness. It is not just life but life lived as long as possible. It is not just liberty but the freedom to pursue as many different experience options as the modern world has to offer. It is not just the pursuit of happiness but the chance to have higher and higher levels of happiness in as many ways as are humanly possible, for as many people as possible, within the constraints of the planet. These are the metrics of progress. They are many and they all count.

Chapter Three

THE CASE FOR PROGRESS

Please don't be alarmed, but almost everything about American and
European life is getting better for almost everyone.
— Gregg Easterbrook, *The Progress Paradox*

The human race is the natural outcome of a process. Like all the other forms of life that came before, humans are both an effect and a cause. They are a natural outcome of their surround, and they are also actors upon that surround. This "surround" includes the land, the sea, and the sky, and all the plants, all the animals, and all the microbial life-forms. In the foreground are all the other humans—parents, peers, children, friends, and enemies, fellow members of our country, and all those others not in our country. The human psychological environment also includes whatever ancestors we are aware of in memory, and even the imagined panoply of gods and ghosts who intrude on our dreams. Change and the possibilities of change are inherent in all these things.

Beginning perhaps twenty thousand years ago, humans began to organize themselves into really large groups, tribes of thousands and tens of thousands, able to take command of large territories. As they gathered into these larger groups, they developed capacities to influence the surround in ever more important ways, consuming significant fresh water and plant resources, killing off many large-animal species and exploiting others for their own purposes. Nobody gave much thought to the rightness or wrongness of these changes. It was just the way humanity was headed, toward greater tribal integration, settlement of villages (and later cities), and territorial conquest.

The Industrial Revolution extended human power over nature almost overnight. This was explosive change, clearly caused by man, for the benefit of at least some men, and presumably subject to the will of those who created and benefited. Since that time when Earth became disturbed by a new form of human conquest, a troubling question has been raised again and again: are humans now changing their world for the *better* or for the *worse*? Are the circumstances of humanity better or worse than they were, say, two thousand years ago, when the Romans ruled the Mediterranean with their Pax Romana and when Jesus lived; or twenty-four hundred years ago, when the Greek city-states thrived, when Pericles led the Athenians, built the Parthenon, and gave cover to all those great thinkers? Or was it two hundred fifty years ago when the Founding Fathers of America lived and wrote, when the Enlightenment was the rage, when we learned the great Newtonian laws about how everything worked, and before all those nasty machines started belching black smoke?

It is obvious that the human circumstance has been changing at a fast rate for at least five hundred years. It may have started with the printing press. Perhaps it was the Industrial Revolution. Or was it the invention of science that occurred about the same time? And now, in less than one generation, we have experienced the digital revolution. The inventions, the changes, the exploitation of resources, the consumption of energy, the explosion of knowledge and communication, all these things are coming at us in a bewildering stream, faster and faster.

All this should be cause for worry. We certainly need to know what is happening to us. Are we headed for doom or deliverance or something in between? Should we try to put the brakes on the kind of progress we have had up to now? A lot of people think so. Perhaps a majority of serious thinkers already believe we are on our way to catastrophe unless drastic action is taken. The view offered here will be much less alarmist and much more hopeful, but we can all agree on one thing: we need to better understand what has been happening. Therefore, let us take a step back and have a good, cool look before we surrender to our fears.

THE POPULATION EXPLOSION
AND WHAT IT MEANS

Doom scenarios frequently start with the population explosion. The statistics can look pretty scary. Consider figure 3.1.[1] World population has been rising rapidly for at least three hundred years, but the most remarkable increase, from roughly 1.75 billion to over 6 billion, occurred during the most recent century. It took one thousand five hundred centuries or more to get to where

FIGURE 3.1.
THE ACCELERATION OF
WORLD POPULATION GROWTH

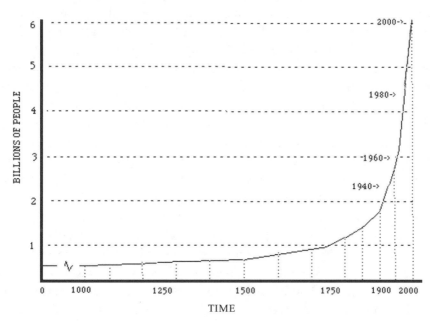

we were in 1900. It has now tripled in just one century. This is a remarkable turn of events for all of us and for our world, by any standard. Considering this fact alone, there is every reason to be alarmed about what is happening to the human race in our time that has not happened in any other time.

In 1798, Cambridge preacher-scholar Thomas R. Malthus in his *Essay on the Principle of Population* proposed that there was an inevitable tendency for human population to advance faster than food supply. Increased population has been perceived by many ever since as an alarming trend. Scientists who pressed this view have often been entomologists, that is, specialists in the study of insects.[2] There may be a reason for this. Population explosions (plagues) among various species of insects have been a proverbial scourge to humanity, not to mention the insects. There is a certain balance in nature such that every species seems to have one or more other species in hot pursuit, thus eliminating the population explosion in a "natural way." Indeed, Malthus also suggested that this was the natural way that human population remained controlled. Disease, starvation, and human-on-human predation would take care of the problem in the long run, he suggested, but it was a dismal prospect, leading to the description of the new science of economics as "the dismal science."

Whereas Malthus lived and wrote in a time long before computer modeling became a popular tool for predicting the future, he should be considered the patron saint of that growing clan of "futurists." When one uses simple mathematical formulas to predict the future of anything important, it can evoke considerable interest, regardless of whether the projection turns out to be right or wrong. Such predictions can sometimes go very wrong, and Malthus was the first, but not the last, to make a doomsday-grim projection that didn't pan out.[3] The most strenuous advocate for population control in our own time has been Stanford University entomologist Paul R. Ehrlich. Starting with his popular 1968 book, *The Population Bomb*,[4] he has continuously sounded alarms about the terrible consequences of uncontrolled population growth. His book, written as a polemic in a popular vein, circulated very widely and made him an academic celebrity for many years.[5] As one after another of his dire predictions failed to materialize, Ehrlich has nevertheless persisted, pushing his doomsday projections just far enough into the near future that they retain scare value while covering the tracks of his previous predictions.[6] Ehrlich and other population alarmists continue to hold a very large audience of believers, and to many in the media and in the public at large it seems like a no-brainer. Uncontrolled population growth is just a bad thing.

When University of Maryland economist Julian Simon[7] started looking at the raw data about the relationship between population growth and relative human prosperity in the last few centuries, he came to a very different conclusion. Looking at a number of indices, he found that human population growth was associated with all kinds of good changes, such as increased per capita income, increased food sufficiency, improved health, and longer life spans. Perhaps the insect was not such a good model for humanity after all. Simon was even so bold as to pronounce that increasing population was a great boon to humankind as a whole, what he dubbed the "ultimate resource." There is no need to embrace Simon's hypothesis that population growth is a *cause* of human advancement, but it is important to note that worldwide food production, of which we will say more later in this chapter, has kept pace and even usually exceeded population growth for all the years since Malthus offered his theory, and there is no trend in the data to indicate that this happy circumstance will change anytime soon.[8]

There are also some puzzling aspects to the population issue that should give us pause. For starters, individual lives are universally valued, once born. Most cultures value human life even from conception. If life is good for me and for my family, then why is it not for you and yours—and, by extension, for everyone else? Life is universally accepted as positive by living humans as applied to themselves, their parents, their children, and their friends. Yet when "life" is described more abstractly as "population growth," it is more often deplored and feared as negating human progress. Simon says they should have no fear because the more of us there are, the better off we are, but it probably isn't quite that simple.

There is another odd twist to the population riddle. As people become more affluent, they tend to want fewer children, even though they can afford to have more. Over the last half century there has been a consistent trend of higher living standards leading to lower fertility rates. This trend applies in all the developed economies of western Europe, the United States, Japan, Australia, and Canada.[9] It now appears to hold also for the demographically challenged subcontinent of India.[10] Presumably for different and less happy reasons, the population of Russia and many of the other states formed out of the former Soviet Union are also experiencing population decline. Where it is rising as a seeming Malthusian juggernaut is in the sub-Saharan African states.

Simon's idea, that population is a resource rather than a drag on progress, may work only in the developed world. Third world increase seems more like a plague. Another entomologist, Edward O. Wilson, suggests that the small, overpopulated, impoverished, and strife-ridden African country of Rwanda is a good model for what we can expect in the future if population is not controlled.[11] Which is the most realistic model of where we are going? Why not pick the equally crowded small country of the Netherlands as the model of the future? Here is a small country with one of the highest densities in the world. Yet their standard of living is among the highest in the world. The Dutch enjoy long lives, a clean environment, low crime, stable democratic political institutions, and many other graces now enjoyed by advanced societies generally.[12] Who is to say that the Netherlands does not offer a better example of what the future holds?

Figure 3.1 seems to show approaching catastrophe, but let us take a closer look. The United Nations report from which the data in figure 3.1 are drawn is not particularly alarmist because it is looking at these raw figures in the context of what else is happening in the world, country by country. Here are some of the other factual items taken from the report summary:

The highest rate of world population growth (2.04 percent) occurred in the late 1960s. The current rate (1995–2000) is 1.31 percent.

In other words, the rate of increase has decreased, if only slightly in recent times.

This is followed by another puzzling item.

Of the 78 million people currently added to the world each year, 95 percent live in the less-developed regions.

So development, per se, is not the culprit after all. In fact, development seems to lead toward population stabilization, albeit at a higher level than some may deem desirable. Clarification of the true state of affairs is given in an accompanying table, reproduced here as table 3.1.[13]

A tremendous amount of information is packed into this table. First, it divides the world into two unequal groups, the "more-developed" and the "less-developed." In the more-developed areas, there is almost no population growth, a finding that clearly breaks the direct link between development and overpopulation. This is not because development has stopped in the more-developed countries. On the contrary, in absolute numbers the more-developed areas are becoming even more developed, meaning more prosperity, longer lives, more leisure time, more of almost everything that can fill a good life.

TABLE 3.1.
CURRENT LEVELS OF POPULATION GROWTH, MORTALITY, FERTILITY & CONTRACEPTIVE USE

	Population size, 1999 (millions)	Population growth rate, 1995–2000 (percent)	Life expectancy at birth 1995–2000 (years)	Total fertility rate, 1995–2000 (average number of children per woman)	Contraceptive use, 1990s (percentage of currently married women)
World	**5,978**	**1.3**	**65**	**2.7**	**58**
More-developed	1,185	0.3	75	1.6	70
Less-developed	4,793	1.6	63	3.0	55
Africa	767	2.4	51	5.1	20
Asia	3,634	1.4	66	2.6	60
Europe	729	0.0	73	1.4	72
Latin America/Caribbean	511	1.6	69	2.7	66
Northern America	307	0.8	77	1.9	71
Oceania	30	1.3	74	2.4	64

From UN Report, The World at Six Billion, table 4, page 11.

The bulk of the world's population is in Asia, where development has advanced considerably in recent years. Life spans have increased markedly and fertility rates have come down. The most troubling numbers come from Africa, by far the least developed region, where life expectancy stands at fifty-one years and probably much lower in the poorest countries. What does this say about development and population? The last column gives a strong hint. Identified here are the technologies of contraception, available only in the twentieth century. For the first time in history, they allowed the fulfillment of sexual urges without procreation. Since their invention and throughout their continuing improvement and refinement, these innovations have diffused rapidly, first throughout Europe and North America and more recently through Latin America and Asia. Innovation diffusion and economic expansion go hand in hand, and the end result is widespread prosperity with stabilized population expansion.

What appeared to be so scary in figure 3.1 is not so scary when we examine table 3.1 and consider its implications. The United Nations report goes on to project future population growth (based on current trends) as leveling off somewhere around the year 2200 at just above 10 billion. This may be a frightening number to many, but it need not be. With the tripling of the world population within the twentieth century we did not see a reduction in life quality or living standards for the majority. All the numbers show that the reverse was actually true by century's end. Furthermore, we have reason to expect that the innovations that made life so much better for most regions during the twentieth century will sweep through all of Africa in the twenty-first century, raising life expectancy and lowering fertility along the way.

There is no simple answer to the question of population growth. Obviously, there is a point at which growth is dysfunctional for one country or another, just as it is dysfunctional for one family or another. The most advanced countries appear to self-limit population growth without coercion, preserving the freedom of individual couples to have the number of children they want. For policymakers, then, the issue should be how to preserve that amount of personal freedom without courting disaster. Their important first step is to *be concerned*. Figure 3.1 is enough for that. The equally important second step is to *understand the problem*—to collect the relevant data and make sure it is accurate, and to analyze that data in relation to other important variables that we care about. Figure 3.1 seems to tell a simple and worrisome story. Table 3.1 takes a lot of the worry away. It shows what happens when we break the story down into elements (as, for example, parts of the world) and relate the raw data to potential causes and consequences (as, for example, levels of development, growth rates, fertility rates, and contraceptive use).

This particular table doesn't tell us everything we want to know, of course. We would like to know if the Chinese coercive pressures to limit family births helped or hindered the explosive growth of the Chinese economy in recent years. We would also like to know how well noncoercive family planning campaigns in India and other countries worked over the same period. We would like to know why the population of sub-Saharan Africa suddenly exploded in the latter half of the twentieth century, after remaining more or less stagnant for thousands of years but without the kind of development and rise in living standards observed in Europe, North America, and elsewhere.[14] These questions weigh heavily upon us and may feed our fears, but the answers are also coming—thanks to better data collection and better analysis—and it is only from these answers, carefully thought through and balanced against other factors, that we can sensibly and nondestructively work our way toward good actions and countermeasures.

The increase in the population of Earth is only one of many dramatic changes that have come about during the last three hundred years, and in the long term it may not be viewed as the most significant.

POSITIVE MEGATRENDS[15]

As the quote from Easterbrook rightly proclaims at the beginning of this chapter, things have been getting better for a lot of people in the world for quite a while now. Just how much better, for whom, and for how long, these are subjects of continuing debate and mass confusion. It is fair to say that most people, even well-educated people, just don't believe it.

(1) Increased Gross Product of Human Activity

The modern economic notion of a "gross product" has proven to be as useful a way as any to summarize and compare the amount of economic activity of one country versus another. The gross domestic product or GDP is comprised of the number and variety of all goods produced in a year in all sectors, agriculture, energy generation, manufacturing, transportation, raw materials, and services. For comparative purposes, GDP divided by population yields a per capita measure. The resulting number is a rough proxy for material well-being. If it is plotted as a trend over a long period of time, the result is something like the following figure, compiled from the work of Angus Madison for the OECD (Organisation for Economic Cooperation and Development) in 2002.[16]

This overall picture does not reflect large regional differences and does not account for enormous individual and group differences in wealth and social circumstances. Nevertheless, the trend holds for even the least developed parts of the world and the poorest classes of people. Supporting this claim, a recent United Nations study reports that average per capita income in the *developing* world almost doubled, from $2,125 to $4,000 in constant dollars, between 1975 and 2000.[17] Such figures signify less hunger, more variety, better shelter, better health, and more and better services—in short, improved lives overall.

(2) The Explosion of Knowledge and Know-how

While the population has increased tenfold since 1700, from an estimated 600 million to 6 billion, our knowledge of the world around us has increased by at

FIGURE 3.2.
WORLD GDP PER CAPITA YEAR ZERO CE TO 1998

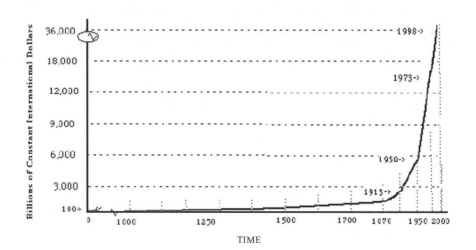

least a hundredfold and probably more like a thousandfold. Moreover, the curve of increase in knowledge is even steeper than the increase in world GDP and is showing no signs of slowing down. This enormous cache of shared knowledge has two large components. One is *scientific knowledge*, meaning verified facts, discoveries, and established fact-supported theories about the phenomena of our environment. This stretches from the farthest galaxies to the smallest particles of matter, to the interaction of matter and energy, to the multiple combinations of chemical compounds, and to the nature, composition, and effects of all kinds of gases and solids. We now collectively know so much that for more than a century it has been impossible for any one person to know everything. There is just too much to know, even though a scientifically literate person can get a good grasp of the essentials.

The related explosion in practical knowledge has been equally astounding and largely accounts for all the other advances listed below. This includes how to fabricate all sorts of materials, how to synthesize chemicals, how to design complex structures like commercial jet airliners, how to kill harmful microbes or render them harmless, how to repair bodily injuries and cure diseases, how to grow food in abundance, and how to distribute all manner of goods and services to millions upon millions of people.

Human know-how has its roots in ancient craft discoveries learned by trial and error and passed on from generation to generation. Only in modern times did the connection between science and technology become apparent. Now we know that each type of knowledge feeds off the other for mutual benefit. New technologies allow us to craft new tools to greatly expand the knowledge base upon which all progress ultimately depends. New science leads to new technology that leads to more new science and more new technology. The net effect of this interaction has been the *acceleration* of knowledge growth in both domains. It is because of this expanding knowledge base that so many favorable trends can be observed at the turn of the twenty-first century. In the balance of this chapter the most important of these trends will be enumerated.

(3) Increased Production of Food

A principle fear of humans since time immemorial has been starvation. Famine was a common scourge of ancient times. Today it occurs only in isolated, underdeveloped areas, usually as a result of persistent use of primitive agricultural methods and tribal land-use patterns, often accompanied by intertribal strife. In contrast, all the densely populated countries of western Europe are now self-sufficient in food production, and many export large percentages of their output. This phenomenon is abundantly clear in the case of the *Netherlands*, one of the most densely populated countries on Earth. The increased quantity and quality of food production worldwide is largely a consequence of the expansion of scientific knowledge and know-how. Everywhere that modern, scientific agricultural methods have been employed extensively, food production soon far outstrips population growth. This is even now true in India and other parts of Southeast Asia where famine was once endemic. So far have we come that Jeffrey D. Sachs was able to assert in 2005,

> The wealth of the rich world, the power of today's vast storehouses of knowledge, and the declining fraction of the world that needs help to escape from poverty all make the end of poverty a realistic possibility by the year 2025.[18]

With increased food production and ever more favorable ratios of production to population has also come a number of problems that environmentalists tend to emphasize. These include deforestation, excessive dependence on pesticides and chemical fertilizers, and the possible but mostly unproved harmful effects of overdependence on "artificial" seeds—including hybrid, genetically altered, and otherwise enhanced varieties. However, agricultural scientists are now working just as successfully to overcome these problems as they have worked on the production issues up to now. The net gain to humanity from advanced agricultural science is enormous and continuing to grow. There is nothing more basic to a positive future than this trend.

(4) Increased Production and Distribution of Energy

To a degree, human progress can be measured in terms of energy expenditure. Our remote hunter-gatherer ancestors had to invest many arduous hours in their quest for game to feed themselves and their families. From the earliest times until the middle of the nineteenth century, the slowly advancing knowledge of farming and the exploitation of animal labor made humans more and more efficient, yet the energy expended was still mostly human with an assist from the horse.

The Industrial Revolution changed all that. By one estimate, by the 1860s the rapidly industrializing economy of the United States had reached a point where the gross output of mechanical energy, generated mostly from coal, began to exceed the biological energy output of both humans and domesticated animals. That trend has escalated over the intervening fourteen decades to the point where today the average individual commands something like two hundred times the mechanical power of his or her laboring ancestor of 1800.[19] That two-hundred-times energy multiplier goes into running vehicles, heating and cooling homes, buying food, running household machinery, building roads and structures, buying medical care, and supplying all the other trappings of contemporary civilized living. That same multiplier will gradually spread to people in other countries and will continue to increase for those already fortunate enough to dwell in western Europe, North America, Japan, and the other most industrialized places on Earth.

There is no question that continued human prosperity is dependent on higher and higher levels of energy consumption. For now and for the next several years, that means petroleum, not because it is the most abundant energy resource but because, for the present, it makes the most economic sense. Coal was the new energy source of the nineteenth century and powered the enormous industrial growth of that era, but when petroleum production began in earnest, its advantages over coal quickly became obvious: it provides more energy for its weight, it's less bulky, and it's cheaper to extract from the ground. In the twentieth century, as the petroleum infrastructure mushroomed from exploration to drilling to transporting to refining and distribution, these natural advantages were compounded and remain to this day. The real reasons that petroleum continues to be the preferred fuel for so much human activity are its convenience relative to wood and coal and its relative cost in a competitive open market for energy. This will not be forever, of course, but the economics of energy supply and demand dictate continued aggressive exploration and extraction for at least another fifty years or until increasing price or other factors make other energy sources more economically sound.

With the enormous increase in petroleum consumption have come two major but somewhat contradictory concerns: (1) that the increased use will pollute the environment in various ways, downgrading the quality of life, and (2) that this same increased use will lead to a rapid diminution of supply, thus starving future growth. Either way, so it is feared, civilization as we know it will surely come to an end. Both concerns are legitimate to an extent. The burning of oil pours particulates and small amounts of gases poisonous to humans into the atmosphere, though not nearly as many as does the burning of coal. This air pollution can cause smog and may also have a cooling effect by increasing low cloud cover and rain over significant areas.[20] The burning of petroleum also produces significant quantities of carbon dioxide, as do fires of any kind and all animal respiration. Pollution of waterways is also intermittently caused by oil spillage from pipes (most notably from the recent BP oil spill in the Gulf of Mexico) but is more common from the huge tanker ships that traverse the oceans in increasing numbers in the race to expand worldwide distribution. In the closing decades of the twentieth century, great strides were made to reduce the particulate discharge of combustion engines and to improve pipeline and tanker security from spillage. This trend continues and grows more effective as the sciences of environmental control become more solid and the public support for environmental regulation gets stronger.

The other great concern, then, is supply. It is widely believed that the world supply of oil is being depleted at a rapidly accelerating rate. There is an intuitive logic to this view. Certainly oil consumption increases enormously as more and more countries industrialize and begin to enjoy the comfort and convenience of private automobile travel and the flexibility and economic advantage of truck versus rail transport for the delivery of goods. It is a substance that comes from deep underground pools unevenly distributed across Earth's surface. No one can yet determine with any degree of certitude how much is really down there, worldwide, but it cannot be infinite. Therefore, simple logic dictates that the more we extract, the less there is remaining.

It is plausible that the supply of oil will run out someday—but what day is it likely to be? As the demand for oil has accelerated over the last century, so has the supply in a jagged up-and-down chase. As of 2009, the *known* oil reserves continue to expand year to year and already exceed the likely demand for some years to come.[21] However, petroleum has some intrinsically undesirable characteristics. Besides being a source of pollution, it is potentially dangerous to handle and is problematic for shipping and storing. Research and development are gradually increasing the efficiencies and reducing the costs of the many potential energy alternatives, such as atomic, hydro, wind, wave, tidal, and solar sources. One or more of these alternatives will eventually become economically competitive and will do to oil what oil did to coal nearly a century ago. Oil will most likely become obsolete and uneconomic for most purposes long before the supply runs out.

(5) Increased Discovery, Transformation, and Use of Raw Materials

One of the truly odd reversals of logic in the tracing of human history is the designation of the Iron Age as an age that was inferior to the Golden Age or the Bronze Age. The extraction and smelting of iron was one of the most sophisticated and important achievements of the ancient world. Throughout ensuing ages, human advancement has been marked by the increased extraction and utilization of raw materials from the earth, from the sea, and from the animal and plant life that surrounds us. This extractive process accelerated greatly in the nineteenth century with the discovery of petroleum, not to mention a host of other new and useful elements and alloys on which our contemporary technology depends (e.g., aluminum, silicon, molybdenum, tungsten, uranium, etc.). We also learned how to separate and recombine oxygen, hydrogen, helium, and a myriad of gases, metals, and compounds to make useful things.

In the twentieth century there was an acceleration of the extraction of all kinds of raw materials to feed an ever-expanding and ever-diversifying manufacturing sector, an acceleration that alarmed many intellectuals who predicted that a world crisis would soon erupt as the limits of material supply were reached. Their concerns were codified and formalized by a group called the Club of Rome in a widely distributed publication entitled *The Limits of Growth*.[22] Building on what appeared to be reliable indicators of current resource supplies the world over and current levels of consumption of these resources, the Club of Rome used the newly acquired capability of computer modeling and simulation to project current trends into the future. In every case they projected dwindling supplies accompanied by a mad scramble to use up what was left, as prices would rise to astronomical heights.

However, none of the Club of Rome projections have even come close to being realized to date. In 1980, economist Julian Simon traced the trends, item by item, over the ensuing years and found that the opposite was true. Supplies of each desired raw material expanded as demand expanded. So convinced was Simon of these trends, seemingly counterintuitive and contrary to Club of Rome projections, that he offered a bet of ten thousand dollars to Paul Ehrlich, a leading proponent of limits, that inflation-adjusted prices of any five commodities Ehrlich would like to name would remain steady over a ten-year period. Ehrlich and colleagues at Stanford took him up on the bet, proposing copper, chrome, nickel, tin, and tungsten. As it turned out, by 1990 the market price of each metal was below what it had been ten years earlier.[23] The same bet could be made now as then for virtually any commodity—from oil to autos to grain to caviar. The downward price trend would also apply to all the important innovations that came on line during the last quarter of the twentieth century, including semiconductors, computers, and all sorts of telecommunications equipment and services so vital to modern economies, not to mention medical progress, safety, and personal comfort.

(6) Increased Worldwide Distribution of Manufactured Goods

Not only have we been able to fabricate an impressive number of new and useful artifacts, but we have also learned how to reproduce virtually any of these items in mass quantities, regardless of their size or complexity. As quantities rise, prices fall, and the bounty they bring in pleasure and utility is enjoyed by more and more people. The process of mass production knows no limits and has continued to advance at an accelerating rate throughout the nineteenth and twentieth centuries. Ever more complex and ever more useful and beneficial products are being brought to market at lower and lower prices, many incorporating the fruits of the latest science and technology.

(7) Increased World Trade

There is much evidence dating back at least to 1000 BCE that early civilizations were greatly enriched by the exchange of goods, sometimes with the traders traveling long distances by land or by sea. The "cities" from which the term *civilization* derives were originally markets and trading centers, gathering places in strategic locations where goods of all kinds were exchanged. Whatever advances occurred in these market places led inevitably to a greater concentration of people in the area, a higher standard of living (at least for some), as well as freed time for more leisurely pursuits. Among the early advances were the invention of the camel and horse caravan, improved roads to support wheeled carriages, and boats with oars and then with sails. The excellence of Roman roads had a lot to do with Roman military advantage, and subsequently the prosperity and the durability of the empire.

With the evolution of larger and larger wooden vessels, with more sophisticated sail rigging allowing sailing to windward, with the compass, and then with the navigational clock in the eighteenth century,[24] worldwide trade became possible on a much larger scale. The invention of the steam engine and its wide-spread use in the nineteenth century on ships and on rails further multiplied this trade volume, lowered shipping costs, and sped up delivery to market.

The great centers of civilization were in every case also the centers of civilized life of their times, as they remain to this day. In the twentieth century, the further expansion of world commerce was again explosive, with much larger ships and air transport for people as well as priority goods. The consistent trend in world trade over several centuries has been more and more, faster and faster, with ever-increasing centralization and ever-increasing wealth accumulation. At the same time, the variety and complexity of trade goods keeps expanding.[25]

(8) Increased World Travel (per person per year: land, sea, air)

It is sobering to consider that a mere four hundred years ago Ferdinand Magellan led the first expedition to circumnavigate the globe, an expedition that took years to complete. Now the same trip can be made in about thirty-six hours for about 10 percent of the average American family annual income. World travel is now commonplace and incredibly inexpensive in historic terms. As carrying capacity and airline technology increase, and as demand and supply both increase, prices per mile traveled continue to fall. The consequences of cheap and rapid travel are many and almost all positive. People become more knowledgeable of other peoples and their places and hence usually more tolerant of their customs and cultures. As they are exposed to the arts, music, architecture, customs, and foods of other cultures of the world, they tend to absorb much of what they have learned for their own great pleasure and life enrichment. The deadly consequences of tribalism wane as people become more and more aware that they live in one world.

(9) Increased Literacy through Wide Distribution of Print Materials

The last five centuries have seen major improvements in the technology of printing and paper production, with consequent increases in distribution as prices drop. Probably the most important consequence of the wider and wider distribution of printed materials was the spread of *literacy*. Even at the dawn of the twentieth century, the great majority of people in the world could neither read nor write. Today the reverse is true, and among the most advanced countries literacy approaches 100 percent. The volume of written material acquired and read by the average person has gone into the thousands of pages, even as alternative media compete for attention. The trend toward greater literacy is continuing the world over, in nearly every country—from the richest to the poorest.[26]

(10) Increased Teleconnectivity through Wired and Wireless Media

Gutenberg invented the printing press in the 1450s, and as this technology and the technology of paper production advanced through the following three centuries, printing greatly increased the diffusion of ideas and technologies through written material that could now be mass produced and widely distributed. By the mid-nineteenth century, the telegraph, invented in the 1830s by Samuel B. Morse, made it possible to transmit coded messages over long distances at essentially the speed of light. Alexander Graham Bell's telephone, invented forty years later, further allowed communication to advance from code to direct voice transmission. Radio, made practical twenty years later, allowed transmission to millions without wires.

During the twentieth century, telephones moved from being a handy luxury for businesses and prosperous individuals to a commonplace of every household in the developed world. Within the last three decades, the facsimile machine has further allowed instant transmission of documents as a standard business practice. Live and recorded moving picture images have now been a commonplace of wireless broadcast for fifty years.

Within the last ten years, millions of people in the developed world have also been linked together through giant computers that add a level of multi-media, multidimensional connectivity undreamed of at the beginning of the century. This interconnective process continues to advance at great speed, doubling the size and power of the meganetwork of humanity yearly or more often. These developments are so sweeping and so profound that no one has yet been able to grasp or even adequately describe their true meaning or consequences for future human life.

To give just one example of the explosive growth of communications in just the first ten years of the twenty-first century, the International Telecommunication Union estimated that mobile cellular subscriptions worldwide would reach approximately 4.1 billion by the end of 2008.[27] In other words, a majority of the entire world's population is now connected through electronic messaging.

(11) *Increased Computational Power*

Probably starting with the invention of money or perhaps much earlier with the growing awareness of the need to count the days before winter came, humans have depended on numbers. The Greeks in particular became number experts and valued mathematics as the most profound area of knowledge.[28] It is thus perhaps somewhat surprising that counting machines came so late in the evolution of technology. Nevertheless, when they came, they came with a rush. Simple adding machines in the late nineteenth century powered merely by spring and finger action were motorized only when electricity became widespread in the early and middle twentieth century. IBM's "business machines" of the 1930s and 1940s were essentially elaborate adding machines supported by punched cards and mechanical sorters. Government-subsidized research projects created the first true vacuum tube computers, using such devices as rotating storage drums in the 1950s. Early uses were for the military and for the constitutionally mandated US census. Private sector demand was largely from insurance companies. The first machines with a few cells of random access core storage were delivered to the Massachusetts Institute of Technology by IBM in the early 1960s and were used primarily for research.

The rapid evolution of semiconductor technology and printed circuits in the later 1960s, spurred on greatly by the computational demands of the space program, expanded computational power tremendously. Power doubled yearly as price per operation dropped to the vanishing point. As these words are written, they are recorded on a laptop computer that dwarfs the power of the IBM 7090 delivered to the Massachusetts Institute of Technology at a true cost of many millions of dollars back in the early 1960s, a mere generation and a half ago. These computer advances have greatly reduced the cost of all commercial activity and have affected virtually every manufacturing sector, bringing costs down while quality goes up. The use of computers for word processing and for assisting design have transformed writing, publishing, and all types of engineering, increasing the accuracy and speed of every transaction.

Cell phone technology has also merged with computer storage technology to provide hundreds of millions of people access not only to each other but also to an enormous and ever-expanding knowledge base including much of the world's stored writing, photographs, and moving pictures. This capability is still too young for us to realize what its potential might be for changing our lives in the long run, but undoubtedly it will be great. Text messaging alone will increase literacy and language facility. Networking will be faster and more extensive, covering more content and providing instant visual, audio, and text access to the entire base of human knowledge, anywhere, anytime. The price of such access drops continuously as the quality of the media and the message vault forward.

(12) Increased Infant Survival Rate

Public health officers worldwide always use infant mortality as an important indicator of overall national health. Here is one index that has dropped year by year throughout the twentieth century. In the United States in 1915 there were one hundred infant deaths for every one thousand deliveries. By 2000 there were just seven.[29] It is a product mostly of improved sanitation, improved nutrition, and other simple steps that are themselves signs of the improved conditions of our times. This trend is the chief factor in producing the worldwide population explosion that the modern Malthusians are so worried about, yet few would deny that this is a very positive development.

(13) Increased Average Life Span

A less dramatic indicator, but one that affects all families, is the increase in average life span by about twenty years in the last century. This is a variable item, affected by wars, famines, epidemics, and "ethnic cleansings." Considering these and various other devastations that have characterized the twentieth century, the increased life span becomes a more remarkable statistic, making us more appreciative of the medical advances of the century as well as the reductions in the most serious forms of environmental pollution: typhoid fever, typhus, malaria, tuberculosis, diphtheria, small pox, and influenza, to name just a few of the major culprits we have now left mostly behind us.

(14) Increased World Standard of Living

Standard of living is a relatively new term in economics that is applied mostly to people in the developed world. The assumption is made that life itself is a given (even though a very big given), but that there is something beyond mere living about which we should be concerned. A higher standard of living means more than the minimum: more food, a more commodious home with more reliable heat and light, fewer roof leaks, maybe even some air conditioning in hot climates. It means adequate clothing for all family members and no worries about paying for doctors and medicines. It also means school for all the children from age five to age eighteen and childcare if mother works outside the home. These are all things that are increasingly becoming standard items in developed countries not only for the privileged person but also for the average person.

Such a notion might have seemed nearly crazy to most people in the 1930s, but it was commonplace by the 1990s. While all this is true for the most developed countries, like the United States, it has also been true to a lesser degree in almost all countries.[30] Whereas we have experienced an abundance of food, the people of the poorer countries have experienced a relief from famine. Where we have expanded our living spaces, they have at least created for themselves more adequate living spaces. Where we have provided twelve years of education for all, they have been able to provide some education and rudimentary literacy for almost all. Where we have been able to provide adequate healthcare for most, they have been able to provide improved sanitation and immunization from some major, killer diseases. All these changes are twentieth-century phenomena. They all owe something to advances in science and technology as well as to advances in a world economic-political system that is slowly taking responsibility for those most in need.

(15) Increased World Quality of Living

Whereas *standard of living* is a relatively new term, *quality of life* is an even newer term, signifying something more than standard of living. *Quality* implies a scale for all the basic items of living, a scale from *minimal* to *adequate* to *better than adequate* to *really good* to *excellent.* We can tell the difference between a meal that is nourishing and filling and one that really tastes good and one that is a memorable culinary experience. So it is with all the items of living, including shelter, clothing, education, health services, and so on. These can all be adequate, good, or excellent. When we add to the list the nonessential and discretionary extras of life experience, such as artistic expression and enjoyment, other types of self-expression, and all manner of "entertainment," we are expanding the idea of what a life means well beyond what is connoted by the term *standard of living.* Yet as regards all these terms, life has been getting better and better during this century, even to the point where we are beginning to redefine upwardly what life is and what it should be.

(16) Increasing Ecological Consciousness

Everything humans do to advance their condition inevitably changes the world in which they live to some extent. If what is "natural" is defined as the world before humans made an imprint, then humans, as they progress, make the world ever more unnatural; and for some, such change is perceived as mostly unwelcome. A common theme running through biblical and other religious traditions is that humans originally lived in a state of nature that was entirely benign, where work was unnecessary and life was forever pleasant. In the Judeo-Christian tradition, this was the Garden of Eden. For the influential early Greek poet Hesiod, it was the "Golden Age." During the Enlightenment of the eighteenth century, this naturalist idea was reinvoked by Jean-Jacques Rousseau (1712–1778). In his *Discourse on the Origin of Inequality*, he proposed that the modern civilization of his time was a condition of total human degradation in contrast to the primitive human existence of the distant past in which people lived the perfect, simple life.[31] Some of Rousseau's ideas were influential in both the American Revolution and the French Revolution, and they are reflected in Thomas Jefferson's idea of a benign democratic society based on pastoral agrarianism.

In our own times, the idea of a completely benign natural state persists and is reflected in the very popular environmental movement. Implicitly and sometimes explicitly environmentalists deplore the human footprint as if the world would be better off without us. As conventional and traditional religions have lost their force in many developed countries, they have been replaced by a fervent belief that the environment itself is sacred. This idea takes its most explicit intellectual form as Gaiaism,[32] the view that Earth itself is a kind of organic whole that needs to be preserved as it is through all future time and without human interference.[33]

While early industrialization in England and elsewhere generally increased living standards, it did so in a very uneven and disruptive manner. The countryside seemed to be suddenly littered in every direction with belching smokestacks, while noisy and dangerous engines roared down newly laid iron rails. For many observers of that nineteenth-century world, Rousseau's admonitions had increasing resonance, and back-to-nature movements multiplied. For the most part, this back-and-forth argument between naturalists and industrialists had a positive impact. The industrialists made important concessions to the naturalists through an evolving political process in which large parks were established and large tracts of land surrounding urban areas were set aside as greenbelt parkland open to the public. Very large areas of nationally owned land were excluded from development and commercial exploitation, and even some of the exploiters used their great wealth philanthropically to make significant contributions to the nature set-asides.[34]

In the early part of the twentieth century, concern for the environment took a back seat as attention turned to the devastation of wars and the crumbling system of colonialism worldwide. However, one of the great political movements of the second half of the twentieth century was environmentalism. It is not entirely clear that the stimulus for this movement had anything to do with science or the progress of science. Rather it was and remains driven largely by Rousseau-style romanticization of nature and by fear of the potential negative effects of the applications of science in the diffusion and utilization of new technologies. Nevertheless, it now took the form of science battling industrial society rather than merely abetting it. Human impacts in the form of smoke or fertilizer or pesticide or working conditions were now measured more carefully, using statistics and a variety of new scientific tools.

These new environmental sciences also spawned new technologies intended to ameliorate or eliminate whatever negative consequences might result from the human exploitation of nature. What has emerged is a new conception of human progress in which further advances in the quality of individual lives are made within an accounting of their environmental impacts as well as their impacts on other humans. In this formulation, science and technology are not the enemies of the environment but rather the watchdogs and guardians of its protection. What may be emerging is a type of research and development process that moves society toward a new kind of progress-embracing "ecosystem."

These sixteen examples of manifest advancement should be more than enough to drive home the point that life for humanity as a whole is getting better and better, largely because of advances in technology which are, in turn, due mostly to advances in science and the scientific underpinnings of technology.[35]

Some Negative Trends

Alongside the examples of accelerating progress listed above, there are some things that don't fit the rosy picture. All is not right with our world. As high as we can list the good things that are happening and that have happened over the last fifty years, there remain mountains of problems confronting the human race. Some millions in Africa are still near starvation. Millions in Asia and Africa suffer from malaria and the AIDS epidemic. The air and the water in many places are thick with pollution, much of it caused by human carelessness. If some things really are getting worse, are human efforts of any avail? Such questions should be faced head-on.

The items that are currently attracting the most concern are global warming, air pollution, water pollution, crowding, and increased production and diffusion of weapons of mass destruction. These are not matters to be taken lightly, and they will not be dismissed out of hand. Rather, the main point here is to suggest that they be viewed rationally and calmly, first with an eye to establishing the empirical fact base and then to considering what countermeasures are appropriate and on what time scale should they be implemented to ensure their amelioration or elimination. In chapter 11 we will take up these concerns one by one and try to provide answers.

What we should not do is be guided by panic. Panic leads to precipitous policy which usually also means poorly thought-out policy. That sort of policy will typically lead to many unforeseen consequences and can lead to disaster. Quite often those most concerned about an issue insist on action now, as in, "Don't just stand there, do something!" If it is a true emergency situation, such as if we see someone drowning or running out into a busy street, that is good guidance. Most times, however, when the problem is complex in both its causes and its possible solutions, it is not such good advice. When we don't truly understand what the real problem is or to what degree it is harmful or to what degree it is urgent, the rational first step is to survey the scene to try to get a preliminary fix on what is really going on. The next step is to consider what actions might be appropriate, following the Hippocratic dictum of *primum non nocere*, above all do no harm. For any problem area that is really complex and in which the immediate situation is not life threatening, the wisest course of action is to investigate further, to collect more data and try to connect the dots, carefully weighing the action alternatives before deciding which action is best to take and when.

Of all the worries that cloud our future, the greatest should probably be the stability of the world social order. Here, again, the role of science and technology is critical and ambivalent. As a result of advancing science and technology, humans have had weapons of mass destruction at their disposal for over one hundred years. It began with the machine gun. Then there was the high-explosive shell, then poison gas, and then aerial bombardment with incendiary shells. Just sixty-five years ago the first atomic weapons were used for explicit military effect. Since that time there has been a lot of research, development, and production of nuclear weapons; and the number of nations possessing the expertise to produce them has proliferated alarmingly and inevitably. Nevertheless, it has been sixty-five years and counting since that one use, and there still has been no other instance. The same applies to chemical and biological weapons, with minor exceptions.

Used or not, these terrible weapons are all products of modern technology. Sadly, our social technologies have lagged far behind. We don't know how to create a truly safe, secure, and mutually beneficial system for world governance to prevent the use of all or any of these weapons. However, some answers to our greatest fears are beginning to emerge. The world "system" is stronger than it has ever been. World trade is more robust. World-circling travel is ubiquitous, and world communications and information distribution is at a revolutionary breakout point. These are positive trends of great importance that should ultimately make our world safer.

We can and should address all these concerns in a rational and deliberate way, looking first at the data, then considering what actions, if any, should be planned. The actions, when taken, should be designed as experiments with measurable outcomes. They should be taken on as carefully conceived and planned world projects, executed on a reasonable time scale to deal effectively with the problem while maintaining and enhancing the general prosperity of the people of Earth.

SUMMARY AND CONCLUSION

The case for human progress has become stronger and stronger during the latter half of the twentieth century. Sixteen important changes for the better are put forward to make the case. There has been a tremendous surge in human innovation and productivity that has resulted from an explosion of knowledge. The impressive results of this surge have been manifested in increased food production and in increased production and distribution of energy, raw materials, and useful manufactured goods. These changes have been accompanied by increased world trade and worldwide travel, very wide distribution of print materials, and wildly increased connectivity coupled with escalating computational power. We have become, in short, one big world brain. At the same time, we have experienced great gains in health worldwide, with increased infant survival rate, significantly stretched average life span, and a great reduction in disease. The result of all these favorable changes is a real improvement in the per capita world standard of living and quality of life. Along with other positive changes, the late twentieth century saw the birth of the environmental movement, with important steps taken to safeguard and preserve the natural surround and to redress the worst side effects of nineteenth- and twentieth-century industrialization, thus further enhancing the quality of life for all. Taken together, all these changes add up to an extraordinary leap forward for humankind. As we move forward into the next century, it is important for all of us to recognize and appreciate this important fact.

The ways in which such signs of progress interact with each other and with population growth are complex and controversial. Many examples can be cited in which population growth has been part and parcel of progress, but the specter of explosive population growth continues to evoke alarm. This is cause enough for concern but not for panic. The human story is changing fast, and the population dynamic is integral to that story in ways both good and bad. To the very positive account of human progress laid out in this chapter there are many counterarguments. Besides population growth, many other scary scenarios are sincerely believed by well-meaning people. Some advocate drastic and immediate action. Their concerns and arguments for a darker future must be taken seriously, and they will be taken up and responded to in a later chapter. Nevertheless, if we look at the total picture, it should be clear that the circumstances of humanity have taken a sharp turn, not for the worse, but for the better—especially over the last sixty years. This is not just a matter of good luck. There are certain forces inherent in the course of human development that are causing these changes. These forces are animal learning, learning externalization, social connection, knowledge platforming, scientific problem solving, and modern global diffusion. Together they form a set to which the forward function best applies. Each of these six forces will be described in turn through the next six chapters.

PART TWO

THE SIX FORCES

The true and lawful end of the sciences is that human life be enriched by new discoveries and powers.
—Francis Bacon, *The Advancement of Learning*

L ife itself is a phenomenon that is still not completely understood. Its most primitive forms have left traces on rocks that go back nearly to the beginning of Earth, four or more billions of years ago.[1] Life appears to be a process of chemical transformation in which small amounts of energy are expended in a slow chain reaction, constructing and then disassembling and reassembling complex molecules. This mysterious process is continuous and expansive, as each collection divides and doubles itself over and over again. Over the ages, many kinds of life-forms diverged from common ancestors. Some successful variants expanded to cover large parts of Earth, leaving their dead remnants and residues to pile up in layers thousands of feet thick. Through mutation and natural selection, some life-forms gradually cohered into larger and more complex systems of living matter until, at some unknown point, there emerged a special variant type that could retain, as reusable memory, some of the experience it gained within its individual life cycle.

We know that crucial evolutionary step as *learning*. It is an attribute of all animal life, from the lowly worm to Albert Einstein. The learning capacity of many lines has been expanding for millions of years, giving successful species greater and greater power to manipulate the environment for their survival and for the perpetuation of their line. One class of mammals, the primates, eventually emerged as the animals with the largest brain size in proportion to weight, and it is fairly certain that our human ancestors belonged to this group. For many hundreds of thousands of years, the pattern of human existence was not much different from that of our cousin primates; but over a period of perhaps four million years, the human brain got larger and larger, far outpacing our cousin primates. We don't yet know why this happened, nor why it happened so fast—and we may never know—but the consequence was a learning and storage capacity for experience that far exceeded that of any other species.

This is where our story begins. After the emergence of the big brain, the evolving nature of the human experience can best be understood as a convergence of six forces. *Homo sapiens* emerged with a huge advantage over other species because it could learn from experience in greater detail; merge different memories; differentiate more sights, sounds, smells, and tastes; grasp and accurately hurl or shape more objects to serve his purposes; and articulate more complicated sounds. The absolutely necessary first step in the making of the modern human was this great capacity to learn.

The next step, externalizing learning, did not begin to happen until a human or a very humanlike ancestor had been walking the earth for perhaps 2.5 million years.[2] This new capacity to externalize is perhaps the least understood and the least appreciated aspect of human evolution. We think of ourselves as actors in continuous motion, but some of our most important supports as civilized beings come from the static and inert residues of our past handiwork and that of our many ancestors long dead. The wonders of our present world would not exist without this enormous backlog of externalized memory tracings.

As humans began to externalize learning, perhaps earlier or perhaps later, they also began to develop and use language to solidify social connections and to share accumulated external learning across generations. Social organization, like learning, is not unique to humans, but in humans it has been developed to a degree of complexity beyond what can be observed in other species. Language is the principal means by which the elaboration of social connections is achieved. Both language and social connection can also be seen as aspects of externalization or vehicles to advance externalization, since what is learned by a particular individual from a particular experience in one generation can be passed on through language and imitation to subsequent generations ad infinitum.

From an accumulation of externalized and socially exchanged lessons within tribes, elaborate knowledge platforms began to be built, formalizing and integrating what had been learned, externalized, and passed on. We can only speculate as to what the earliest knowledge platforms were like. No doubt they contained stories of exploits in hunting and in warfare against enemy tribes, together with admonitions and speculations as to what the world was really like and what controlled human destiny. As tribes fought and as larger kingdoms and empires were established, the winners determined which knowledge platforms would hold sway, but, as often as not, winners would adapt and adopt elements from the losers' platforms as they were perceived to be useful or potent. For the better part of the last four thousand years, a few giant religion-based knowledge platforms have competed with one another for dominance in different parts of the world, sometimes in open conflict, other times in semipeaceful coexistence. Each asserted its preeminence as the one true religion while borrowing extensively from the others.

The invention of science just three hundred years ago changed the shape of the age-old competition for truth. Science was a new way to solidify and validate acquired knowledge. Thus it now became possible for humanity to have a single secure and integrated knowledge platform. As science has begun to prove its value and its superiority over folk knowledge from all the older platforms as a basis for problem solving, it is gradually displacing the older platforms as a guide to action in all spheres of human conduct.

Along with the rise of science have come many new modes of social interaction that have accelerated both the accumulation and the spread of knowledge and its blessings. Soon thereafter, new modes of mass production and new media of communication allowed for the diffusion of the fruits of science to every corner of the globe and to every level of society. Modern diffusion started with the printing press and the mass production of paper, but in the nineteenth century, the telegraph and the telephone advanced communication to the speed of transmission on electric wires. The twentieth century brought radio, television, and, most recently, the Internet—with its many modes of instant-message packaging and delivery. The spread of important information from a single source to a billion or more receivers can now be achieved in a matter of seconds.

It should be obvious that each of these changes represents a giant step forward for humanity. As new forces of science and diffusion have emerged, the old forces of learning, externalization, social connection, and platform building have remained as the base. Thus the learning process continues to be fundamental. Externalizing learning is also fundamental and occurs every time something is made with the hands or written down or photographed and/or recorded. The social connective process also continues to play a crucial role in all forms of progress, becoming ever more complex, multilayered, and extensive. Tribal, cultural, and religion-based knowledge platforms continue to compete, sometimes in deadly combat, even while the platform of science gets larger and stronger. The process of science itself also continues to change and grow. New information collection and analysis processes are invented continuously so that the science of today is far advanced beyond the science of even fifty years ago. Diffusion similarly expands and transforms itself as new media are added to the mix, the latest being the ubiquitous cell phone and its world-integrating partner, the Internet.

The forward function of today is far from being the perfect engine of human progress, but it is the best we have been able to do so far, and it will get better. No doubt, more forces will be added beyond these six, but they will emerge from these six just as science and diffusion emerged from learning and social connection. In its present form, the forward function advances human welfare at a variable rate, sometimes seeming to stall or unravel, as when we engage in wars or bring other calamities upon ourselves. Ultimately, however, the forward function is unstoppable and will continue on into the far future as long as humanity as a whole survives.

Here, then, in six separate chapters are explanations of the six forces: how they came into being, what they do, how they build on one another, and how they contribute to progress.

Chapter Four

ANIMAL LEARNING
Forward Function Force #1

It is not accidental that all phenomena of human life are dominated by the search for daily bread—the oldest link connecting all living things, man included, with the surrounding nature.
　　　　—Ivan Pavlov, pioneering Russian psychologist, 1849–1936

Man's power to change himself, that is, to learn, is perhaps the most impressive thing about him.
　　　　—Edward L. Thorndike, pioneering American psychologist,
　　　　　　　　　　　　　　　　　　　　　　　　　　1874–1949

Progress can be explained in large part simply as *learning*, which just means adding more and more new behaviors and experiences to an existing intelligent being, making him or her more skillful, more adaptable, more able to function within Earth's environment. Yet how we learn is not so simple. Experimental psychologists have been studying the basic principles of learning for over one hundred years. They are still not quite sure how it works, but they have learned a great deal about the basic principles of how all animals, including humans, learn.

WHAT IS LEARNING AND
HOW DOES IT COME ABOUT?

Even though we do not yet have a good idea about how life began on Earth, we know a lot about how living things work. Every living thing has certain features in common with every other living thing. We are all composed of millions of molecules, many of them extremely complex, containing thousands of atoms arranged together in semipermanent structures. If all these structures have a "purpose" it appears to be to maintain a kind of energy chain

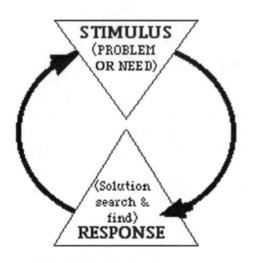

FIGURE 4.1.
THE CONTINUOUS
S-R CYCLE
THAT SUSTAINS LIFE

reaction at a low level. To achieve this chain reaction, these complex structures are organized together in such a way that they are continuously taking new elements in, processing them into their internal structure, and then expelling the unwanted remnants.

Living systems thus exist in what might be called a dynamic equilibrium, always coming apart and coming back together again; restoring the stability, then losing it, then restoring it again in a cycle that is nearly endless. Despite its inherent complexity, the essence of this process can be depicted as a simple interactive pattern between two poles, as suggested by figure 4.1.

The destabilizing event is the "stimulus" (S), and the stability-restoring event is the "response" (R). Whatever constitutes a threat to the survival of the organism is a stimulus because it requires a response if life is to go on. For any complex organism, this cycle repeats itself continuously in every cell, in every tissue of the body, and in the organism as a whole. The same repeating cycle is observable in the manifest behavior of all animals. Cellular life requires a continuous input of food and water. The stimuli that we experience as thirst and hunger are signals sent up to the brain through neural pathways from the cells of the body. Through another set of neural pathways the brain responds, and the response that is most observable from the outside is action in search of that food or water.

Almost all these billions of S-R loops are *automatic*, meaning that they are governed by a code that is locked inside the DNA protein molecule. No thought is involved. The stimulus demands the response, and if it doesn't

FIGURE 4.2.
THE RUDIMENTARY
LEARNING PROCESS

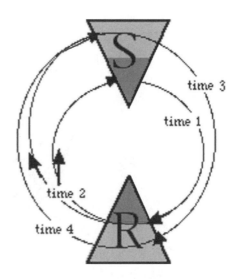

happen, life eventually stops. Even at the level of the manifest behavior of complex organisms like mammals, most responses are automatic in this way. The behavior is built into the organism and it will repeat itself in exactly the same way every time that stimulus appears.

Somewhere along the evolutionary path, something happened to change that automatic pattern. It was probably an error to begin with, as most if not all evolutionary changes start out being. A normal stimulus triggered an unusual response, or, one might say, an "error." If, by chance, this aberrant response turned out to be more satisfactory than the normal response in various situations and more reliably life-sustaining, it would eventually replace the original "normal" response and survive as a piece of the altered genetic material. This is how heredity works. The DNA can be thought of as a long sequence of errors that turned out to work better. But that is not what happened in this instance because the organism giving the erroneous response managed at the same time to retain the original response as part of its repertoire. So there were now two response possibilities. If the stimulus then varied slightly, the response might now come in two alternative ways: (a) in its original form or (b) in the newly acquired variant. Over repeated trials the animal would build up a memory of which response worked best in which situation. That is the rudimentary model for the wonderful process we call *learning*. It is partially depicted in figure 4.2.

At "time 1," the normal preprogrammed S-R cycle (indicated by the

FIGURE 4.3.
EXPANDING STIMULUS AWARENESS
AND DIVERSIFYING RESPONSE IN THE
ANIMAL LEARNING PROCESS

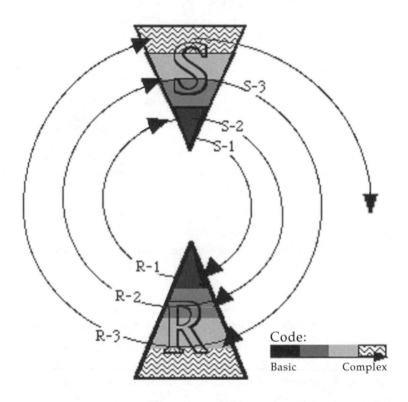

darker shade) is initiated. At "time 2," a new "erroneous" response is triggered. At "time 3," a new S-R cycle is initiated from a slightly more complex stimulus (suggested by a lighter shade), having been altered by the erroneous response. At "time 4," the new response is reinforced by successful repetition, now dropping into the animal's "habitual" response repertoire. Learning represented a revolutionary step in evolution because it allowed for change and variation *within an individual lifetime.* In effect, the animal could become smarter and smarter throughout its life, depending on the number of varied stimuli it was exposed to and its ability to generate more and more of these "erroneous" responses. Figure 4.3 is drawn to suggest this elaboration and diversification of responses.

In the early days of the twentieth century, psychologists began to focus on the learning process in animals. Behaviors were measured in precise, observable quantities, and conditions and interventions were varied in systematic ways. Both procedures and results were then reported in meticulous detail so that they could be replicated[1] by other investigators. By midcentury there was a substantial knowledge platform on the topic of learning, a set of coherent theories supported by thousands of research studies conducted on many different types of animals, including humans in many different situations. The core findings of learning research remain as valid today as they were fifty years ago.

All organisms, including bacteria, plants, and fungi, are equipped with a set of automatic responses inherited over hundreds of millions of years of evolutionary development. Yet from the moment of birth, animals, as distinct from other life-forms, are able to move beyond this fixed set of inherited behaviors. As they are exposed to various stimuli and conditions, they make incremental additions to their inherited behavioral inventory. They do this through two or three types of processes. Pavlov used dogs to demonstrate what could be called S-S-R learning. An automatic inherited stimulus-response connection is extended by pairing the stimulus with another stimulus previously inert to the given response. For the dogs, the originating S-R was food (S) and salivation (R). The introduced stimulus was a bell ring. After a certain number of pairings of the bell with the food, the bell alone elicited the response. Anyone with a dog has probably observed the same type of effect in uncontrolled conditions. Pavlov went on to demonstrate that the bell itself, once established as a potent secondary stimulus, could be paired with a third stimulus and then a fourth. Thus more and more complex chains of association could be built up.

Other psychologists soon went beyond Pavlov's paradigm, paying closer attention to the *response*. In simplest terms this could be called R-S learning. Responses could be shaped in various ways by altering the stimulus and its presentation. What counted was the stimulus that came *after* the response, in the form of a reward. Change the presentation of the reward, altering its frequency and its difficulty of attainment, and the behavior changes accordingly. The most prominent and prolific theorist-researcher of this school was B. F. Skinner, who believed that all behavior (including advanced forms of human speech and "thought") were ultimately explainable in terms of these simple principles. Virtually all animal training today is based on Skinner's methods.

Many psychologists have objected to Pavlov and Skinner's reductionism and have offered alternative theories to explain human learning as distinct from animal conditioning.[2] These critics note that humans are capable of learning much more at much faster rates than any animal. Humans also seem to have more sophisticated strategies of learning, comprehending *patterns*. Psychologists promoting this view adopted the German word *Gestalt* (meaning "form" or "configuration") to identify their work as distinct from individual stimuli. Many theories of learning lay greater emphasis on presumed human mental qualities, such as "insight" and "imagination." Nevertheless, the most persistently convincing evidence stems from Pavlovian and Skinnerian roots. Experimental evidence to support claims for alternative theories is mixed at best.

Suffice it to say that, whether in small increments or in larger jumps, humans learn and learn throughout life, a process that stops only at death. It may not always seem that way, but it is a fact that as we get older, we also get incrementally wiser simply because of this animal learning process that we inherited from our ancestors and will possess until we die.

It is also true that we lose a lot of what we have learned along the way. Memories of what was learned long ago tend to fade or are contaminated or obliterated by new learning. Therefore, the net gain from each episode of new learning may become smaller and smaller with age. It should also be kept in mind that animal learning is a nearly random process. It is entirely the result of proximity and association in time and place. If two things occur one after the other, the brain connects them and preserves that connection in memory. Animals and people are all victims to their widely varying immediate environments and the particular stimuli they are exposed to at specific moments in time. What is learned is largely conditioned by the particulars of that immediate environment, and environments may be radically variable and unstable for some, while monotonously stable and redundant for others. Furthermore, what is learned in this automatic animal way may not fit into any coherent larger design. Such new "learning" may sometimes even be dysfunctional and self-defeating.

BRAIN CAPACITY

It undoubtedly helps that we all have large brains and a lot of neurons to work with. The most obvious change that occurs as we move up the phylogenetic ladder is brain size, both in absolute numbers of neurons and the ratio of neurons to body size. In that sense, larger is smarter. However, within a species it is more difficult to attribute individual differences to brain size alone. All humans have nearly identical brains in the strictly physiological sense, and the capacity for learning is nearly the same for all of us. Yet clearly there are enormous individual differences in the amount people learn, the eagerness to learn new things, the capacity to remember what is learned, and the capacity to use what has been learned and to transfer that learning to new situations.

HOW LONG IS THE LEARNING LOOP?

Apart from sheer brain size and number of neurons, humans differ from other animals in the number of steps that can be sustained in a learning loop. Pavlov first paired the bell with the food to get the salivation response from his dogs. He then paired the bell with a light, and then the light with another noise, and so on, to see how far the stimulus could be stretched to still achieve a response. In his long and productive experimental career, Skinner likewise stretched out the schedules and patterns of reinforcements to see how far and in what directions behavior could be modified. They both found that there was a limit beyond which animals could not go in extending the connections between stimulus and response.

However, in humans there seems to be nearly no limit to the extension of a response loop. Some humans will persevere (responding) in pursuit of a single goal (the stimulus) for hours, days, years, and even lifetimes. It is often said that the ability to postpone gratification is a sign of maturity. Some of the greatest social rewards provided by any society go to those who have shown the greatest ability to postpone gratification and to sustain extraordinarily long and complicated arcs of learning. Learning to read and write certainly belongs in this category. Then consider the trials involved in becoming a physician. For a doctor, gratification as performance in the desired role comes only after twenty-two years of arduous study and apprenticeship.

It is reasonable to assume that such individual differences in learning ability were just as prominent among our ancient ancestors. Every tribe probably needed to have a few hunters who were especially clever at tracking and killing game or fending off and killing invaders. Their offspring were undoubtedly cherished above all others. Thus, through selective breeding, these learning skills were passed on through the favored DNA. Nevertheless, all the knowledge and skill of the great hunters would die with them if it were not for some other very important factors that will be discussed in the next two chapters.

THE ENORMOUS GAP IN UNDERSTANDING OUR HERITAGE

It is too bad that the story of how humans acquired such an enormous learning capacity must end here. The fact is that our evolutionary roots are a nearly total mystery, and we are left to speculate and argue endlessly about what might have happened to us along the way to bring us to our present civilized state. There are at least five sources of evidence: social anthropology, physical anthropology, DNA analysis, inferences from ancient writings, and artifactual remnants.

Social anthropology is the study of human cultures with a special emphasis on isolated groups that have been shielded in one way or another from modern influences, particularly those stemming from the Industrial Revolution and the socio-intellectual traditions that dominate modern culture. Such studies have an intrinsic fascination and add enormously to our understanding of humanity in all its variants. They can also provide some suggestive clues as to our origins, but these clues are only suggestive. Isolated cultures show a strangely exotic mixture of customs, beliefs, mores, and rituals. Each tribe seems to have its own language, partly conditioned to its unique environmental circumstances (e.g., the number of words for *snow* in Eskimo tongues). Some are more warlike than most modern cultures, some less so. Some appear to exalt the status of women and children while others do not. This great variety is better explained by special environmental circumstances than by hereditary differences. What may be most remarkable is how much these isolated cultures are like the rest of us. They are nearly identical to us in a physical sense. Their brains are the same size and they seem to learn the same way. They eat more or less the same kinds of foods. They organize themselves into groups in much the same way. They all use tools. They nearly all fight and use weapons in hunting and fighting. They all have fairly elaborate belief systems involving a combination of dead ancestors and gods and cosmologies that explain the earth and the sky and the origins of animals and humans. It therefore seems doubtful that they are the missing links to our evolutionary past.

In some respects, social anthropological clues may lead down the wrong track. The so-called primitives, aboriginals, and isolated tribal groups that are the favorites of study may be the last people we should be looking at for evidence of our own remote past for the mere fact that they are isolates, outriders on the human ladder of advancement, people who have made very special adjustments to special and often especially difficult environments (dense jungles, deserts, arctic wastelands, remote islands, etc.). The lives and circumstances of our ancestors who were on the main track toward what we now call *civilization* are almost completely unknown to us prior to about seven thousand years ago.

Physical anthropology is the study of how humans evolved as a species from a common ancestor among the great apes. There is no longer much mystery about evolution in gross terms. We know how eyes, ears, legs, arms, and other manifest physical characteristics evolved. We can see from careful anatomical observation that humans are similar to other primates, and all primates are similar in physiology to all other mammals, down to the lowly mouse. Yet the gap between the great apes and modern man in intellectual power, brain size, and learning capacity seems to be enormous.[3] The gap is so great that it would seemingly take another several million years of evolution to explain it. How did it happen so fast? It had to have happened within only a few hundred thousand years, a mere twinkle in life's multibillion-year climb. And how did it happen from such a small population base of humanlike animals? The fossil record is shockingly flimsy, a jaw bone here, the piece of a skull there, no signs of massive kill-offs, few signs of intermediate forms, no signs that humans expanded into great numbers or even lived in anything like high-density concentrations until perhaps six thousand years ago.

MYSTERIES OF LANGUAGE ACQUISITION

Above all, what all the humans on Earth share is language. Every known human tribe has a way of expressing itself in special noises made by the mouth, larynx, and windpipe (with an assist from the nose), all made comprehensible through complex structures in the ears. These organs seem to be especially adapted to this purpose, suggesting that there is a strong genetic basis for speech that is matched by a specialized sensing apparatus in the ears and also possibly in the eyes. There is something oddly anomalous about this gift of speech from an evolutionary point of view, however, and it involves the learning process. Whereas the capacity for language is almost certainly dictated by our DNA, language is universally observed to be a *learned* phenomenon. Babies are not born with words rolling around in their heads. Even the ability to form all the complex sounds involved in any language do not fully develop until the second year of life.

From the little we can glean from studies of early language development in twins and children with nonspeaking parents, it appears that they all develop an ability to speak, even if the language is partially invented. It is also universally observed that all hearing children brought up in normal environments have a working vocabulary by age two and are more or less fluent in their parents' language by age four.

IMITATION

Primates all seem to have a gift for imitation, observing complex behaviors of others and copying them into their own behavioral repertoire. However, humans appear to be far more adept at imitation than their primate cousins. This is a skill that is retained throughout life but may be most pronounced and most vital in the first years, partially accounting for rapid language acquisition. It is also a process that goes well beyond Pavlovian or Skinnerian learning in its speed of acquisition and its complexity.

EVOLUTIONARY GUESSING GAMES

Language acquisition is not the only important puzzle left buried in our most recent evolutionary past. It is widely speculated that something happened among the prehuman population to greatly accelerate the evolutionary process. An obvious possibility is selective breeding. We have plenty of models for this in our domesticated animal populations. Dogs, cats, cows, pigs, chickens, turkeys, horses, corn, wheat, other varieties of grain—all these and many more animal and plant varieties are essentially human genetic inventions. These human-manipulated species are barely recognizable in their Darwin-derived ancestors. We also see this in the rapid evolution of bacterial strains that sometimes run ahead of the antibacterial efforts of modern medicine.

Humans clearly also have the ability to breed *themselves* selectively. A powerful tribe leader could presumably take any wife he liked and favor any child he wanted. Thus if there were a long succession of powerful leaders with particular wants and particularly brutal inclinations, they could have shaped the DNA of their offspring in significant ways after just a few generations. In lieu of any real evidence for what happened, we are left to speculate on what might have happened. The topic is intriguing because there is so much that is not explained. Language acquisition is perhaps the most important of these mysteries. However, more speculation has centered on how this rapid evolution shaped the human psyche or mind as distinct from the physical size and structure of the brain itself. How did we come to have the beliefs and inclinations that we have? Why have we been nearly constantly engaged in warfare? Why is there a nearly universal taboo on incest? Why is there a widespread taboo on nudity? Why is there a nearly universal belief in gods, in an afterlife, and/or in the power of dead parents and ancestors to influence our lives? Are these all residues of several thousand years of brutal gene shaping, or was the process more benign, shaped by evolutionary mechanisms that we still don't understand at all? It would be nice to know the real story. Perhaps we will never know, but as we progress, we keep on finding new ways to examine our past. As a result we now know more about our origins than we did even a decade ago, and we will continue to know more and more about our past as we advance into the future.

DNA ANALYSIS

The salient question as it pertains to this chapter is how much of the all-important human "mind" is actually controlled by our DNA versus controlled by ad hoc learning from the physical and social environment. Clearly the specific content is learned. Whether you believe in Jesus or Mohammed or some other god idea depends entirely on what you are taught by those around you. Soldiers fight because they learn how to fight and because they learn to obey their leaders. Children learn to speak and to read and write in a particular language because they are taught that language and no other. None of these specifics that characterize particular human minds comes directly from the DNA. What then must come from the DNA of modern humans is the capacity to be shaped in almost endless ways by the social and environmental influences they are exposed to from birth. In theory, if we understood our DNA completely, we could unravel the nature-nurture conundrum once and for all. Whatever traits and behavioral elements can be traced directly to DNA are inherited, and that is that.

We are not remotely close to making such a determination. However, even with what we know now, the DNA of modern humans tells its own special story. It is a new kind of story that is far more complex and much longer than any we can derive from studying cultures or history or even from comparing ancient skull fragments and stone tools. The human genome has now been "mapped," showing up with a surprisingly small number of genes (about thirty thousand) strung out on a human DNA molecule of about three billion base pairs.[4] We can see the pattern of these pairs even if we don't know what they mean.[5] In fact, the pattern could be observed long before the genome was mapped in the year 2000, and knowing the pattern has proved to be extremely useful in a number of ways. Every human, it turns out, has a *unique* pattern, far more discriminating than, let us say, the fingerprint. Moreover, since this pattern is contained in every human cell, alive or dead, including hair and sloughed-off skin cells, it is very useful in crime detection. It is also useful in tracing our past back to very remote ancestors. We know to a certainty, for example, that we have common ancestry with the great apes because we have so many genes in common—even though that common ancestor existed something like 6 million years ago.

But what about other humans? If every human has a unique DNA print, what can be said about individual differences and where they came from? Most individual differences are explained by environment and learning, but many are not, and these must be in the DNA. Evolution can be thought of as the accumulation of billions of mistakes that worked. DNA molecules are fairly robust in the sense that they can carry life in one form for thousands of generations without any significant change. However, despite this robustness, DNA is changing all the time, primarily because Earth and all its inhabitants are being bombarded constantly by cosmic rays that can break up molecules and reorder them in a more or less random fashion. Every such hit may be a catastrophe for a particular strand of DNA. It may render a particular offspring unviable, but even if it doesn't, it is a "mistake" from the point of view of species purity. However, the mistakes are generally so randomly spread out and the number of species individuals so large that they have little effect.

Nevertheless, the bombardment is constantly changing our DNA, and mistakes get passed on in a cumulative fashion. Not only does this make people different from one another genetically, but it also makes for a unique "history" for every human tribe. This is how we know nearly for certain that we are all descended from people who once lived in Africa. We can also trace the ancestry of the various tribes that migrated out of Africa to Asia, to Europe, to the South Asian archipelago, to Australia, and even to the remote islands of the Pacific. We also know that humans crossed the land bridge from far eastern Asia to North America during the last ice age, and over the next few thousand years came down through the Americas even to the southern-most tip. All this happened in the mere span of about forty thousand years, and the cumulating mistakes in the DNA tell the whole story. As we learn to decipher more and more of these mistakes, we will be able to get a better picture of where and when our ancestors migrated from one place to another and probably how they mixed across races to form our currently diverse genomes.[6] It is important to know all this, and it gives some clues as to what we were actually doing, but it does not tell much about how we lived and what we learned along the way. For that we need to examine another trail of evidence.

INFERENCES FROM ANCIENT TEXTS

True believers of most of the world's religions have no doubts about where we came from: God or various gods created us. For evolutionary scientists, such explanations are no longer very satisfactory, but some thinkers have specu-lated on our origins from examination and interpretation of ancient texts. Most noteworthy among these was Sigmund Freud, who devoted two major works to such efforts, trying to show that the unconscious roots of the modern personality descend from prehistoric events and cultural patterns that were translated into myths, repeated orally from generation to generation, ending up in various scraps of scripture after writing was invented.[7] There are several difficulties with this kind of speculation. First, for evidence it depends on materials that were created long after most of the supposed formative events happened. Written records cover no more than two hundred and fifty out of the approximately five thousand generations since humans started migrating out of Africa. Add to that perhaps as much as twenty generations for scraps of oral history to pass down in some form through memorized recitations, and we are still not very far along into our known past existence as fully formed humans. Furthermore, there are few consistent details across the many different ancient cultures of which we know, if we include the Aboriginal Australians, the North and South American native populations, the East Asian cultures, the Germanic tribes, even the Greeks and their contemporaneous Hebrews, Egyptians, and Persians. All the differences and similarities among these cultures are interesting and informative on various grounds, but they shed little light on the formative events of human nature.

ARTIFACTUAL REMAINS

As humans traversed the ages, they have left behind material traces, but not nearly as much as would tell us how they lived and what they learned. We have a scant fossil record, but we do have many items of stone that show a purposeful human impact. Some of our ancestors made tools. By inference we also know that they made boats because of the extent of travel indicated by the DNA migration across fairly extensive bodies of water. Stone tools are not easy to make. Chipping rock to make sharp edges takes skill and practice as well as know-how, and it can be assumed that along with stone tools, humans were able to fabricate various kinds of wooden tools that, as organic remnants, left no trace after hundreds of years of exposure to the elements.

We leave this important subject of artifactual remains here and return to it in the next chapter, where its enormous significance will be considered in detail. As far as learning is concerned, the fact of tool making shows a human ability to learn and to problem solve that goes beyond that of any other animal.[8] Very early humans used tools, perhaps even before they had much language capacity. Tool making suggests an extended learning cycle, the postponement of action until a tool could be fashioned, grasped in the hand, and then employed in the pursuance of the ultimate goal. Gratification had to be postponed until these intermediate tool-making, tool-preparing, and tool-using steps had been taken.

LEARNING ERRORS

Most of what animals learn is good for them. The red berry satisfies hunger and it tastes good. The green berry looks similar but tastes sour. So the animal learns to choose red berries over green. But nature plays nasty tricks and along comes a red berry that tastes bad or, worse, that actually poisons the picker. An individual animal now stuck in a patch of red berries may be in deep trouble just because of a past lesson learned. Learning is a long sequence of stored associations that the animal interprets as cause-and-effect relationships. If *A* happens and *B* happens right after *A*, then *A* must cause *B*. Much of the time this works. *A* really does cause *B*. But often it doesn't. There is frequently no real connection between *A* and *B*, even though they seem to be paired. The environment of living things is filled with random events, but the learning process takes no account of randomness. If *B* follows *A*, then *B* gets associated with *A* in the brain. As a result, the brain fills up with a lot of "learning" that is erroneous and is therefore potentially dysfunctional for survival.

There is a process that clears mistaken associations that the behavioral psychologists call *extinction*. It is similar to learning, but the extinction process is slower than learning and is less reliable. Bad habits are hard to get rid of. What gets learned earliest tends to hold on longest. It also takes a lot of experience to make the fine distinctions between genuine and random associations, true and false clues. This is why older means wiser much of the time. Older people have just had more time to experience their environment, more exposure to more diverse stimuli, and more time to observe what really connects to what. One of the hereditary advantages of humans over all other mammals is a longer average life span. This means more time for learning to take place, more items learned, and better discrimination between real and false associations.

THE IMPORTANCE OF INNOVATORS AND OTHER SPECIAL ROLES

In the parable of *Groundhog Day*, it was only Phil who learned from day to day while everyone else acted exactly as they had the previous day. So it is in everyday life that some will extract new learnings from a given experience while others will respond to the same experience in exactly the same way they responded to previous similar experiences, without learning much of anything. They fail to observe the special details that make the new experience different from the prior experience. Progress therefore depends heavily on the number of people who fall into the category of acute learners, fast learners, discriminatory learners, and skilled appliers of learning. Human progress depends on a special category of acute learners who could be called *innovators*, people who are capable of inventing new behaviors that have superior outcomes, which, in turn, can be copied by others. Undoubtedly in prehistoric times, thousands of such innovators lived in one tribe or another, leaving their progressive impact on emerging cultures in increments of which we now have little trace.

The special role of innovator was a necessary but insufficient cause of progress in prehistoric and ancient times. By their very nature, innovators defy preexisting common practice. Overcoming resistance to change was therefore another prerequisite for the survival of any progressive innovation. Diffusion to, and acceptance by, others was required and could happen in many ways. It could come through cross-generation copying, father to son, mother to daughter. It could also happen through acceptance and promotion by powerful tribal leaders, or perhaps by the manifest advantage of the innovation itself. Without wide acceptance, however, innovations would not pass on to others but would disappear with the death of the innovator. More will be said in the following two chapters about how innovations survive beyond the life of the innovator.

LEARNING DIES WITH THE LEARNER

Human beings are undoubtedly the best learners on the planet. They have the largest brains and can sustain the longest and most complex problem-solving loops. Furthermore, as they age and gain more and more experience, the total amount that they know gets greater and greater. There are also periods of development, built into the DNA, in which learning is extremely rapid, boosted in unknown ways by poorly understood but built-in mechanisms. All individual humans who live into adulthood therefore get wiser and more skilled as they get older up to a point, and certain types of learning keep going on until death, accumulating inside the skull of the learner. Yet all this learning, by itself, cannot explain progress over time and over generations because all this learning is lost when the learner dies—unless other things also happen.

It may well be that humans experienced no progress at all over the first several thousand years of their existence. From time to time there may have been great innovative learners, people who learned all kinds of skills, who saw associations quickly, and who were able to develop very long learning cycles.

Some of these great ones may also have been fortunate enough to live into relatively old age, but when they died, all their skill and wisdom died with them. Something more than learning was needed to move humanity up the ladder, and it had to be something that outlasted any lifetime. In the next three chapters we will propose what these other preservative forces were.

Chapter Five

EXTERNALIZING LEARNING
Forward Function Force # 2

Scene A-11

A small warthog ambles past the group of browsing humanoids without giving them more than a glance, for they had never been the slightest danger to its species. But that happy state of affairs is about to end. The big male suddenly bends down, picks up a heavy stone lying at his feet—and hurls it upon the unfortunate pig. The stone descends upon its skull, making exactly the same noise that Moonwatcher had produced in his now almost forgotten encounter with Big-Tooth. And the result, too, is much the same—the warthog gives one amazed, indignant squeal and collapses in a motionless heap.

Then the whole sequence begins again, but this time it unfolds itself with incredible slowness. Every detail of the movement can be followed; the stone arches leisurely through the air, the pig crumples up and sinks to the ground. There the scene freezes for long moments, the slayer standing motionless above the slain, the first of all weapons in his hand.

Scene A-14

One-Ear merely looks up at the raised club until the heavy thigh bone of an antelope brings the darkness down around him. The Others stare in wonder at Moonwatcher's power. Moonwatcher surveys the scene. Now he was master of the world, and he was not sure what to do next. But he would think of something.
        —Excerpts from screenplay of *2001: A SPACE ODYSSEY*[1]

The wonderful brain is at the center of animal life. It receives all the messages from the senses and commands all the actions taken in response to those messages. More than that, it stores what it senses and what it does for future reference. In humans this storage capacity is enormous but still finite, and as we have noted in the previous chapter, its entire contents are destroyed upon death. The learned stimulus and the learned response lie there inside the brain waiting for later use, less permanent than the stimulus-response patterns that are laid down in the genes, but, unlike the genes, expandable up to the brain's storage capacity. The human brain is by far the largest of all animal brains in proportion to body size and thereby probably has a much greater capacity to store learned elements than any other animal brain. This greater brain capacity is just one aspect of forward functioning, however. Just as important as larger brain size is the capacity to store knowledge *outside* the brain.

Some higher animals besides humans have this capacity to a very limited degree. Adult birds and mammals are certainly able to model hunting and fishing behaviors for their young, although it is hard to draw the line between the genetic inheritance and what is truly learned. In humans, however, the teaching-learning relationship is far more developed and intricate and far less dependent on patterns laid down in the genes. Humans transfer what they know by both *show* and *tell*. Humans can show other humans what they have learned by demonstration, and they can also tell others what they have learned through symbolic language.

HOW IT WORKS

The most rudimentary form of external memory is just a marker, a reminder to the brain that a particular kind of stimulus requires a particular kind of response. If an early human picked up a stone to break open a coconut and then left the stone in a particular place, the stone itself could become a marker for its next use. The next time there is a coconut to open, the sight of the stone signals what should be done: pick up the stone and smash it into the hard shell. The rock has now entered the problem-solving chain. It is not only a tool, crude as it may be, but also a visual and tactile symbol for the act of cracking, a necessary step on the way to using the coconut as food. Thus, this external

FIGURE 5.1.
AN EXTERNAL ITEM ENTERS
THE PROBLEM-SOLVING CYCLE

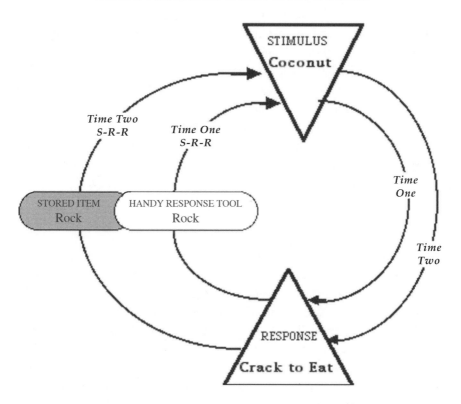

item has become an integral element in the problem-solving cycle, substituting for a small element that otherwise would have been held in memory.

Figure 5.1 suggests how this works. At "time one," the person is engaged in learning, advancing from basic to complex learning by means of experience and memory. However, every time a successful response is made, the person puts out an external marker representing what the response was. In the simple case of the coconut cracker, the marker was the stone. There it is, sitting where it was before, waiting for the next coconut. The next time the individual feels a need for coconut, he sees the stone and grasps it, immediately then looking for another coconut. This stone is now an external stimulus for the whole cycle of coconut cracking. It has become a very simple but nonetheless real tool.

TOOL USING

Ancient humans were probably tool users in this sense for hundreds of thousands of years.[2] They made use of various items in their environment, stones, sticks, shells, and animal bones and hides, all to assist in problem solving. They undoubtedly gathered these items around themselves, safeguarded for future use. Such crude artifacts had instrumental value of an immediate sort, but they also had symbolic value as jogs to memory about how to do various things. This first phase of tool collecting and using would have left no archeological trace that would be easy to follow, but for early modern humans they represented a kind of progress toward more sophisticated types of problem solving that would not depend so exclusively on remembered learning.

TOOL MAKING

The next big step was the shaping and modifying of these simple tools first to better suit their original purpose and then to serve new purposes. A straight stick could be shaped at one end to a sharp point that could then be used for killing game. Bones and rocks could be shaped for various types of cutting, stabbing, and scraping, as well as cracking and crushing. All these new artifacts, though seemingly obvious and simple to us today, probably did not come along very rapidly. Close examination of ancient shaped stone arrowheads indicates that their fabrication required considerable skill not only in shaping the stone but also in selecting the appropriate types of stone for the task.

These more and more elaborately fashioned artifacts are the first evidence we have from archeology of how our earliest toolmaking ancestors lived their lives. They tell us that they hunted various game and that they had certain skills that must have been passed from generation to generation. There were undoubtedly many more artifacts that did not survive to our time because of natural decay. These would include articles of clothing, wooden tools, wooden structures, rafts, and primitive boats. We know they also had the very important tool of fire from a very early time.

These modified tools would have told their own story to other humans long after their creators had passed on because the know-how is implicit in the object. If one picks up an arrowhead left by another, its potential use is quickly evident, so the finder can begin to use it in a hunt as soon as it can be affixed

FIGURE 5.2.
EXTERNALIZING MULTIPLE LEARNINGS

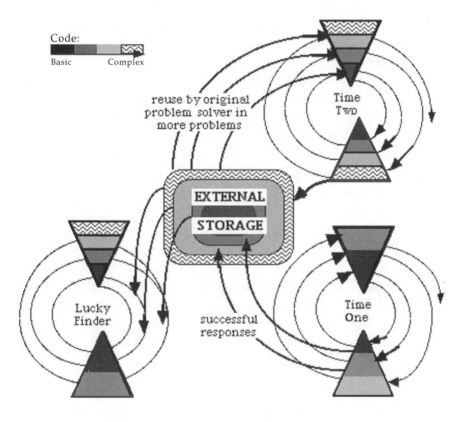

to a new arrow shaft. The finder does not need to know how it was made to find good use for it. Yet the arrowhead also contains essential information about how it was made. It came from a particular kind of stone, perhaps similar to rocks that the finder has noticed in his immediate environment. The fact that the arrowhead exists in this shape also indicates that another stone can be shaped similarly with a little effort and skill.

Thus it may come to be that the finder can fairly quickly replicate the process of arrowhead making without ever knowing the original maker. The knowledge of both use and fabrication are inherent in the object!

Figure 5.2 diagrams this process of externalized knowledge building, starting from the simple process of figure 5.1. Externalized knowledge storing builds on itself just as learning does. A crude tool can undergo many refinements until it is far more useful. It may eventually acquire multiple uses and acquire new significance to its users along the way. Thus by drawing on the external source, the problem solver at "time two" can make a jump into a more complex and differentiated set of learnings suggested by the progressively lighter-shaded areas of the figure.

On the lower left there is another problem solver who is not socially connected to the first. He is the "lucky finder" who stumbles upon the stored artifact (e.g., a well-shaped arrowhead, an empty hut, an unused boat, or a discarded clay pot). The utility of these objects is clearly indicated in their fabrication, and much about their manufacture is also indicated. The lucky finder has skipped many steps of arduous learning, making a great leap forward in problem-solving ability.

The external storing of learning can take place without direct human-to-human contact if that learning can be embodied in an artifact. This was the case for the lucky finder in figure 5.2. By merely discovering the artifact, this finder could move to a much more sophisticated level of problem solving. It is an important point in explaining the continuity of knowledge building over the ages. The story of ancient civilization is saturated with the violence of intertribal warfare. The object of the victors was most often the total destruction of the vanquished. There was little, if any, social interaction remaining. However, the artifacts of the vanquished would have largely remained, including tools, hooks, weapons, pottery, clothing, and huts. Some of these items would have represented something new to the victors, something worth adopting into their own lives and their own modes of problem solving. Thus, even though lives and much of the culture of the defeated is lost, significant elements of progress remain and are passed on to the victors.

BEHAVIORAL MODELING
AS A MEANS OF EXTERNAL STORAGE

While external storage in artifacts is a universal attribute of humans and expands problem-solving capacity enormously, it has some severe limitations. Again from figure 5.2, compare the circumstance of the originator of the stored item at "time two" with that of the lucky finder. When the originator reuses the stone ax or other stored item, he knows exactly what it has been used for before. The lucky finder can only make a guess. The originator further knows more or less exactly how the item was made because he made it. The lucky finder can look over the item and do some mental reverse engineering, guessing how it was made and how he might replicate that effort, but he will not know exactly how that particular artifact was made just by looking at it, feeling it, and using it. The process of rediscovery that must take place before there is a complete transfer of this highly useful technology may take hours, days, or years, depending on the complexity of the artifact.

If, on the other hand, the second user has a chance to observe the first in the acts of manufacture and use, then the entire process of transfer becomes simple and rapid, and the transfer is precise. There is no guessing involved and no chance of error. This is what modeling is all about: observing another in an act of problem solving, with the end result that the observer can then replicate the act with precision. This is also a situation of storing learning outside the body, in this case not in an artifact but in the body and mind of another person.

Modeling takes place in many other animal species to a certain extent, so it is not a uniquely human attribute. Humans seem to be unique, however, when it comes to their expansive ability to use modeling. They can observe long sequences of behavior, hold them in memory, and then act them out with uncanny accuracy. This is enormously significant for cultural progress because it allows what has been learned by individuals in one generation to be passed on to the next generation and the next, and so on. The inventive skills learned by a person of one generation become the commonplace adjuncts to problem solving of the next. The inventors in that next generation, as they make modifications and refinements, build on learnings of those long dead, and their progeny have the same advantage over them. By such a process, succeeding generations appear to become more "intelligent," better problem solvers, without any change whatsoever in their genetic makeup.

ANCIENT LANGUAGE AS A STORAGE MECHANISM

Animals have communication systems that are sometimes impressively sophisticated, but they neither invent them nor teach them to others.
—Edward O. Wilson, *Consilience: The Unity of Knowledge*

The transfer of more complex information, ideas, and concepts from one individual to another, or to a group, was the single most advantageous evolutionary adaptation for species preservation.

—Donald Ryan[3]

We know very little about how language evolved or even what its purpose was in the very beginning, but its purpose must have been very important because language capacity is so firmly lodged in our DNA today.[4] If it was that important, it must have had strong survival value. Some individuals could talk better and listen better, and those were the ones who survived.

For language to work, each sound had to be associated repeatedly with an object, an action, or an event until the mere sound could evoke recall of the particular associated item, just as the bell caused Pavlov's dogs to salivate. For language to become a useful adjunct to human problem solving, such associations had to be repeated over and over again for hundreds of sounds, and the associated sounds had to be easy to articulate and had to be consistently applied over and over again throughout the tribe.

Language thus emerged as another very important type of knowledge transfer; but for a long time, perhaps thousands of years, it must have been an awkward and fragile storage medium. Word noises are easily confused, and the sequence of words can be difficult to remember. If the father wanted to explain to the son how to make a spear and hunt with it, he would have to engage in a series of show-and-tell exercises that would be composed of a lot more show than tell. Holding the spear, he would use hand gestures along with verbal symbols to explain how it was shaped and tipped, and then he would use more gestures with words to indicate the act of throwing. The artifact is still center stage while the words flow around it.

The words come into their own when the objects and actions can no longer be conveniently displayed, when the hunter returns to tell the tale of the hunt, or when he recounts episodes of past hunts, triumphs, and tragedies. These stories, important remnants of cultural knowledge that need to be passed on from generation to generation, are extremely prone to distortion and error in the retelling. Furthermore, as memories of real events mix with remembered dreams, accuracy falls off further, even though entertainment value is enhanced.

THE POEM AS A MEDIUM
FOR KNOWLEDGE TRANSFER

Entertainment value is not to be dismissed lightly. The difficulty of preserving cultural memories in language depends partly on sustaining the motivation to remember words in sequence on the part of the listener. Twice-told tales may have been the first entertainments of our distant ancestors, perhaps embellished by props of sticks and rocks. These long stories preserved word pictures of the past as both experienced and imagined. Memorization was aided by repetition of key phrases and by casting the word strings in a semi-fixed formula of recitation. These stories gradually evolved into the epic poem. Memory was also aided by setting the verses in musical form, probably the origin of music. This oral heritage allowed the storage and transfer of remembered events long after their occurrence. However, it was an unstable and inaccurate medium because, as with the DNA, mistakes were inevitable in the passage from one reciter to the next. Things that happened would gradually be merged with things that were merely imagined or perhaps dreamed. Feats of past heroes would be merged or reattributed to others.

PICTURES AS A STORAGE MEDIUM

The earliest-known pictures created by humans are cave paintings in northern Italy that date to about thirty-six thousand years ago. Although these were crude pictures of barely recognizable humans and animals,[5] their significance is enormous from a memory storage point of view. A painting is a symbolic physical product of a human observing, composing, and rendering. The fact that we can now observe this thirty-six-thousand-year-old relic and even derive a trace of its representational meaning is truly an example of stored knowledge, transferred directly to us over that thirty-six-thousand-year chasm. If we discover one such remnant in one known human habitation, it is reasonable to assume that there were many more. From some of these ancient cave paintings we get pictures of hunting scenes that might have had a functional didactic purpose in addition to glorification of past victories. Most obvious, a pictorial or statue rendering of an important person could have special significance as a totem of that person and a symbol of his or her importance. It would be a notification and reminder of the existence and power of that person whenever he was absent and, ultimately, after he was dead. Such human-form artifacts would have had important social purposes, as will be further discussed in the next chapter.

WRITTEN LANGUAGE AS THE ULTIMATE STORAGE SOLUTION

Abraham Lincoln, one of the great self-taught intellects, once said as follows:

> *Writing*—the art of communicating thoughts to the mind, through the eye— is the great invention of the world. Great in the astonishing range of analysis and combination which necessarily underlies the most crude and general conception of it—great, very great in enabling us to converse with the dead, the absent, and the unborn, at all distances of time and space; and great, not only in its direct benefits, but greatest help, to all other inventions. . . . Its utility may be conceived, by the reflection, that to *it* we owe everything which distinguishes us from savages. Take it from us, and the Bible, all history, all science, all government, all commerce, and nearly all social intercourse go with it.[6]

The first writings were probably just pictures in a row, scenes that tell a story that the creator wanted to have memorialized. In addition to storytelling, the ancients had a need to keep track of ancestors in written as well as oral form. Thus some of the earliest "writings" are genealogies, lists of important ancestors going back several generations. However, the current consensus among archeologists is that early language was associated with early agriculture. Permanent settlements appear for the first time in the Fertile Crescent about ten thousand years ago, based on the cultivation and harvesting of grasses in that region. With permanent settlement it became important to keep records of such items as land boundaries, grain storage, the counting of days, and the number of members of a tribe among whom the grain harvest could be divided. What we find, dating from about nine thousand years ago, are "counting tokens," small tablets on which are inscribed marks suggesting a numerical accounting process.[7] This is probably the precursor to writing because it is the first indication of a purely symbolic system of representation other than speech.

The first samples we find of what appears to be a recorded formulation of spoken language comes several thousand years later in the same general region. This "writing" began as a series of pictures, which gradually evolved into "pictographs" or stylized picture elements strung together and inscribed in brick or clay tablets. Pictographic representation was highly developed in Egypt by about 4000 BCE, but what happened soon after in Mesopotamia proved to be much more important for the development of writing. The cuneiform script, which also had pictographic roots, evolved into a set of abstract symbols that probably represented consonant speech sounds. The lineage of the subsequent scripts of Hebrew and Phoenician probably derived not from cuneiform but from a Semitic language spoken in the northern part of the Fertile Crescent some time before 1000 BCE. Greek script added letters to the alphabet for vowel sounds, creating for the first time a written language that corresponded, sound for sound, with the spoken language of oral culture.[8]

A great architect or sculptor or painter can leave a permanent, nearly immortal but wordless imprint on humanity, and this heritage is treasured by all as a mark of advancing civilization. However, the significance of written language as a forward step for the storage of knowledge cannot be exaggerated. Whatever a person experiences in a lifetime, no matter how extraordinary his or her exploits, no matter how wise he or she becomes, no matter how important his or her discoveries, all these great things die with the individual if there is no written record—or at least so it was until the very recent discoveries of audio and video recording. With the beginning of writing, humanity now for the first time had the capacity for endless accumulation of retrievable and reusable material from the experiences of other humans, regardless of when they lived. All the creative insights and discoveries from the wisest people of the post-writing past then became accessible in the present and in the future as long as we survive on the planet.

DYSFUNCTIONAL AND FALSE LEARNING PASSED ON

Unfortunately, not everything that gets passed down to following generations by poetic recitation or by writing is true or helpful. Just as errors are passed on in the genes, so are they passed on in the cultural inheritance. Scribes on whom the accuracy of ancient texts depended for the better part of two thousand years made few mistakes, but the precise origins of sacred texts are often obscure. Thus, inadvertently, names and places are sometimes confused or merged, while sayings are attributed to people who never said them and acts to people who never performed them.

Knowledge stored as artifact always had a reality test. It worked or it didn't, regardless of who made it. The hut withstood the weather or it didn't. The boat floated or it didn't. The spear with the shaped stone point killed or it didn't. There was no such reality check for a string of words. Indeed, the more fantastic the story, the more interesting it was and hence the easier to remember. Yet transcribed word strings from the time of their invention onward have cast a mysterious spell over humanity and have preserved cultural rituals and beliefs nearly intact for thousands of years. Holy texts—despite their manifest inaccuracies, their deviations from their sources, their fabrications, and their errors—form the bedrock of all major religions, the platforms on which belief systems, cosmologies, customs, rituals, laws, family life, and worldviews are based. The fact that there are many such holy texts supporting many different religions and cultures is a source of endless strife throughout the world. It is an irony that this greatest achievement of humanity, the invention of writing, has also been the source of such enormous delusional thinking, human suffering, and multiple failures in human problem solving.

THE DESTRUCTION OF STORED KNOWLEDGE

Considering the potency and potential falsity of the written word as passed on through the ages, it is not too surprising that humans have from time to time gone to great lengths in attempts to destroy or severely censor the writings of the past. The further back in time we go toward the invention of writing, the more successful these attempts probably were. In its early stages, writing was undoubtedly a rare skill, and writing materials scarce and fragile. The Greek city-states of the sixth and fifth centuries BCE were known to produce prolific writings. Numerous observations and ideas on all manner of subjects (from mathematics to astronomy, history, the arts, medicine, politics, morality, and even religion) espoused by the great thinkers of that time were duly recorded and thus preserved for later generations. Taken together, these writings represented the first really rich compendium of "knowledge" as distinct from the epic poems and sacred tribal texts passed down from the oral era. Yet very little of this rich outpouring of written material has actually carried down to our time. Why?

One reason may be the fire that destroyed the great library of Alexandria some six hundred years later. It is also possible that many writings were destroyed deliberately by people who thought that such writings were dangerous. In numerous writings, for example, Plato rails against assorted others who were professing ideas that were antagonistic to his own. That so much of Plato survives and so little from his enemies does is a suspicious fact that might be attributable to deliberate suppression by Plato's followers, who became dominant in Athens and then throughout the ancient world as Alexander—Aristotle's most illustrious pupil—and his successors established their empire.

Book burning has been a habit of many religions down even to our present day, and we should also take note of the notorious efforts of Adolf Hitler to destroy certain writings and cultural artifacts during his brief reign of terror. However, after the printing press was invented and print materials were widely disseminated, total suppression of any writings became a virtual impossibility.

Throughout the nineteenth and twentieth centuries, many new means became available for the external storage of knowledge. Photographic recording of images began in the 1840s. Voice recordings began in the 1880s. Motion-picture recordings became possible before the turn of the century. All these innovations evolved steadily throughout the twentieth century, becoming vastly more refined and accurate as prices per unit tumbled. The digital revolution of the late twentieth and early twenty-first centuries now allows the recording of all human output, including the permanent and accurate preservation of pictures and facsimiles of all retrieved human artifacts back to the earliest crude stone tools. This is a great human triumph from which all future generations will benefit enormously.

All these records of human creative output exist outside the minds of their creators. They are as inanimate as fossils. Yet they are the very bedrock of civilized life. Generation upon generation, we depend on this inanimate residue, the traces of our creative ancestors, externally preserved remnants of what went on inside their brains. They speak to us, loud and clear, as if their creators were still standing next to us.

SUMMARY

Humans differ from other species in having the unique ability to pass on what they have learned in one lifetime to later generations and to other peoples who might benefit. They can do this both intentionally and inadvertently. The earliest evidence of this transfer ability comes from the stone tools, many samples of which have been found dating back many thousands of years. Such tools tell their own story, providing visible and tactile evidence of both their manufacture and their purpose. Tool making may have been the first medium of transfer, but it was undoubtedly accompanied by behavioral modeling from one generation to the next.

The most important of all transfer skills was the acquisition of language, a trait universal to humans that appears to be learned but that has a strong hereditary propensity. The origin of language is still a matter of speculation and may always be so, but the consequences are clear. With language, the contents of one brain could be spilled over into another and another, ensuring the preservation of much that was learned or invented by particular individuals.

Language and tool making go back many tens of thousands of years, but only within the last three thousand have humans learned to write, thus preserving in exact form what once had to be memorized and was often distorted or forgotten. The externalization and hence the preservation of all human knowledge then became a possibility.

Chapter Six

SOCIAL CONNECTIONS
Forward Function Force #3

When several villages are united in a single complete community, large enough to be nearly or quite self-sufficing, the state comes into existence, originating in the bare needs of life, and continuing in existence for the sake of a good life.

—Aristotle, *Politics*

Man is a social animal. Without society he is nothing but animal. Yet many consider themselves "self-made."

—B. J. Gupta, *Philosophy of Life*

A baby's presence exerts a consistent and persistent domination over the outer and inner lives of every member of a household. Because these members must reorient themselves to accommodate his (or her) presence, they must also grow as individuals and as a group.

—Eric H. Erikson[1]

The human is a social being to a greater extent than any other animal species. This is an obvious truism, but it is worth considering some of the specifics as they relate to the creation and advancement of culture. Today we are all linked in a vast network on which billions of sounds, pictures, words, and ideas connect billions of people to one another all around the globe. This is a very great achievement, but it has its roots many thousands of years back in our prehistory.

We have already discussed the fact that language ability is a built-in advantage that humans have over other primates, so it is reasonable to assume that language, a special medium for social connecting, is where the complex social relations of the historic period had their beginnings. In early prehistoric times, communication even between just two individuals must have been a complicated business, constantly prone to error, misunderstanding, and conflict. As language evolved, many of these difficulties were resolved by negotiated or dictated agreements on more and more precise meanings.

Like the learning process, social organization is not unique to humans. Mothers of all advanced species play a critical role in both nurturing and training their young, and fathers also play a protective and educational role. However, social organization among humans has evolved in a very special way, becoming elaborated and differentiated far beyond what has been observed among other animal species. This elaboration of social organization has played a critical role in increasing human capacity for problem solving. Once knowledge is shared among a number of humans through artifacts, modeling, and language, it becomes available for *collective* problem solving and for *passing on* from one generation to the next, even from one culture to another. All this sharing and passing on depends in turn on the very social nature of the species. Social connectedness is integral to all types of problem solving, to language, to the accumulation of knowledge, and to the making of progress in general.

The earliest social organization had to be the family, as it is for most advanced species. The family, to a large extent, is a biological necessity in creatures whose young are defenseless and grow slowly to adulthood over a period of fourteen to sixteen years. We do not know, but we can suspect that the original nuclear family consisted of one father and one or perhaps two or three mothers. Many key functions were dictated by biology. Birthing, nursing, and protecting the young belonged to the mother almost exclusively. The father's role had to be primarily the protection of the family as a whole, the gathering of food by whatever means, and the seeking and impregnating of fertile females in what was often a deadly contest with other males.

CONNECTING TWO INDIVIDUALS: THE DYAD

The dyad is the simplest form of social organization. It grows out of the initiation of communicative channels between two individuals. A "channel" is simply a connection between two entities that allows messages to flow from one to another. Channels become strengthened through use and through the transfer of rewarding stimuli from one side to the other, just as occurs in animal learning. In fact, channel building and networking can be viewed as special cases of S-R learning. Some degree of stability and commonality of expectation between sender and receiver must be established either genetically or through learning to sustain channels and networks.

Animals communicate in various ways but mostly through rituals that are

FIGURE 6.1.
ANOTHER HUMAN AS AN EXTERNAL RESOURCE

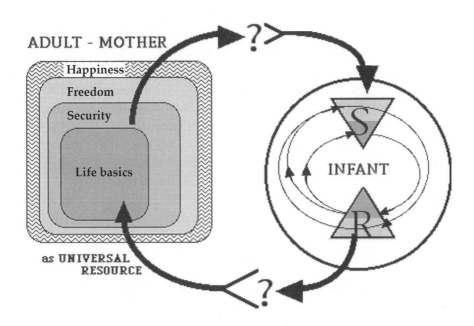

firmly implanted in the genes. These rituals serve the life-sustaining activities of mating, food gathering, and defending the brood, the herd, or the flock. No doubt, human channels have similar origins, and many human communications serve these same purposes. Babies need no teaching to attach to their mother's breast, but therein lies the first and most basic of all human social connections. From that most satisfying of stimulus-response cycles soon emerge hundreds of learning cycles that bond the child to the mother and then to other rewarding humans in the immediate environment. Like the rock in the coconut cycle, these others become potent symbols for actions that will bring rewards.

THE ANATOMY OF A SOCIAL CONNECTION

Let us begin this analysis of social connections with what may be the simplest example of one-on-one human connection. Figure 6.1 takes the framework of the inanimate external resource of figure 5.1 and substitutes a human being.

This other human being is vastly more complex than the rock but is nevertheless at first an undifferentiated object to the infant, a universal problem solver. Whenever there is a need, the solution is right at hand. As time goes by, a more varied set of responses are required. Unlike the rock, the human-object is not always there in the same place the next time it is needed. This variability of the external human-object has several important consequences. One is the development of social connecting skills. In the figure, the connecting arrows are intentionally drawn in two segments, an "out" half and an "in" half. Between the two the figure shows a big question mark to indicate the problematic nature of the connection. Over time and through countless repetitions of the connecting cycle, the developing human learns to fine-tune both sending and receiving skills so that the tracking of the continually changing behavior of the external human-object (usually the mother) can be maintained.[2]

Figure 6.2 diagrams the key elements of the new dyadic relationship that now emerges. The exchange builds over hundreds or thousands of loops

FIGURE 6.2.
ANATOMY OF A HUMAN DIALOGUE

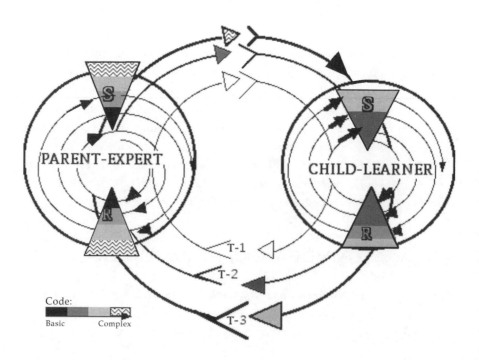

between the learner and the expert. With each exchange ("time 1" to "time 2" to "time 3"), the link between sending and receiving signals becomes more focused, more precise, and potentially more valuable to the receiver. The question marks in the previous figure are now filled in with the crucial details of sounds and gestures, visual and verbal signals that allow a stronger and stronger connection to emerge. It seems clear that this process, while generally characteristic of how animals learn to relate to each other, is far more developed in humans, especially with the crucial addition of language.

In addition to learning how to make better and better use of the external expert through more accurate and more complex exchanges, the dialogue process teaches the new learner some other important lessons. One is that the expert resource cannot always be relied upon. This external resource person is often out of sight or unable to respond. It moves about and becomes increasingly unreliable in its responses while, simultaneously, the infant's own capacities for locomotion and resource acquisition grow by leaps and bounds.

When the adequacy of the external resource person inevitably and eventually falters, the learner has two choices: (a) to reach out to *another* person, perhaps another parent or an older sibling or another member of the tribe, or (b) to acquire the needed and necessary resource on his or her own. Thus both self-reliance and extended sociability emerge from the same dialogue process. Up to a point this is a good thing. The external universal resource can be maintained for only a limited time. What was once external must ultimately become internal, ending the many cycles of infantile dependency. This is weaning, a process that all infants must go through and that all humans must go through symbolically as they grow up and learn to live on their own.

Along the way to full independence and socialization, the growing individual learns more and more about other humans as potential external resources. He or she learns, for example, that the external human also has cycles of need and fulfillment that correspond in both parallel and complimentary ways to their own. This insight represents a huge step forward in intellect.

Language learning begins in the second year of life and progresses rapidly to fluency in little more than two years thereafter. While it is clear that the underlying neural mechanisms to make language are built into the DNA, it is equally clear that the immediate social environment is the carrier. The ear of the learner connects to the sounds emanating from the mouth of the mother over and over again. The infant soon learns that it can emit nearly identical sounds. Hearing these same sounds from one's own mouth no doubt reinforces the realization that these others are similar to the self.

Many wonderful things flow from the human dyad. It is the foundation of all relationships, the family, the tribe, even the nation-state and the largest associations of religions and common cultures. At the same time, errors and distortions in the early development of the dyad may be responsible for some of the worst human woes. Anger and aggression are nearly universal responses to the frustration of a failed dyad, one that does not produce positive rewards, in which the cycle is disrupted at crucial moments. Dyad failure or poor development may also be responsible for the well-known characteristic of some humans to treat others not as fellow human beings like themselves but as objects to be manipulated and even destroyed, without any recognition that these others are like themselves.

The realization that externally perceived and engaged humans are like the self leads to an ability to simulate the other in the self, to copy not only single acts and instrumental behavior but also entire sets of behavior, as if absorbing the other person's identity and personality as a whole. This also carries on into a sense of coidentity and fellowship, the very source of family and tribal connections. These connections routinely become so strong that they overwhelm the instinct for self-preservation so that individuals can go gladly into danger to risk sacrifice of their own lives for the sake of the group.

This sense of common fate with other humans is also the cornerstone of human morality, as will be discussed more fully in chapter 10, but it entails many contradictions because it has definite limits. At first it applies only to the immediate family, and even then not reliably. The myths of many cultures are filled with intrafamilial conflict, fathers killing sons and vice versa, brothers killing brothers. The settling and stabilization of extended family networks and their transformation into tribes was originally an awkward and bloody business that is reflected in folklore.

THE EMERGENCE OF COOPERATIVE PROBLEM SOLVING

Of the many reasons why humans might have first gathered together in groups, the one that has the most relevance here is the purely *instrumental* one: group problem solving. It must have been evident from a very early time that coming together in tight-knit groups was advantageous for safety from predators (human and otherwise), for protection from the natural elements, and for hunting and foraging. In chapter 5 we already discussed socialization and language learning as a form of knowledge transfer. Figure 6.3 illustrates the next important phase in the development of a complex knowledge base, the generation of cooperative relationships that are coordinated and reciprocal to achieve common ends.

The three problem solvers at the bottom right of the figure are intended to represent the collective efforts of any number of individual problem solvers who have managed to pool their knowledge and labor to achieve a common end. Such an instance of cooperation might go unrecorded and unremembered, to be repeated over and over again by creative clusters of individuals for hundreds of years. However, at some point, some member of such a group

FIGURE 6.3.
COOPERATIVE PROBLEM SOLVING

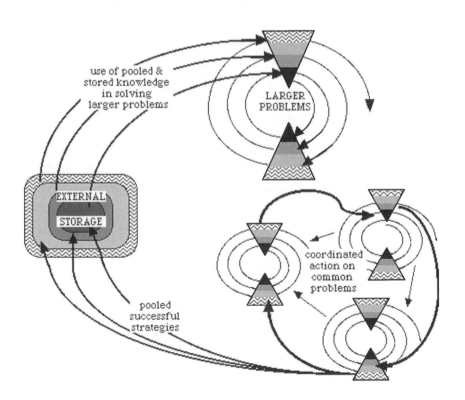

will externalize his or her understanding of the successful social arrangement, either by composing a poetic recitation or picturing the story on a cave wall or, in later times, creating a written record. Thus it enters the external knowledge storage bin suggested by the rectangular box on the left.

Drawing from the same externalized memory sources, later generations will know how to engage in particular tried-and-true forms of collective action, thus taking important new steps toward human progress.

MULTIPLYING THE NUMBER OF PROBLEM SOLVERS AND DIVIDING THE LABOR

In addition to more and more extensive networking, the evolution of human social organization has also involved *larger and larger groupings* organized for common purposes. The larger the social organization in terms of sheer numbers, the more potential problem solvers there are available for a common end, no matter what that end might be. Organizational size also requires leadership and coordination that go well beyond simple networking. As size increases, the mechanisms of command and enforcement of group norms become progressively more elaborate, and the possibilities for new kinds of problem solving also proliferate. Furthermore, efficiencies arising from divisions of labor free up time and labor for new purposes and possibilities.

The prevailing purpose of larger social organizations (originally and for many thousands of years) was probably warfare, defensive or offensive or both. Warfare required a division of labor, first and most simply between leaders and followers and then between various kinds of specialized fighters, armorers, shipbuilders, sailors, and so forth. Each of these labor divisions reflects a problem to be solved and a means of solving it.

LEADERSHIP AND POWER RELATIONS

Hierarchical relationships are observed in many species, and early humans were no exception. The larger and more complex coordinated problem-solving efforts described above could be managed only through some kind of leadership, whether voluntary or coerced. Since larger numbers working together could achieve more, especially in battling and conquering other tribes, the trend was toward larger and larger tribes and more coercive leadership. Nevertheless, size without the adequate social technology of organization tends to become unwieldy and unstable, particularly at moments of inevitable leadership transition. The leader dies in battle or from natural causes or from mutiny among strong underlings. The consequence is an endless series of social "experiments," rearrangements of the social connections in which different patterns are tried out: coleaderships, triumvirates, female leaders, committees, participative governance, and so forth. From the earliest recorded times, history has been filled with examples from this struggle to find the most workable and durable forms of social structure.

The most common resolution of the succession problem is through familial generational linkage, a kind of social mimicry of DNA's multibillion-year rule of succession. This seems to work best when an exceptionally talented and charismatic individual advances to tribal leadership. A large part of the success of such a dynasty-forming leader is mastery of the externally stored knowledge of the tribe, as described in chapter 5. The leader thus becomes the dominating symbol of the tribe and its collective knowledge. He may seek to magnify his power in the eyes of followers by adopting a totem to symbolize himself and the tribe together with their acquired knowledge. This aggrandizement frequently extends to declarations of immortality and the construction of elaborate memorial tombs as living reminders. When this leader is succeeded by his son or by another, the totem and the tomb remain as visible, tangible evidence of the great leader. By copying the father's ways, the son also gains immortality and the awed obeisance of other tribe members, inheriting and perhaps elaborating on the totem and erecting an even more magnificent tomb for himself. In Egypt, such a process was extremely successful in maintaining a stable social system for over two thousand years.

SPECIALISTS AS CUSTODIANS OF SHARED-STORED CULTURAL KNOWLEDGE

The earliest successful leaders were probably also the experts. They were the ones who knew the most about how to make weapons and other tools and were the most skilled in how to use them. But as the external knowledge base expanded, this became impossible, and the first specialists came into being, persons with expert knowledge about the specific technologies of weapon making, tool making, trap making, brick making, house building, leather making, and so on. Notable among these specialties eventually would be *farming*, a complex enterprise involving gathering seeds, preparing soil, planting, protecting the field, weeding, watering, harvesting, milling, storing, and distributing. Each of these specialties required its own technology, externalized knowledge that had to be passed down across generations in as accurate a form as possible.

These specialists, to preserve their craft, also began to form social networks, subsystems within the larger system and often with an uneasy connection to the larger system. Specialized networks are critical for progress because they can cut across geographical, political, and cultural boundaries, bringing together experts working on the same types of problems. From its beginnings, European science has been sustained by simple networks, originally the sending and receiving of letters written in Latin, the shared international language of the European Middle Ages. As such networks have evolved over the last four centuries, other languages have displaced Latin, and letters have mostly been displaced by a journal system, but the basic rules of communication and the assumptions of open distribution and exposure to critical review remain the same to this day. Such social networking has become very important in the acceleration of scientific discovery and the application of scientific knowledge in all spheres of human problem solving.

Fast forward to our own times, and one finds an intricate division of labor among societal problem solvers. Knowledge building itself has become highly specialized, segmented into thousands of specialties. Within each specialty there exists a complex structure in which power and influence are widely dispersed, as between universities, private organizations, and government offices. Such power and influence can be quite centralized and hierarchical *within* many of these same social entities. All are held together by their specialized networks that also have a kind of hierarchy of journal editors, influentials, and gatekeepers of various sorts. Of particular importance for the refinement of the forward function was, first, the creation of *faculties* of science, medicine, and engineering within universities; and later came specialized scientific research and development *laboratories*, some affiliated with universities, others created within commercial enterprises, and still others serving as adjuncts to government agencies.

The human facility for social connection is one of the keys to progress. Social connection is not only a critical carrier for preserved knowledge but also the main means by which knowledge gets shared both within and across cultures. Furthermore, this facility seems to have no practical limits. Social networking even in primitive times could involve thousands of people working in unison, but with the advent of modern communications it now can involve hundreds of millions through whom knowledge flows in ever-increasing torrents.

SUMMARY

Social connection has always been the primary means of transmitting cultural knowledge from generation to generation. It starts with the relationships between parents and children. Over time the modes of connection have become ever more complex and more efficient, as reflected in the growth of languages. Family and kinship relations were probably the original basis of culture and the source of subsequent tribal groupings. Tribes, in turn, were able to maintain cohesiveness through the relative advantage of cooperative problem solving in food acquisition and defense. The acquisition and preservation of a common language added to cohesiveness and made problem solving much more efficient.

The fact that all cultures, however isolated from others, develop a language, suggests that this capacity is not learned but is dictated by genes. The nearly infinite capacity of different cultures to expand language with new words and new word-string structures (complex sentences and paragraphs) indicates that language is not only the prime carrier of culture but also a prime vehicle for innovation and progressive change. Language is the primary means of externalizing what is going on inside the brain, namely, memory of past learning and what we call "thought," but the motivational force that drives this externalization and subsequent transfer to others is social connection. Talking and listening are the prime means by which social relations take place and the prime means by which they can expand and create culture. The externalized results of this expansion are knowledge platforms that are further considered in the next chapter.

Chapter Seven

KNOWLEDGE PLATFORMS
Forward Function Force #4

We are like dwarfs sitting on the shoulders of giants. We see more, and things that are more distant, than they did, not because our sight is superior or because we are taller than they, but because they raise us up, and by their great stature add to ours.
—John of Salisbury, 1159 CE

All the aspects of any civilization arise out of a people's religion: its politics, its economics, its arts, its sciences, even its simple crafts are the by-products of religious insights and a religious cult. For until human beings are tied together by some common faith, and share certain moral principles, they prey upon one another.
—Russell T. Kirk, *The Roots of American Order*

Just as there are complex and varied connections among people, there are also complex and varied connections among the artifacts and words people create. The "knowledge base" of a culture is the sum of (1) all the technologies they create and use, plus (2) whatever artifacts and possessions they are able to preserve and pass on to following generations, plus (3) their unique language and dialect, plus (4) religious or other beliefs and memories such as they are able to preserve and perpetuate in some form. Because people are always learning throughout their individual lives, are always continuing to store externally what they learn, and are always extending and expanding the social connections that allow knowledge to pass from person to person and generation to generation, this knowledge base is always expanding, as long as the particular culture remains intact.

A MINIMAL KNOWLEDGE PLATFORM FOR HUNTERS: SPEAR CULTURE

In chapter 5 we suggested how stone-pointed spears and other primitive hunting tools might have been developed. Now consider the number of different learned-and-stored elements that must have been understood together and integrated to allow that knowledge to pass from one generation to the next. These necessary elements must have included at least the following:

1. Identification and mining of the right kind of stone for the purpose;
2. The tool needed to chip the stone to the right size, shape, and degree of sharpness;
3. The manner in which that tool had to be held and used to shape the spearhead;
4. Selection of the right kind of sapling or tree branch to make the spear shaft;
5. The cutting and shaping of the shaft to fit the head;
6. Attachment of the head to the shaft by vines or bark strands or grass;
7. Technique for throwing the spear to have the desired effect;
8. Tracking and observation procedures needed to prepare for the kill; and
9. Knowledge of the type of animal (or human) most vulnerable to this kind of spear.

Assuming that a linguistic capability was available, there would also be at least one word for each of these nine items.[1] There might also be a picture story showing various stages in the process and perhaps an oral word string prepared in a form that could easily be remembered to describe each part of the total process. In addition there could have been a division of labor within the tribe such that some were spear makers, others were spear users (hunters), while still others were food and pelt preparers. All the separate pieces of knowledge—the artifacts created and preserved, the words, pictures, and stories—all these items go together in an integrated way to make a minimal knowledge platform about stone-tipped spear hunting.

Yet that is merely the technical aspect of the platform. There is usually much more to it than that. For early man, hunting was surely a chance affair. Sometimes it worked and sometimes it didn't. Sometimes the game got away.

Sometimes the game wasn't there. Sometimes the game just got mad and came after the hunter. Through trial and error the hunters would gradually become better at finding the game, making better spears, and so forth. This is the learning process in action. But along with all this functional learning would come a lot of random connecting. Certain incantations and prayers would seem to be important because they were uttered just before a successful hunt. Perhaps an invocation to a deceased father or leader would lead to success. Important but randomly connected events, such as deaths, droughts, storms, plagues, floods, and accidents, would be ascribed causal meaning. From this

FIGURE 7.1.
CREATING KNOWLEDGE PLATFORMS

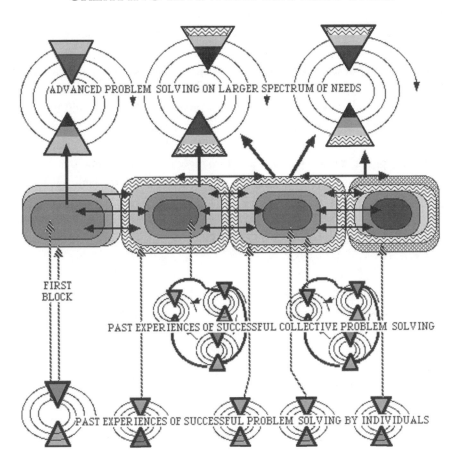

could come the anointing and blessing of spears and the preservation of certain spears as sacred totems. All these ideas, in word form and in story form, are then added to the platform to be carefully preserved and passed on, generation to generation.

Of course, the technology of stone-tipped-spear hunting would not be the only item of cultural preservation. What children would have to learn to be socialized into this culture would have to include all the technologies developed and preserved by this tribe, including the hunting and trapping of a variety of species, the gathering of edible plants, food preparation, clothing manufacture and wear, and shelter construction. Boat construction, boat handling, and navigation would also be central technologies for seafarers. For each aspect of these technologies there would also be words and word stories. On top of the technology, the newly socialized member would have to know all the norms of conduct with peers, elders, and children—and perhaps from men to women and from women to men. To each of these more words and stories would be attached. Topping off the bundle of knowledge would be the remembered works and deeds of ancestors and the supposed workings of gods and spirits of all sorts, who animate every important feature of the human environment, including the land and the sea, the sun and the moon, the plants and the animals. Every tribe ever studied seems to have a cosmology, a way of explaining everything that humans observe and experience. This cosmology exists or is invented to pull all the strands of the culture together, all the technologies, folkways, rituals, stories, preserved monuments and artifacts, and the language itself.

HOW KNOWLEDGE PLATFORMS COME INTO BEING

Building on the discussion of the last three chapters, we can imagine how knowledge platforms come into being. Figure 7.1 provides a schematic of how this might occur. A platform starts with the very basic connection and externalizing of two bits of learning in an individual, let us say the realization that a sharp-pointed stick can kill a pig if thrust in a certain way at a certain distance. As described in chapter 5, the learner preserves the stick and demonstrates its use to his son, thus ensuring the external preservation of his discovery. In figure 7.1 these acts of cultural preservation are suggested by the activity to the far left, identified as "First Block." As this newly stored knowledge filters up to the next generation, it adds to the family's ease and complexity of problem solving: "Grandpa figured out how to make a spear and use it. Let's see if we can make the point sharper."

As we move to the right in the figure, collective problem solving facilitated by ever-strengthening social connections adds to the storage base and integrates with it (horizontal arrows) to increase its strength and power. This process of adding and strengthening connections goes on and on as long as the culture of the tribe survives. As knowledge accumulates and as it is overlaid by language, it gets shuffled, integrated, and reorganized in innumerable ways. Some of these organizing efforts are particularly elaborate, inclusive, and persuasive, with the result that they come to be seen as a new basis for understanding *everything*. The results of successful synthetic efforts could be described as new or emergent *knowledge/know-how platforms* because they serve as a floor or foundation for a multitude of diverse thinking and problem-solving efforts for all who come after.

THE CLASH OF PLATFORMS AND THE BATTLE FOR TRUTH

The first knowledge platforms of prehistoric times must have been tribal. The boundaries of shared and stored knowledge and technology were tribal boundaries. Thus each tribe developed its own ways of doing things, its own spears and houses, and created its own gods, probably based on ancestors, dreams, and the random events that intruded most into their lives. Yet tribes existed alongside other tribes, and both cooperation and warfare among tribes must have been common. Whether through cooperation, warfare, or both, knowledge platforms inevitably became shared to some degree. In cooperative arrangements, gods and cosmologies would have to be shared. In warfare, the triumphant tribe enjoyed the dominance not only of its technology but also of its gods and cosmology.

It was also up to the victors to decide what remnants of the loser's knowledge and technology would be worthy of inclusion in their new and expanded platform. It might be most, some, or none at all. From the earliest historical times, diverse cultures have struggled with each other for dominance. Some of the vanquished have disappeared without a trace. Others have left mute testaments to their greatness—mostly in stone, the least perishable of their artifacts—but the extent and nature of their knowledge platforms can only be guessed at. At various times, some of the conquerors became more creative, learning valuable lessons from those they conquered. An early step, oddly enough a turn that we should probably think of as progressive within its time context, is *slavery*, which was the decision to make use of defeated enemies instead of just killing them off and looting their habitats.

An outstanding example of cultural transfer through military success is provided by the Roman conquest of the entire Mediterranean by the beginning of its imperial period, about the first year of the Common Era (CE). Upper-class Romans were known to take Greeks as slave-tutors, thereby absorbing and eventually valuing and copying much of Greek culture. The Greek political system was destroyed along with the autonomy of the Greek city-states, but the language was preserved. The Romans even adapted the Greek pantheon.

In European history, many examples of all types of cultural transition can be seen, as Germanic tribes overran the crumbling Roman Empire in the west and as Asiatic tribes pressed in on the other Roman Empire from the east. The Anglo-Saxon tribes obliterated Roman influence in Britain, implanting a language that had strong Germanic roots. The Germanic tribes known as the Franks occupied what is modern France and preserved much more of the Roman artifactual and architectural remains, developing a new language based largely on Latin (i.e., Roman) roots. The Byzantine remnant of the Roman Empire resisted invasion for a thousand years, thus preserving its knowledge platform but doing little to build on it during all that time.

HOLY TEXTS AS SEMIFROZEN SYSTEMS OF THOUGHT

Despite the capacity of individuals to learn and to build on the stored knowledge created by others in the past, there is a very strong yearning in all people for permanence and solidity in the principles that govern their lives. This desire for permanence and resistance to change is clearly on display in the reverence held for ancient texts that is consistent across all religions. As time goes by, however, and later generations of revered leaders, scholars, and holy men of various sorts arrive on the scene, writings by and about them are added to the Holy Writ. In the Roman Catholic Church there has evolved a system for incorporating the later contributors, which is known as canonization. One cannot think of the Roman Church without including its many saints as an integral part of that system of belief. In addition, it is hard to think of Roman Catholicism without adding the ritual and iconography of great paintings, sculptures, and cathedrals. They are all part of an overarching and all-embracing way of life that ties present to past in layer on layer of an evolving eighteen centuries of art, architecture, music, ritual, and intellectual thought.

The Protestant Reformation in the West has evolved in a somewhat similar fashion but with less elaboration. The original intent of the founding fathers of Protestantism in the late Middle Ages was to get back to basics. They wanted to scrape away the overlay of more than one thousand years of the canonization process, returning to what they believed to be the original teachings of Jesus in the Gospels. Yet even these Gospels were mostly written long after the life of the historical Jesus. The back-to-basics impulse of Protestantism has persisted into the present and has led to the continuous fracturing of Protestantism into separate denominations, each rejecting the symbols, artifacts, and theological overlay of prior sects.

The same pattern of reverence for original Holy Writ followed by a long period of revisionist additions by holy men, wise men, or powerful rulers can be observed in Judaism and Islam. Followers of these religions assert that there is only one system of truth because it is the word of their god. It is not subject to doubt. The articulation of doubt even about the smallest article of belief can be taken as a crime, punishable by death and perhaps even eternal damnation. Nevertheless, the words recorded by the ancients are typically obscure in their meaning. Therefore, they require interpretation. Thus it is the interpreters who now rise to holy status as their words of interpretation are added to scripture.

TOLERANCE AND DUALISM

It must have been evident to the earliest tribes that had contact with other tribes that their own tribal gods and rituals were different from those others in some degree. If it is correct that the earliest gods were common ancestors, then clearly the god or gods of other tribes must be different. How they eventually merged is an important but mostly unknown story in the rise of civilization. Usually, it was the conquerors who determined the prevailing religion ever afterward for the people who lived in the territories they controlled. The

Greeks and the Romans appear to have been fairly tolerant. The Romans had an official religion that became Christianity after the conversion of Constantine, but the Romans generally allowed the practice of different sects within their domain before and after. In the eighth and ninth centuries, Islam spread across the Middle East and North Africa in a way comparable to the spread of Christianity in Europe a few centuries earlier. Yet many temporal and religious rulers, Christian and Muslim, tolerated the continuing practice of other religions within their borders so long as they were not disruptive of the majority and did not challenge state power.

An important advance toward tolerance of alternative worldviews came with the idea of separating religious and state powers. In the Christian Bible (Matthew 17:21), Jesus is supposed to have said, "Render therefore unto Caesar the things that are Caesar's, and unto God the things that are God's." This can be interpreted as an avowal of the principle of separation of church and state, although there are many contrary interpretations among Christian theologians. Throughout the Middle Ages, the Christian world was confused and divided about the separation of powers. It was thought that temporal rulers had some authority over church matters and that church authorities had authority over temporal rulers, but which had what and how much was never resolved, and the relative tolerance of one time and one set of rulers and clerics was frequently followed by the intolerance and massive persecution of the next set. To some extent, these swings reflected the ambivalence about the possibility of dualism, the idea that two systems of truth could exist side by side.

In modern times this ambivalence persists. In the political realm it is played out as church versus state, but in intellectual circles the debate is between the various religions on the one hand and science on the other. Which is the really true platform of knowledge, and can there really be more than one true platform? For many if not most scientists, dualism is a convenient dodge. If we can all accept that there are two kinds of "truth," one scientific and the other spiritual (sometimes rendered as "mental"), then the scientists can continue with their sort of discovery and truth-building activity governed by the rules of science, without worrying about any inconsistencies with religious people and their elected representatives. One suspects, however, that many accept dualism only as a practical convenience, something that allows them to get their work done. However, there are crucial dividing points where that just doesn't work, particularly when the topics of human life and the nature of human beings is at issue.

KNOWLEDGE PLATFORMS IN WESTERN THOUGHT FROM THE GREEKS AND THE HEBREWS FORWARD

For the ancient world after 300 BCE, the platform for what later became "science" was formed from the writings of the Greek philosopher Aristotle. Indeed, Aristotle remained a leading authority (and for many the only authority) on all matters scientific right through the Hellenistic, Roman, and medieval periods, also greatly influencing Islamic thought. Over the ages since Aristotle, many other knowledge platforms have been extremely influential, particularly the holy scriptures that have served as the bases for major religions.

In the late Middle Ages, many of the most important holy texts dating from early Hebrew times to late Roman times were brought together in one set of books that was thought of as the "canon," an inclusive compendium of all the wisdom of the ages. This term has continued into our own times as including not only the Christian Bible but also the major writings of all the major wise men of history, ancient and modern, eastern and western.[2] The canon as a concept is a conservative idea. It suggests that most of what is worth knowing is old; and by implication the older the knowledge, the more it is valued. However, the canon concept can also be viewed in a progressive light if it is taken as the platform on which we stand as we reach for the future. To make genuine progress, humans must build on past knowledge and past experience, just as Phil in *Groundhog Day* was able to add on to his experience of each recycled day to make himself a wiser and ultimately better person.

Building surely on the past is more easily said than done. There are two big complications. The first is that our supposed knowledge from the past is a mixed jumble of facts and myths. Some past assumptions may be taken as true within certain limits, representing perhaps a consensus among the most educated people of a given time. The overall base of any culture's knowledge platform includes billions of observations and experiences, some that are fully validated and authentic but many more that are poorly documented, and more still that are spurious or that are drawn from the pure inventions of creative minds.

Until modern times, the custodians of knowledge platforms were religious institutions. Sometimes the religious leadership was merged with the political. At other times it was distinct and occasionally even antagonistic. Universities emerged in later medieval Europe as institutions intended first and foremost to train priests. A large part of that training involved under-standing ancient texts, which meant learning Latin and Greek and, in the process, becoming exposed to pre-Christian Roman and Greek thought. Thus, the comprehensive writings of Aristotle formed a framework for what was thought of as science, completely integrated with Christian theology. Thus the knowledge platforms that were dominant in all of Christian Europe, including the Byzantine Empire, derived from the same ancient sources. The process of knowledge building consisted mainly of interpretations and com-mentaries on older texts as well as the laborious hand copying of all that had been written and preserved previously. The belief in ancient texts was absolute. This was the canon, presumably dictated by God himself.

Thus, for example, the writings of Copernicus could not be accepted by the church and could not be incorporated into the Christian knowledge plat-form from the mere fact that they contradicted the writings of the much more ancient and therefore more "valid" theories of the Alexandrian astronomer Ptolemy, even though Ptolemy was not a Christian and Copernicus was! Like Christians, Muslims created and solidified a knowledge system based on old texts. The Qur'an was their central guiding document, but they also acknowl-edged older texts as part of their canon, including Aristotle and the Greek philosophers, mathematicians, and astronomers. Indeed, through most of the Middle Ages, the Muslim knowledge platform was more coherent and more scientifically accurate in the modern sense than the Christian version was.

We have only gradually come to realize that most of the old platforms of what was once widely thought of as "knowledge" are very wobbly indeed. The Reformation was an extremely unstable period in which the Christian knowl-edge platform was challenged from within by priests like Martin Luther, who reinterpreted Christianity. This was in many respects a battle of competing knowledge platforms derived from different interpretations of the same ancient texts. It was very serious business. Many were tortured, beheaded, and burned at the stake simply for advocating views that were inconsistent with those of the prevailing ecclesiastical and political leadership. None of the competing knowledge systems could be described as in any way secular, yet from the cauldron of disputation emerged the foundations of a new way of looking at knowledge and truth, which we now call "science."

A discussion of what science is and how it emerged apart from and in par-allel to preexisting religion-based knowledge platforms will be reserved for the next chapter. It is interesting to note that all the early scientists of the Renaissance, from roughly 1450 to 1750, were priests or monks or religious figures of one sort or another, and they all thought that what they were doing was simply revealing or enhancing the existing knowledge platform of their time, which they knew was God's truth.

To a large extent, knowledge platforms are coincident with and equivalent to culture or civilization. Thus, when S. P. Huntington speaks of the "clash of civilizations," he is also talking about the clash of two systems of belief within which both "knowledge" and "truth" receive their definition and value. Huntington is thoroughly Hegelian in seeing history played out as a series of great conflicts that are never resolved. In his formulation, the "West" is a civilization in direct and irreconcilable conflict with Islam and other Eastern influences including China. While he identifies himself with this "West" and suggests all kinds of ways it can defend itself against further decline, he sees decline as inevitable and continuing. He also rejects the idea that there are any universal truths deriving from Western culture, including "Western" science. He calls such ideas "false," "immoral," and "dangerous."[3] In making such a bold assertion, he sets himself up as hostile to the main thesis offered here, that science-based progress is inevitable and postcultural.

THE KNOW-HOW PLATFORMS

From the earliest times to the present, the most critical platforms for progress have not been stores of scientific knowledge but remembered and recorded ways of doing things that have had proven life-enhancing value. This began more than one million years ago with how to make crude stone tools and weapons, how to trap and kill game animals, and how to light fires. By historic times, these know-how platforms had become quite sophisticated and included how to build and navigate boats that could carry cargo and people long distances; how to create pottery in all shapes and sizes; how to plant grasses with edible seeds; how to crush the seeds and cook them to make bread; how to make weapons and ornaments of bronze, gold, silver, and iron; how to quarry stone; and how to build large, protective structures of both stone and wood. Not the least of these technological achievements was that of statecraft, how to put together large numbers of people in coordinated enterprises for hunting, farming, building structures of wood and stone, fighting off enemy hordes, and dominating territories.

By the early Renaissance of the fourteenth and fifteenth centuries, a flood of innovations extended humankind's reach and power. These included glass-making, mechanical clocks, horse harnesses, printing, ocean-going ships, firearms, and many others. By the late Middle Ages, craft guilds were also pro-tecting many separate know-how platforms and supporting the invention of ever more elaborate and sophisticated tools and artifacts. New measuring and record-keeping schemes secured and solidified each platform.

After just another two hundred years, there are steam-powered mills, presses, carriages on rails, and ships. There are mass production of clothing, firearms, iron and iron products; deep shaft mining of coal and other minerals; and the beginnings of mechanized, high-production agriculture and food dis-tribution. There is also the beginning of what will become a mighty alliance of technology and science, with the first serious use of telescopes and micro-scopes to redefine the natural world and the first uses of physics and chem-istry applications in electricity and materials refinement.

Advancing into our own times, each of these technology know-how plat-forms has become firmly wedded to a background in a particular applied sci-ence that in turn is derivative of a more basic science. The guilds have given way to schools of engineering, agriculture, and medicine, each with its associ-ated set of applied "sciences." These know-how platforms are now each ener-gized and expanded by thousands of experts in thousands of university departments and laboratories, tied together by an elaborate network of asso-ciations, journals, professional meetings, annual conferences, and countless interchanges by electronic media.

The infrastructure that has evolved in support of these modern know-how platforms is exceedingly complex, yet it is also robust to the point of indestructibility. Each subsystem is set up in such a way that new discoveries are being made continuously, adding to or strengthening the knowledge floor, filling in the holes, and affirming, clarifying, and extending discoveries.

THE KNOWLEDGE PLATFORMS OF THE ARTS AND HUMANITIES

This book is primarily concerned with the emergence of science and tech-nology and how they will affect our future, but it should be understood that the growth of knowledge, building on the past, also applies to all the creative output of humanity, whether it be in the form of fiction, painting, sculpture, music, architecture, or any other arts—including the modern forms of photography, cinema, and television production. Those people who live within a given era may be able to partake of the creative output of their own time and a sampling of all previous recorded time, but they are allowed nothing of any works that come after their time. When romanticists imagine themselves back to another past age and think, for example, how wonderful it would be to have been present when Handel himself was conducting *Messiah*, they tend to ignore the obvious fact that they would thus have no knowledge of Mozart or Beethoven or all the classical and romantic composers who came later. Nor would they have had an opportunity to hear that great piece over and over again in their own living room. If they had been lucky enough to have been present when Shakespeare first offered *Hamlet* at the Globe Theater, they would also have been unlucky enough to have no knowledge of any later playwright, not to mention Dickens, Tolstoy, and on and on. Each generation adds a layer of culture that enriches the whole, and to the extent that each addition is made accessible to all, it enriches each person to an extent that was not available to anyone ever before.

SUMMARY

The sum total of stored human knowledge is very widely distributed, existing not only in the heads of the few billion living humans but also in books, photographs, magnetic tape, discs, and many other storage media. It is partially collected and cross-referenced in libraries, and now much of it is available to many millions of people through the Internet. Access and availability differ very widely between individuals and between cultures, as does the capacity to absorb and make meaningful use of the contents. Conservation over many generations has always been problematic. Continued storage of particular files is not guaranteed, and there are circumstances in which much of what has been stored can be permanently destroyed or erased. It is worth recalling that in the third century CE, the great library of Alexandria, Egypt—up to that time the greatest library in the world—was destroyed by fire. Great stores of knowledge are lost continuously as people of wisdom die and as their writings, notes, and files are assigned to the garbage heap. Nevertheless, what remains is so vast and the redundancy among knowledge holders is so great that total loss is becoming less of a threat than it was in the past.

How this storehouse of knowledge is put to use is another big problem. Much of what is now stored so easily in electromagnetic files is used for entertainment with only limited consideration of its educational value. It is also used, in distorted ways, to advance various beliefs and values having little to do with human progress. Nevertheless, a significant fraction of the total constitutes the knowledge base of all the empirical sciences as well as the engineering know-how that generates useful products and practices in every sphere of human need. Sorting out those segments of stored knowledge that are actually applicable to human problem solving is itself a major task on which many thousands of people labor their whole lives through.

Chapter Eight

SCIENTIFIC PROBLEM SOLVING
Forward Function Force # 5

Francis Bacon's method, as explained in Novum Organum (1620; "New Instrument"), consisted of three main steps: first, a description of facts; second, a tabulation, or classification, of those facts into three categories—instances of the presence of the characteristic under investigation, instances of its absence, or instances of its presence in varying degrees; third, the rejection of whatever appears, in the light of these tables, not to be connected with the phenomenon under investigation and the determination of what is connected with it.
> —Encyclopædia Britannica, "Francis Bacon"

A science is any discipline in which the fool of this generation can go beyond the point reached by the genius of the last generation.
> —Max Gluckman, Politics, Law, and Ritual in Tribal Society

When Kepler found his long-cherished belief did not agree with the most precise observation, he accepted the uncomfortable fact. He preferred the hard truth to his dearest illusions; that is the heart of science.
> —Carl Sagan, Cosmos: A Personal Voyage

There is a single light of science, and to brighten it anywhere is to brighten it everywhere.
> —Isaac Asimov, Russian-born American biochemist and author

The four forces discussed in chapters 4 through 7 could stand alone as the forward function up to the year 1700, but we have moved very far forward at a much faster pace since that time for two reasons: science and modern diffusion. These new forces began to emerge out of the existing knowledge platforms about that time and largely explain the great acceleration of progress in our own time. In a real sense, everything starts with and builds on the animal learning process, so perhaps the way humans learn new things in the twenty-first century is just an elaboration on how all living things, including jellyfish, have always learned: confronting obstacles and opportunities in the environment and changing behavior accordingly, all the while storing the new behavior for future reuse. Storing knowledge outside the body, organizing socially to solve problems, and creating a summation of all individual and collective learning as a knowledge platform for further learning—all these elements follow naturally from that basic learning process, even though physiologically only humans seem to have the complex nervous system that can do all these things together.

However, humans have achieved much more in recent times by extending the learning process and expanding their social organizations for the preservation of knowledge out of all semblance to the core functions that they derive from. Modern learning is not just simple trial and error. It involves a complex and highly refined series of steps that go together to produce both certain knowledge and reliably useful artifacts on a mass scale. There is no one individual principally responsible for this great advance, but William Gilbert (1544–1603) may have been the first person to employ the rigorous experimental method through a series of studies on the nature of magnetism.[1] Francis Bacon (1561–1626), cited above, was the first to articulate what came to be known much later as "empiricism," and Galileo (1564–1642) was one of the first to stress the requirement that theories had to be tested repeatedly with experiments using carefully recorded measures. All subsequent investigators who followed these rules deserved to be called "scientists." What these pioneers had discovered was a new and more certain way to sort out what was true, what was doubtful, and what was not true within the knowledge platforms of their times; but their rules have continued to serve us well ever since. Moreover, these new rules apply to all natural phenomena, whether observations and theories come from Christian cultures, Islamic cultures, or the many cultures of south and east Asia. In other words, these rules are universal.

It is common to view historical development and particularly the history of science and technology as a series of jumps for which a succession of great men are responsible, but this may be quite misleading. The roots of science certainly go way back, perhaps even as side-by-side problem solving with the first tools. The conceptual elements of the scientific method were certainly not new with Gilbert or Bacon or Galileo. Rather, it was a number of ideas and behavioral patterns that had to be brought together in an organized form and then established by consensus among many scholars from many different parts of the world. This did not happen either all at once or in one specific set of events involving just one set of individuals. The conceptual elements of scientific problem solving that evolved over hundreds of years were as follows: naming, connecting, ordering, quantifying, thinking causally, formalizing the elements of a problem-solving cycle, and synthesizing. In the pages that follow we will consider each of these elements and how they fit into the larger pattern that is scientific knowledge building.

Over thousands of years, humans have learned to invent new patterns and to modify old patterns in order to solve problems more surely and easily.[2] As suggested in chapter 5, the first of these new patterns could have been pre-verbal or nonverbal, as in the fashioning of wood or stone tools, constituting the first examples of what we might call "know-how" knowledge. However, new patterns really began to take off after humans began to talk, using words as symbols for objects, needs, and actions. These word strings were used both to communicate with others and, reciprocally, to understand what others were saying. Constant repetition and rehearsal led inevitably to internalization of problem-solving sequences in what we now call "thought."

NAMING

The seemingly simple act of attaching a name to an object was a great advance in human development. Attaching a verbal designation to each of the things that surround us allows two important additional steps to take place. The first is the storage of a memory of the object in a compressed and abstracted form, thus greatly expanding memory capacity. Second, such verbal labeling allows individually discovered information about observed objects to be passed from one brain to another. Thus, naming things is the basis of language, which in turn becomes the basis of all advanced forms of communication and much of the substance of human memory and thinking.

We have no idea today how naming began. It must have been a long and tortuous process with many failures and confusions along the way. Consider the possibility that you began life without language but with full language capabilities to the extent allowed by your genetic makeup. Then suppose that you are clever enough to start naming things just to make it easier to remember them. Now you come across another person who had the same idea, and you start to talk. Immediately you realize that you have different names for everything. You start pointing and naming so the negotiating can begin. Whose word do you use? Somehow this all got worked out long ago, perhaps sometimes by negotiation, probably more often by force. Fortunately today all that negotiation and struggle is mostly behind us, but the naming goes on and on and will continue to go on as long as humans continue to discover and invent new things.

Naming may have begun with objects, but it eventually spread also to actions and to the relationship between objects and actions. It also spread to the parts of objects, to the acts of people, and then to objects and people who were not seen or heard but only inferred or imagined. Humans discovered that a person could be identified by a name and that the name could still be used to describe the person after he was dead. By invoking the name of a dead person, that person was brought back to life in memory. It was perhaps in this way that religious ideas about dead souls and then gods had their origin.

Naming was followed eventually by the external recording of names. It is no accident that much of the earliest writing was in the form of lists: lists of rulers, lists of genealogies, lists of goods, lists of ships and ship inventories. It was not very exciting stuff as literature, but it is suggestive of the critical importance of naming things even in early historical times. From recording lists, it was then an easy step to sorting (segmenting the list into types of things and parts of things), and then separating actions into episodes and phases. In our own time, the naming goes on, perhaps at an accelerating pace. While outsiders complain of "jargon," members of any specialty know that they have to keep on naming and naming, differentiating one object from another, simply for the sake of accuracy and to communicate more clearly with colleagues within the same specialty. Scientists and technologists now create name after name for things that can be seen only in electron microscopes or through telescopes. Names are also created for objects, processes, and concepts that are not seen directly but are only inferred from what is seen (such as "dark matter" or "black holes"), existing entirely in a theoretical realm while being considered completely "real" nevertheless.

The process of naming has not stopped and will never stop. As new discoveries are made, new names are coined automatically, usually building on the platform of old names and the naming systems of language. Naming is thus another extremely useful and utterly necessary element in human progress.

CONNECTING

From naming naturally follows the connecting of named objects and actions to one another. The most primitive form of connecting is simply grouping. *Oak, elm, ash, cedar* and *pine* are all somewhat alike, so all can be called *trees*. *John, Jim, Joan,* and *Alice* are all *people*, *John* and *Jim* are *men*, *Joan* and *Alice* are *women*. By attaching such labels, we are making connections between objects by clustering them on shared attributes. In learning to assign these attributes, we are generalizing and abstracting aspects of each object, enabling us to say they are the same in this way and different in that way. In so doing, we are also subjecting the objects to more detailed scrutiny, observing and then distinguishing certain features and then collecting the common features under one umbrella name.

ORDERING

Associative connecting, taken one step further, can lead to ordering. This refers not just to setting one object and one group apart from another but inferring qualitative distinctions between pairs and between groups. The trees are now *hard wood* and *soft wood*; the people are *young* or *old*, *tall* or *short*, *strong* or *weak*. Age grading, size grading, weight grading, brightness grading, loudness grading, speed grading—anything from which our senses can detect variation becomes an important target of grading. The ultimate form of conceptual connecting is the taxonomy, a complete system for ordering objects and concepts in a given domain. Aristotle was the earliest-known master of taxonomies, and his orderings of all phenomena were accepted as "final" for nearly two thousand years. The traditional disciplines of botany, biology, and geology were all founded on taxonomizing: collecting specimens, naming them, sorting them by various attributes and ordering them in meaningful arrays according to some unifying principles.

As naming goes on and on with each new observation and discovery, so the process of connecting quickly follows. A new species of bird is found and given a name. What group does it belong to? What hereditary pathway connects it to other similar species? How is its habitat similar to or different from other bird species? Not only is there no end to this process, but the types of connections become ever more refined, more sophisticated, and more extensive. Furthermore, what is connected also becomes progressively more complex, as human knowledge and problem-solving capacity expands. Connections are made among connections, among patterns, among theories, and among all manner of problem-solving processes. There is no end to connecting any more than there is an end to naming.

QUANTIFYING

The problem-solving powers of naming and connecting were enormously enhanced when names began to be counted and the counts began to be connected and further manipulated through what is now known as "mathematics." Quantification undoubtedly began with simple counting of named items but eventually became elaborated into measuring, arithmetic summing, and further manipulations, such as the quantifying of associations and connections. By the late nineteenth century, the mathematical specialties of probability and inferential statistics put the act of prediction on a secure platform for the first time.

The simple operation of counting was the important first step on the road to quantification. "In many inquiries, counting the individuals who possess a certain character is the only possible method of avoiding vague ideas."[3] So say Cohen and Nagel in their classic treatise on logic and the scientific method. They go on to say that counting "is undertaken not for its own sake but because we suspect significant connections between the groups counted."

Measuring is a feat that not only builds on counting but also goes beyond it. Whereas counting is limited to discrete entities, measuring moves us into fractional quantities and the possibility of ever-increasing accuracy as the tools of measurement are refined. Precision of measurement is a hallmark of modern engineering and advanced forms of problem solving. Increasing accuracy is also a never-ending process that often leads to new discoveries concerning the nature of matter and energy. For example, it was only after the measurement of the speed of light was made for the first time that Einstein was able to derive his brilliant formula for the relationship between energy and matter.

From the abstracting operations of counting, connecting, and measuring evolved the endless series of abstract manipulations and game playing that became mathematics. Pure mathematics concerns itself only with relationships among abstract entities without reference to any real phenomena or any assumption that there is such a thing as a "real" object or a "true" proposition.

In this sense, it is not a true science and is not concerned with problem solving in the real world.[4] However, it has been discovered over and over again that when mathematical and logical principles[5] are applied to real phenomena, such as counts and measures, they are extremely useful and become an integral part of all discovery and problem-solving processes.

Quantification, including counting and ever more precise measurement, has overwhelming importance because it paves the way for the most thoroughgoing application of mathematics, a field that has made great strides in the last three centuries and that continues to grow like all other fields of inquiry. Differential calculus, invented by Leibniz and Newton in the mid-seventeenth century[6] "immediately became the mathematical instrument for all understanding of variables in motion and hence of all mechanical engineering."[7] By the end of the nineteenth century, another mathematical specialty, probability theory, was wedded to statistical analysis to become a powerful tool in many applied fields. It had an especially profound effect on agriculture, where the efficacy of new methods and new seeds could be validated by statistical analysis. When these scientifically validated findings diffused, the consequence was an enormous boost in food production and the end of famine throughout most of the world. Further applications of statistical mathematics were soon dominating the new fields of psychology, sociology, economics, public health, and pharmaceutical research. Mathematical statistics continues to be the critical tool in expanding the frontiers of science and problem solving, especially in the direction of accurate prediction of future trends.

CAUSAL THINKING

Causality as a commonsense notion has been with us since at least early historical times. The Old Testament of the Bible, for example, provides a complete cosmology in vague, causal terms, starting, of course, with God: "... and God said, 'let there be light,'" and so on. In such ways did early humans come to understand and explain their world, very often by invoking spirits and developing a pantheon to explain such crucial elements of experience as birth and death, light and dark, fire and water, storms, disease, and so forth.

The exploration by psychologists of animal learning is also an exercise in causal analysis. If a certain stimulus is associated with another that causes a certain response, then, upon repetition, the first stimulus will come to evoke the same response without the second stimulus being present. It is reasoned that the stimulus pairing alone caused the first stimulus to gain this attribute. From the animal's point of view, there is no cause and effect because the animal presumably does not think in these terms. The great human advance over the animal was the ability to look at the sequence and to abstract the elements from the ongoing action. Humans have now been doing this for thousands of years. What changed over time and especially with the scientific revolution was the increasing specificity, accuracy, and credibility of causal propositions.

The Scottish philosopher David Hume, writing in the mid-eighteenth century, gave a prominent role to causal analysis, asserting, "The only immediate utility of all science is to teach us how to control and regulate future events by their causes."[8] Kant added the idea that causal connections could be further formulated into general rules or universal laws, and these propositions could then be subjected to both deductive and inductive logical reasoning.[9] The writings of Hume, Kant, and others gave a philosophical and logical foundation for what later became experimental science. Causal connections could be proposed and then tested by carefully restricting the number of observable elements allowed to vary. Propositions could also be connected to one another in causal chains, and the causal chains connected to form more elaborate theoretical constructs, tying together millions of empirically observed and quantified elements.

PREMEDITATED ACTION

From causal thinking it is a small step to causal action, making decisions based on sure knowledge that if *A* causes *B*, then, by doing *A*, one can make *B* happen. This is what might be called "premeditation," that is, thinking through what one will do, based on an understanding of what really works. Though a small step in logic, it is often a big step in a reality test because the action taken has real consequences for the actor. Even tested propositions are often incorrect when applied in a different time or circumstance. Thus the safe actor must test and retest the knowledge at hand to make sure it will work. The most prudent strategy, if it is available, is to begin with a trial, evaluate the results of the trial, and then proceed with an expanded action, perhaps modified from further information obtained from the trial.

Premeditation is almost infinitely expandable. Consider the chess player who looks at all the pieces on the board in contemplating his next move. In his head he imagines all the countermoves that might be taken by his opponent and then his own moves that might result in response. Great chess players can extend these mental rehearsals in dozens of directions that extend many moves ahead. Only the clock determines the end of this process, dictating that one move and one move only must now be taken. So it is with life. Thoughtful humans undertake action based on their knowledge of the number of possible moves and the number of possible external circumstances that would result from each move. We are continuously doing thought experiments, making mental rehearsals of possible action and contemplating the results in our heads before committing ourselves to the manifest act.

Each mental rehearsal involves a series of steps in a cycle, starting with a perception of the need stimulus, followed by the act-as-imagined, followed in turn by an imagining of the consequences. The brain then reviews the imagined need-action sequence and its imagined consequences. This review then leads to an action decision, and only after that decision is made will action be initiated, if at all. The decision taken is quite often and quite sensibly a decision *not* to act but to either ignore the impulse or to try thinking of another alternative action. In the case of the tournament chess player, another move is contemplated and its effects mentally played out, and then another and another until the clock strikes and an actual move decision is forced to be made, based on what seemed to have been the most satisfactory of all the mental scenarios played out.

With the development of language, humans were able to expose their premeditation to each other and make plans for action in coordination with others, thus greatly expanding their powers. With the invention of writing and the ability to record action sequences, the usefulness of premeditation took another leap forward. Now plans could be externalized, reviewed in written form, shared among a number of premeditators, then revised and rewritten before action decisions were undertaken. After histories of past actions were committed to a written record, past planning and action sequences could then be reviewed and incorporated into new plans. We know, of course, that such advanced forms of planning are far from foolproof. They depend on having a complete grasp of the relevant facts, the proper application of the truly relevant historical example, and the validity of the causal analysis contained in that example. Without hard empirical evidence and validated scientific analysis to determine true causation, the action decision will forever stand on a shaky foundation.

FIGURE 8.1.
TWO-STEP PROBLEM SOLVING:
THE BASIC REACTIVE MODE

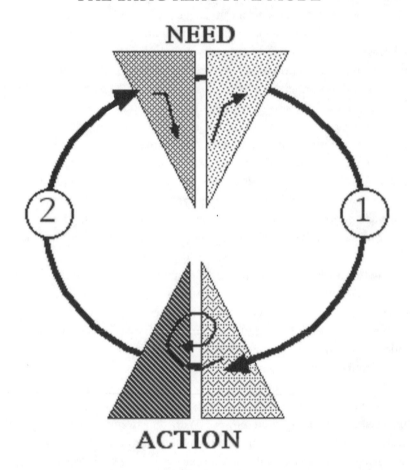

HOW ALL PROBLEM SOLVING WORKS:
THE BASICS

As was more fully described in chapter 4, cyclical problem solving is a fundamental of life itself and the subtext of the process by which progress is made.
All living systems up to and including very complex human organizations with
millions of individual members function according to this same cyclical principle. Figure 8.1 recaps figure 4.1 with minor relabeling. Every person and every

social organization must have many kinds of problem-solving processes in order to survive in a changing world. This does not mean that everyone is an expert problem solver, and it does not mean that everyone finds innovative solutions when there is a problem. However, everyone has multiple ways of coping with change. The two-step cycle of figure 8.1 is the most primitive form, but it is also the most common. We are hungry, so we eat. We are cold and wet, so we seek shelter and warmth. An enemy or a predator attacks, so we counterattack. A good deal of what passes as problem solving among humans who should know better is of this reactive two-step variety. It is impulsive, reflexive, and, one could even say, mindless, as is too often heard in expressions such as "Don't just stand there! Do something!" or "Do anything! Just do it!"

Dialectic reasoning is an advance on two-step problem solving in that an alternative action is offered for comparison and an analysis precedes the action. This pattern is depicted in figure 8.2. Some sort of thought process has intervened between need and action. Here the "thought" process is merely the posing of two alternatives. The simplest choice would be between doing a particular action and doing nothing. Doing nothing is sometimes a rational choice, especially if the need level is too low to justify any action or the action alternative is too difficult, too costly, or judged to be ineffective with respect to this need.

Assuming that choice *B* in the figure is something other than doing nothing, the figure leaves a number of questions hanging. The most prominent might be how the ideas of action *A* and action *B* were arrived at in the first place. Action *A* might represent the old way of doing things, what worked for us in the past, or what we were given in our hereditary makeup, which was supposed to work. The possible action *B* has a much more interesting origin. Perhaps it was an alternative already given in our complex heredity, just another way to resolve the situation. Or perhaps it is something suggested by another person. Conceivably, it could also be something newly imagined by the problem solver, a true innovation, a creation out of memory, or perhaps a combination of many things. The possibilities are endless.

The real key to effective problem solving is to get beyond the two-step mode. Advanced problem solving starts with adding steps to the cycle. The simplest addition is the stutter step implied in the expression "stop and think." Stop and plan what you are going to do. Stop and think about the consequences of your action for different people, for the longer term, for the system as a whole. Stop and think about whether you know what the problem really

FIGURE 8.2.
THREE-STEP PROBLEM SOLVING: ALTERNATIVES

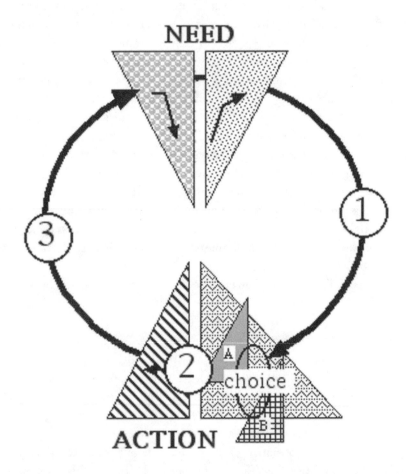

is. Stop and think about who is really being helped or hurt by this action. Stop and think about whether you have considered enough alternatives for what should be done or how to go about doing it.

"Stop and think" can be extended from *B* to *C* to *D* and to a near infinity of alternative choices. All advanced animal species can make thousands of such choices, depending on the extent of the learning they have been able to store in memory. In this respect, because of their very large brains, humans have the clear advantage over other species in making decisions informed by the widest set of alternatives. Whether or not the best alternative is chosen in any given instance of need is another question. Human history is in many respects a story of good and bad choices. To clarify the nature of this problem and to see where scientific problem solving diverges from traditional problem solving, consider figure 8.3, which poses a more complicated cycle of four stages that might intervene between need arousal and need reduction.

As in figure 8.1, we start with the need panoply as the initiator of the action cycle. But need is rarely if ever a simple unitary sensation requiring a single, simple response. There are multiple and conflicting needs. There are needs that are obvious and highly articulated for which solution tracks are more or less obvious, and then there are other needs that are poorly articu-

FIGURE 8.3.
ELEMENTS OF ADVANCED PROBLEM SOLVING

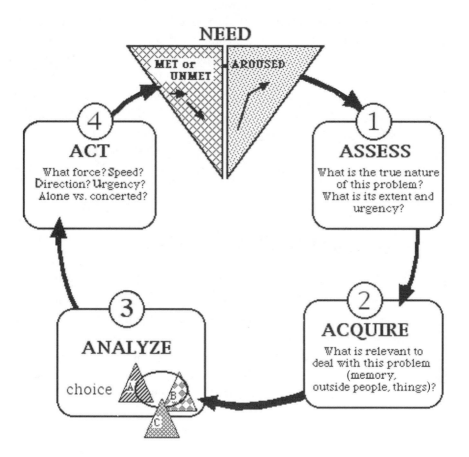

lated, complicated, and not framed well enough to invite obvious solutions. Effective problem solving thus requires a distinctly separate stage 1, *Assess*, to sort out what is really going on and what is most urgent. With stage 2, *Acquire*, the problem solver searches memory and may sometimes reach out to bring to bear whatever information might be relevant to a possible solution. As noted earlier, the platform of knowledge has become exceedingly large, now requiring many kinds of "search engines" to guide us sensibly to an absorbable subset of possible actions.

Stage 3, *Analyze*, requires a sifting of all the acquired information, assembly of alternative action strategies, and determination of which strategies show the most promise in the given situation. Much of this, like acquisition from memory, is probably automatic, dictated by a combination of genetic inheritance and relative saliency of separate memories. Yet in humans there is the possibility of thinking through a number of alternatives, just like the chess player, before settling on a particular action. Analysis requires the merging of various action ideas, adapting and altering others and even inventing some new ones. It also involves planning, laying out a strategy and a time line for how the action is to be implemented.

In stage 4, *Act*, the action has been settled and must now be implemented in overt behavior. Once decided upon, there are many ways in which the action might proceed. The problem solver must decide which form of action is likely to be most effective in the given circumstances. This final stage may even require a rethinking of the entire process to include the possibility that no action at all is the wisest course.

USING THE KNOWLEDGE PLATFORM

Few human actions are guided without the help of some knowledge platform, no matter how limited and tribal it might be. We have seen in previous chapters how these knowledge platforms are built up over the ages, pertaining to nearly every aspect of living. Therefore, advanced problem solving requires adequate access to as much of the platform as possible, and the knowledge gained may enhance solutions and actions at every stage, from assessment to acquisition, to analysis, to action. Figure 8.4 is intended to convey the over-riding importance of such access.

As *Homo sapiens* has become a better and better problem solver, strategies as well as action possibilities have multiplied. They have been greatly advanced through copying, one tribe to the next, one culture to another; and by recording and examining history, providing more and more specific detail on what worked and what didn't work in the past.

Such is the nature of advanced modern society that an immense infrastructure of problem solvers and problem-solving systems are readily available (sometimes for a price) to cover a very wide spectrum of needs. As social problem solving becomes more sophisticated, each of the stages displayed in

FIGURE 8.4.
HOW KNOWLEDGE PLATFORMS
ENHANCE PROBLEM SOLVING

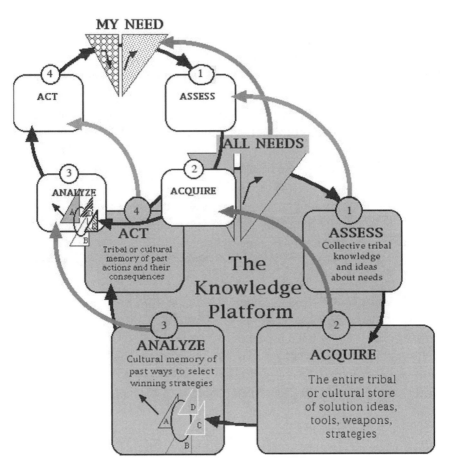

figure 8.3 fills in with more detail and refinement. In stage 1, at the leading edge of this ever-expanding infrastructure, old problems are redefined and new unmet needs emerge on a continuous basis. Problems that were previously unknown or unrecognized now get names attached and levels of concern aroused. Gaps in the knowledge base now become apparent, initiating new cycles of action. It is on this leading edge that the processes of science-based research and development (R & D) come into play. When they do, the forward function is most in evidence.

COUNTERPROPOSITIONS AND DIALECTIC REASONING

Over the last few centuries many attempts have been made to improve the analysis process so that outcomes could be made more reliable and more beneficial. The most venerable of these, perhaps dating back to Socrates in the fifth century BCE, is the dialectic, in which a proposition is put forward and then questioned, usually by another person. The other person may merely question the truth of the proposition (a form of the null hypothesis) or may advance a counterproposition, or both at the same time. The dialectic form of reasoning and approaching the truth through a back-and-forth dialogue has advanced through the ages and is today embedded in the common law of most countries as the "adversarial system." Science also incorporates this adversarial dialectic up to a point, in that any asserted discovery must be open to factual challenge, the final arbiter (as in law) being a majority judgment of what the weight of the evidence seems to show.

The problem with pure dialectic reasoning is that it is static. It assumes that there is one truth that can be discovered by a debate between two parties, each having equal access to whatever facts are available. It does not allow for the intrusion of a third or fourth alternative, and it does not allow for compromise or merger between the thesis and the antithesis. Thus, dialectic is not a process that allows for much in the way of progress. The historical philosopher Hegel proposed a kind of dialectic between social systems and social movements in conflict. Each such movement, as it becomes dominant in a particular historic epoch, tends to engender a countermovement that arises to challenge and eventually overwhelm the original, thus establishing a new hegemony, which in turn is eventually challenged. In such a pattern a kind of progress or, more properly, a progression occurs throughout history. Despite the almost absurd simplicity of this model, it was given great credence throughout the early nineteenth century and was adapted by Karl Marx at midcentury as the basis of his dialectic materialism. Neither Hegel nor Marx were really scientists, so their theories required scant proof, but their impact on history is undeniable. We also see an echo of such dialectic reasoning in Thomas Kuhn's notion of the structure of scientific revolutions, mentioned earlier, according to which a particular theory becomes dominant until a pre-dominance of contradicting facts leads to its overturn.[10] It is then replaced by another theory, which in its turn is also challenged and supplanted, ad infinitum.

SYNTHESIS, NEGOTIATED TRUTH, AND THIRD-WAY CREATIVE REASONING

We might suspect that in the long early advance of humanity, life was very often a zero-sum game. In battle there is a winner and a loser. The winner, by killing or enslaving the loser, wins everything, including the right to pass on dominance to offspring, controlling the hereditary line thereafter. This is a very ugly form of dialectic that has nevertheless characterized the endless wars and conquests that represent our human heritage. Perhaps we are learning how to go beyond this savage dialectic, yet it is clear that many of the world's people retain such a mind-set, and we continue to see it played out through endless cycles of violence in such places as the Middle East and the giant central African state of Sudan. Even the current "war on terrorism" has been framed in such starkly primitive terms as *good* versus *evil* and *us* versus *them*. In other words, it is polarized such that our truth must be dominant because theirs is manifestly and totally false.

Such thinking is also prevalent in the American legal system. In the case of a legal trial, if the defendant is declared innocent, he or she may or may not be truly innocent, but the process either stops there or goes on to some other potential suspect and another adversarial process, also with only two outcomes. In the civilized nonlegal world there are, thankfully, many more options. The thesis and the antithesis both may be utterly false, or they both may be partly true, in which case a compromise can be arrived at, incorporating some of the truth or justice adhering to each position. A creative nego-

FIGURE 8.5.
PROBLEM SOLVING IN SCIENCE

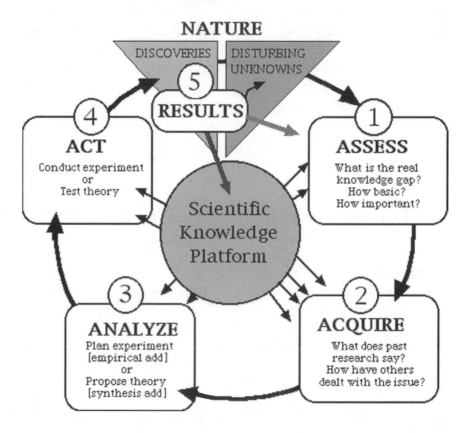

tiation can thus result in a synthesis representing the best elements in a new formulation that advances the truth represented in each and arrives at a new truth. Beyond synthesis is the recognition that there are many alternative solutions and partial solutions that could apply to any problem. This is where new discoveries in both substance and process come into play and true progress can be made. A major aspect of the forward function is the expansion and elaboration of the problem-solving process to extend way beyond the two steps of the dialectic.

THE RESEARCH PROJECT AS A MODEL
FOR THE FORWARD FUNCTION

Figure 8.5 suggests how the generalized problem-solving model works in the context of scientific research. A typical research project or a doctoral dissertation in a scientific field conforms nicely to the same stages as were laid out in figure 8.3. Such a project begins with the delineation of an aspect of the natural world that is poorly or inadequately understood. The investigator must establish the importance of a particular unknown within the larger context of the particular field and define and delimit the question that calls out for solution, all stage 1 (*Assess*) activities. Then the doctoral candidate must conduct an exhaustive review of the scientific literature, that is, the knowledge platform for his or her subject, which is clearly a stage 2 (*Acquire*) activity. The search defines the topic area more precisely and identifies the gaps in the platform, the places where some pieces of knowledge are missing, and eventually focuses on one particular piece, which, the candidate argues, is especially critical for one reason or another. Then the candidate sets up the framework for the particular project (stage 3, *Analyze*). This might be an experiment or a survey or an observational exercise. It might also include control groups, randomized assignment of conditions, double-blind ratings, and so forth. There are a great number of possible research designs. The main purpose of all of them is to ensure that the outcome being measured yields data that is both reliable and valid, in layman's terms, "true." Stage 4, the *Act* phase, is the actual conducting of the experiment.

Once the project is completed and before it can become a potential candidate for inclusion in the scientific knowledge platform (the "results" downward arrow in figure 8.5), it must be written up and summarized (stage 5). This write-up must include not only the findings but also the literature review highlights establishing the knowledge gap and the precise conditions of the study or experiment, the subjects or data observed, the experimental and control conditions, the instruments used, and all the conditions related to the study that might have affected the outcome. This write-up is then submitted for publication in one of the journals that is recognized as authoritative in the field. Then the submitted article is reviewed by an anonymous panel of recognized experts, each rendering an independent judgment without knowledge of either the study author or the organization under whose auspices the study took place. Only after passing this review and subsequent publication do the findings of the study make their way into the knowledge platform of science; and even then, there is no guarantee that the particular findings will become established in a significant niche, changing the platform and strengthening it to a meaningful extent. A most common and important result of any experiment is a failure that may lead to a reassessment and initiation of a new cycle (the "results" gray arrow in figure 8.5). Science typically involves numerous recycles of theory and experiment before a solid piece of new knowledge can be added to the platform.

SYNTHETIC RESEARCH

Considering what a tortuous path any piece of research must follow to get onto the great platform of scientific knowledge, it might seem amazing that there is much of a platform at all. In reality, this classic route is often bypassed. Established researchers who work in prestigious organizations, principally universities, may supervise hundreds of research projects, many simultaneously. While many of their students go on to become full-time researchers and experts in their own right, thus multiplying the number of studies ad infinitum, the originating research professors synthesize their work and that of their students in book form in the hope or expectation that the results will come to constitute a nice, big, new block in the platform, perhaps replacing some significant old blocks. If the synthesizer's new formulation is taken by many to be a revolutionary contribution, casting a lot of prior research in a new light, as in a "paradigm shift," a Nobel Prize may be in the offing.

Such synthesizing work can also be considered as true knowledge building and problem solving, and it readily fits the stage model of figure 8.5. With a synthesis the scale is larger. The synthesizer introduces the subject by pointing out how important it is in the larger scheme of things (the need assessment, stage 1). Then the literature is reviewed, reminding the reader of what the current state of the knowledge platform is in this particular sector (the search, stage 2). The synthesizer now explains the various conditions of new studies that have been undertaken in recent years, no doubt highlighting those undertaken by his or her own students (choose and prepare, stage 3). Then the quantitative findings are laid out within the framework of the new theory, and their implications and significance are spelled out in terms of the knowledge platform (evaluation, stage 4). Unlike the raw research study, the synthesis now goes to a book publisher who ideally also employs an expert review panel blinded to the author's name and institution. Then, as a book, the synthesis has its chance in the marketplace of knowledge and may become the new platform block that the author hoped for.

Many types of syntheses can contribute meaningfully to the platform. One very important type of synthesis is the textbook, the primary medium for passing important sections of the platform from one generation of specialists to the next. The university course, composed of a series of prepared lectures on a given topic combined with readings and usually some form of dialogue between professor and students, plays a synthesizing role similar to the textbook. The professor who teaches a course covering a specific range of subject matter also follows the four-step model, beginning with the determination that the course is needed and that it fills a significant gap in the curriculum. In course preparation, the professor will likely do a substantial search of the literature (stage 2), prepare lectures (stage 3), and then deliver the lectures and assign the readings (stage 4).

A particularly interesting form of synthesis has been under way for many years under the aegis of US National Institutes of Health. At irregular intervals usually numbering half a dozen per year, the institute's staff picks a medical topic of some urgency in which a large number of new findings have been accumulating and convenes an advisory panel of about twelve people to reach a consensus on what the major findings are and what might be their implications for practice. The panel includes several researchers along with at least one statistician, a medical ethicist, and one or two consumer representatives. Substantial review summaries are read by each panel member, then they are discussed, and finally a consensus document is prepared, usually without dissent but sometimes with individual qualifiers. The result is then presented to the general public via a news conference, and arrangements are made for publication in a prominent medical journal, thus contributing in some way to the platform of medical knowledge. Unlike the professor's course or the textbook, the consensus document gives explicit recommendations regarding what procedures and medicines are effective and what should be the standard of care in a particular area of medical practice.[11]

ONE PLATFORM OR MANY PLATFORMS?

With the explosive growth of science in the last century has come a new kind of concern. There is now too much in the knowledge base—too many facts, too many specialties, hence many different platforms. This compartmentalization has distinct advantages for the separate specialties of science and practice. The limits of a field allow those working in that field to prosper and to move further without being concerned with larger issues, such as the meaning of their work in a political context or how what they have learned could be applied for good or otherwise. However, there is an overarching scientific platform that encompasses all specialties, and as we learn more, the need for integration across specialties becomes increasingly obvious. The basic integrative facts of this larger platform can be mastered by most educated people and can be easily taught at the high school level. The American Association for the Advancement of Science (AAAS) has been working on such a curriculum project for several years.[12]

A very laudable science-synthesizing effort was undertaken in the late 1990s by biologist Edward O. Wilson.[13] Wilson tried to show a wide audience of educated people that scientific knowledge is all of one piece and depends on a foundation of mathematics and physics. He drew on the rare term *consilience*, coined by nineteenth-century English scholar William Whewell, to refer to the bringing together of different areas of knowledge "by the linking of facts and fact-based theory across disciplines to create a common framework of explanation." Wilson adds that trust in this consilience "is the foundation of the natural sciences."[14]

The AAAS authors make it clear that to be scientifically literate means to be standing on this platform of modern science, a platform that starts out with mathematics and physics but stretches out to include all the biological and social sciences. The AAAS has an objective more ambitious and more all-encompassing than Wilson's. They want this new platform to serve not just for scientists seeking new discoveries but for all people. The analogy to literacy is clear; all adult members of contemporary society are now expected to be literate, to know how to read and write in their own language. AAAS says they should also know some basic information about science because such knowledge is necessary for them to be fully engaged and participating members of a modern society and to derive full benefit from the wonders of modern technology.

HOW KNOW-HOW DEVELOPMENT
DIFFERS FROM SCIENTIFIC RESEARCH

It is important to keep in mind that the forward function is not just about the continuing growth of knowledge. More directly it is about the production, distribution, and utilization of knowledge to improve the human condition. The previously mentioned medical consensus conference model is but one of many attempts to bridge the gap between research findings and practical benefit. Medical research is by definition applied research, always aimed at outcomes that are practically useful. It is about building knowledge and improving practice in any and all ways to extend the life and improve the health of humans individually and collectively. However, the world of medical research includes many kinds of problem-solving activity that go beyond the research model as described above. Medicine is also about the invention and production of medicines, as well as techniques, procedures, protocols, and devices of all kinds, all with the same general aim of promoting life and health. Until the mid–twentieth century there was no term that easily covered all these disparate but important problem-solving activities and connected them to the knowledge platform where they truly belong. Now we can group them all with scientific research under the big umbrella designation *R & D*, for "research and development."[15]

Development, as distinct from basic and applied research, is focused on the creation of all kinds of artifacts and procedures that will have a demonstrated utility. In 1959, a publication of the (US) National Science Foundation set forth a semiofficial definition as follows: "Development is the systematic use of scientific knowledge directed toward the production of useful materials, devices, systems, methods, or processes," which includes "the design and development of prototypes" but excludes "quality control or routine product testing."[16] Perhaps what was most important about this new definition of *development* was the strong link that was explicitly made to mainstream science. Humans had been inventing useful things since the first stone was shaped into a blade, but until the mid-twentieth century the thought that such activity was necessarily connected to what scientists were doing was rarely put on the table. Great inventors like Bell, Edison, and the Wright brothers had some scientific knowledge to go on, but they were basically tinkerers who hoped that their inventions would become popular and make them some money. The new view of all technology as having grounding in science is also reflected in the

AAAS curriculum reform efforts that afford a prominent place to technology and what the AAAS refers to as "the designed world" of modern agriculture, energy, communications, and materials technology.[17]

Granted the important distinctions that can be made between research on the one hand and development on the other, it remains noteworthy that all types of development fit the basic cyclical model of figure 8.3 just as well as any scientific knowledge–building activity, as suggested by figure 8.6. Development is manifestly need-driven. Developers are not trying to fill gaps in knowledge directly but rather are trying to address some real and explicit need, perhaps an urgent need. The source from which each development project springs is both a knowledge and a know-how platform, and ideally such a project starts with a clear definition of what is really needed (stage 1)

FIGURE 8.6.
PROBLEM SOLVING IN APPLIED SCIENCE AND TECHNOLOGY

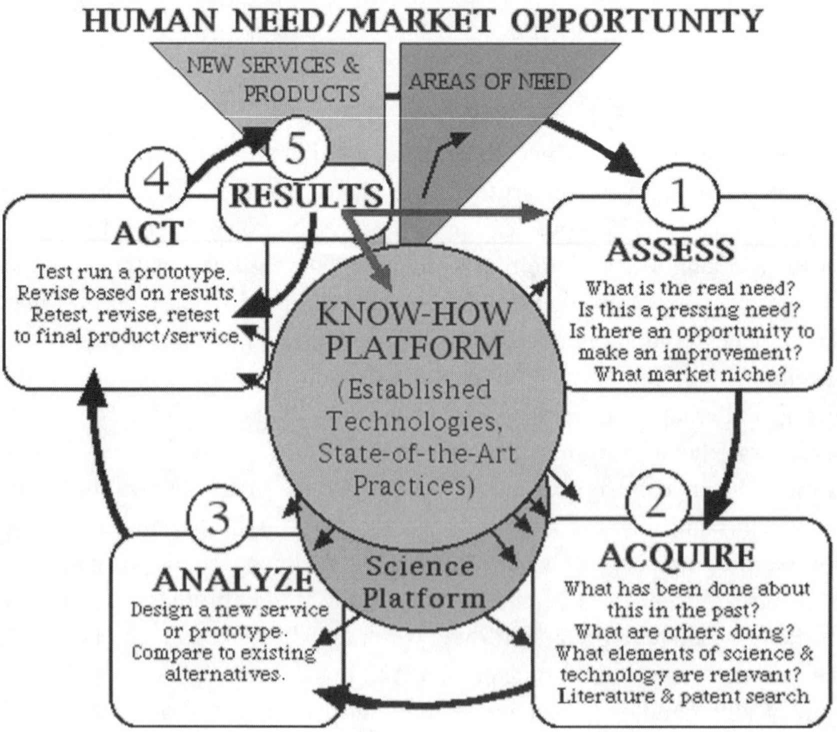

HUMAN NEED/MARKET OPPORTUNITY

NEW SERVICES & PRODUCTS   AREAS OF NEED

5 RESULTS

4 ACT
Test run a prototype.
Revise based on results.
Retest, revise, retest
to final product/service.

KNOW-HOW PLATFORM
(Established Technologies, State-of-the-Art Practices)

Science Platform

1 ASSESS
What is the real need?
Is this a pressing need?
Is there an opportunity to make an improvement?
What market niche?

3 ANALYZE
Design a new service or prototype.
Compare to existing alternatives.

2 ACQUIRE
What has been done about this in the past?
What are others doing?
What elements of science & technology are relevant?
Literature & patent search

and a review of all previous attempts to fill this need which either failed or only partially succeeded (stage 2). If commercial viability is sought, the platform acquisition activity will also have to include a patent search. From this platform an invention takes shape, a new device or product or procedure that is first imagined, then conceived on paper, modified, and shaped into a prototype so that obvious design flaws can be corrected (stage 3). Then the prototype is submitted to a real-world real-time test, perhaps even in the form of an experiment or a comparison with other types of products already in use (stage 4). The "results" phase, stage 5, now becomes a critical feedback loop that may be repeated many times until the product or service is ready for full introduction into the market or service sector. The outcome of the new product or procedure may be evaluated in various ways. Early prototypes need to respond to the question "Does it work?" For later test models the question becomes "How well does it work?" or "What is this item's relative advantage over existing alternatives?" or "Does it succeed in the marketplace (i.e., return profit to the inventors)?"

Development cycles are deliberately iterative, meaning that the cycle repeats itself, each time seeking a stronger and more reliable impact. In successive cycles, each of the four stages may have to be repeated: Have we made the right assessment of need? Have we done an adequate search? Have we made the correct analysis? Have we fabricated the product in the best way or implemented our trial in the most appropriate way? Various refinements and modifications are added to prepare for entry not into the knowledge platform but into the marketplace. The proprietary nature of many development outcomes is such that they may only partially enter the "public domain," the know-how knowledge platform that is open to all. Thus, while commercialization is a strong force for innovation and human advancement, it can also be a drag for as long as the know-how is kept as the secret property of a privileged few, however worthy their claims may be for priority.

Of special importance for the forward function are those invented and developed technologies that enhance the problem-solving process as a whole. Telescopes and microscopes, although developed long before anyone conceived of development as a process in the modern sense used here, deserve special mention as problem-solving accelerators because they opened windows on macro- and microworlds heretofore unseen and therefore unknowable. With these wonderful new discovery devices, the knowledge platform quite suddenly became both larger and more solid. Their further development and nearly unceasing refinement and widespread use are continuing to expand the knowledge platform, as are many other types of devices for measuring and recording sound, radiation, motion, heat, weight, and so on.[18]

In the electronics and communications explosions of the twentieth century, all types of instrumentation for science took another leap forward. Data precision and reliability improved many times over. Computers, computer programs, electronic messaging, and networking continue to speed up the processing and statistical manipulation of data, also making scientific observation more precise and deep. The use of computer modeling of designs prior to actual field tests under realistic conditions sometimes allows for thousands of simulated tests before there is commitment to the expense of the actual test.

THE MERGER OF SCIENTIFIC AND KNOW-HOW KNOWLEDGE

Know-how, once established and proven, has never been controversial. The church fathers did not deny that Galileo's telescope magnified far-off images. They just refused to accept his interpretations of what he saw. Likewise, both Christians and Muslims were both glad to use the new technologies of firearms that traders had brought from China in the early Middle Ages, despite their contrary worldviews and hostile relations. Nor was there much controversy over the usefulness of horses, carts, plows, seeds, spears, pots, boats, and so on. Even as the technologies in all these and sundry other areas advanced over the centuries, there was little controversy over their utility and little resistance to their acceptance, regardless of their source. This kind of knowledge passed readily from the hands of the European invaders and settlers to the native populations of North and South America within two or three generations of the first European landings. The history of technology strongly suggests that no important, useful technology remains the property of one tribe or one nation for long, even when desperate attempts are made to keep it secret. This is as true of lasers and transistors as it is for atomic weapons. The genie always comes out of the bottle.

The same cannot always be said for the overall knowledge platform or for the knowledge platforms of science. Galileo is perhaps the most memorable instance of this. The church leaders of his time believed, quite reasonably, that there could be only one truth about the universe, and for them that was God's truth as revealed through scripture and the interpretations of scripture by holy wise men through the centuries. Having incorporated Plato, Aristotle, and much of Hellenistic science into their Christian framework, they had what they thought was a thoroughly rational and consistent framework for understanding everything. Their thought system included a cosmology consistent with Genesis that incorporated the motion of all the observable heavenly bodies, sun, moon, stars, and planets. They were not dualists. There could be only one system.[19]

As the different spheres of scientific exploration began to adhere in the nineteenth century, they suggested a very broad and logically coherent view of empirical reality that was sharply at odds with the biblical texts. For those who came to accept this new perspective on science, dualistic thinking was the only way to preserve their religious heritage. There was the truth of science on the one hand, and the truth of God as revealed through scripture on the other. Dualism will always work pretty well as an intellectual dodge. Furthermore, the brain is not constructed to be a logic machine: it is possible for any brain or any number of brains working together to hold many logically contradictory ideas at the same time, and for most people this causes little if any cognitive dissonance. On the other hand, solid knowledge platforms must work like logic machines. They cannot tolerate the dissonance of contradictory propositions. All through the nineteenth and the early twentieth centuries, the pieces of the cosmologic puzzle were coming together with the table of elements, the enormous space and time extension of the new astronomy, and the enormous expansion of the microworld of atomic particle physics, atom-based chemistry, and chemical-based life. Dualism, especially after Darwin, was becoming a real intellectual challenge for the world's religions. Their own cherished knowledge platforms, based on holy writ, were under increasing threat.

What happened mostly in the latter half of the twentieth century was a new kind of knowledge integration, not across fields but between science and know-how. This came about partly through the growing realization that the scientific method could serve as a universal problem solver. Any practical problem could be framed in precise terms and subjected to test and evaluation, regardless of what field it came from: medicine, agriculture, building construction, metallurgy, animal breeding, and even animal and human behavior modification. Suddenly there was just one knowledge platform for everything. It was huge, it was expanding at an enormous rate, and scientific methods and proven theories were at its core!

WORKING ACROSS KNOWLEDGE AND KNOW-HOW PLATFORMS

The knowledge system's intricate differentiation and complexity has long since passed the point where it can be fully grasped by a single mind.[20] Therefore, synthesizers like Wilson and umbrella organizations like the AAAS are needed to bring it all together and demonstrate to a larger public that there is, indeed, an overall pattern. It is especially important to recognize that the know-how platforms stand alongside the scientific knowledge platforms. Galileo first copied and improved his telescope from a crude model that some spectacle makers from Flanders were trying to sell to the Venetian government. He then demonstrated its value to the Venetian Senate by showing them that they could see ships approaching the harbor from many miles away, an astounding demonstration that gave him great credibility and widened his fame. Only later did he turn it up to the sky to observe the moons of Jupiter for the first time, what we would today call a scientific application.[21] Thus we have one practical use (spectacle making), leading to another practical use (identifying ships at sea) preceding the first scientific use of a new technology. Subsequently, the telescopes and microscopes that derived from the glassmakers' craft transformed our scientific understanding of both the macrouniverse and the microuniverse, establishing and expanding the sciences of astronomy, physics, chemistry, and biology. The know-how knowledge feeds the science just as much as the science inspires the technology to the enormous benefit and expansion of both.

PLATFORM SOLIDITY

Ideally there should be just one integrated megaplatform for science and technology, a platform that is both solid and reliable, one that covers all subjects and shows the connections between subjects. This is more or less the case between astronomy and physics, physics and chemistry, chemistry and biochemistry, biochemistry and biology. However, there are huge gaps and many of the curators of the subplatforms hardly communicate with each other unless forced to do so, despite the efforts of cross-discipline synthesizers like Wilson. Isolation allows specialists to concentrate on specific problems, free of distraction and free of politics. Academic science is also shielded from the pressures of the marketplace and the flood of human needs that continually cry out for solutions. Of the platform gaps, the most glaring are in the so-called social sciences. Despite valiant efforts over the last hundred years to tie social phenomena to the methods of scientific inquiry, there is still no really stable platform of social science knowledge. There is no coherent theory that binds the social sciences together or ties them to sister disciplines in the natural sciences. Nor is there even any set of data points that are widely accepted as the basis for empirical study.

The weakness of the social sciences is especially unfortunate when the task is to understand the world of science itself. How scientists work together to build the knowledge platform is primarily a social science issue. The patterns by which knowledge flows through these labyrinthine networks toward practical applications are primarily social phenomena. A more detailed understanding from social scientists of how this system really works would provide important guidance on how to make both basic and applied science work better for greater public benefit.

Some social scientists have gone so far as to propose that all knowledge platforms are illusory. According to Thomas Kuhn, for example, the theories that bind together a particular field of study are under constant challenge from observations and countertheories. Eventually the opposition gathers enough strength to upset the apple cart of established wisdom. Kuhn refers to each dominant theory of a particular time as a "paradigm." When the tipping point occurs, there is a "paradigm shift," meaning the embrace of a new paradigm by the great majority of scientists within the given field. The old order with its associated base of fact-theory is thus broken.[22]

Kuhn's model may well apply to the shaky platforms of psychology and the social sciences,[23] yet it may be somewhat misleading as it applies to the hard sciences and to their applications in medicine, agriculture, and engineering. As scientists look ever more closely at certain fundamental phenomena, let us say, the nature of the atom or of the living cell, new patterns and new explanations emerge, but these discoveries are almost always embedded in a larger fabric of understanding that becomes progressively stronger over time. Thus biologists have seen the cells of life in their microscopes for about as long as astronomers have been seeing the stars through their telescopes, and they have long since established the basic fact that all living things are made up of cells. They are also learning more and more every day about what goes on inside a cell, how it works, and how it takes in and transforms energy in tiny amounts to keep life going. These added findings will surely lead to new insights into what a cell really is, but they do not change the fundamental realization that cells are the building blocks of life.[24]

The same solid founding structure applies to the nature of matter itself, which is the basis of all chemistry and chemistry's applications in material science and biochemistry. The periodic table of elements is basic. The existence of atoms, though mostly submicroscopic, is now entirely established. The relative weights of all atoms are known, as is their formation into the basic compounds that we know as solids, liquids, and gases. No new finding is going to upset this apple cart, even though our insights into the nature of the atom's nucleus, its binding of energy, and its other features and effects continue to be explored by physicists. Kuhn would probably agree with all this. He was looking primarily at the workings of scientific specialties, but the paradigm-shift idea has often been invoked to obscure the relentlessly progressive aspect of scientific knowledge building. Through all the paradigm shifts that inevitably take place, the platform gets stronger and stronger, and its underlying validity and integrity prove more and more solid.

With few exceptions, the separate knowledge and know-how platforms expand continuously without end. While they are expanding, these platforms also divide as the knowledge building becomes more differentiated. Even as divisions multiply, the connections between separate platforms become more evident. Thus the overall platform becomes stronger. Fortunately, the expansion has also proceeded in parallel with improvements in the capacity to store both knowledge and know-how so that, in the modern era at least, virtually nothing is lost along the way. No modern version of the catastrophic fire at the library at Alexandria is going to obliterate what is now known or what will be added as the years roll on.

Even though the physical size of the human brain has not been expanding in step with the expansion of the knowledge platform, the ability of scientists and technologists to pull together and integrate knowledge strands has been enormously aided by advances in information technology and communication, as well as in the continuing reorganization of the science and technology enterprise. We have no need to fear the Tower of Babel scenario in which taller structures of knowledge lead to separations of language and purpose that end in chaos. Even language itself is not the barrier it once was, as more and more works now appear in translation. The language barrier in science will virtually disappear as automated technical translation software improves. Instantaneous computer-assisted translation is just around the corner.

Even though there is this continuous expansion of the base, it is unfortunate that not every discovery, not every new problem solved, and not every synthetic insight gets added to the worldwide knowledge storehouse. Many great and insightful discoverers labor on in isolation and silence, never known outside their own circle. Many "discoveries" can thus disappear without a trace, perhaps occasionally to be rediscovered by later scholars but more often not. In the ancient world, this was even more the case. One suspects that stone axes, wheels, and sundry other labor-saving, life-enhancing devices were discovered multiple times and then lost, retarding the advance of humanity by who knows how many thousands of years. Natural disasters and political misfortunes have also played a role in limiting the spread of the platform. Many have suggested that the Alexandria fire set back modern science by two or three hundred years. After printing was developed, this kind of catastrophe could not happen again, even though some ambitious book-burning projects were undertaken in the twentieth century.

SUMMARY

With the invention of the scientific method, a new type of knowledge platform came into being. For the first time, the critical thought processes of naming, connecting, quantifying, and causally analyzing could be knitted together in ways that continuously ensured their empirical validity. The real human environment was beginning to be mapped in its entirety. The new platform had and still has enormous gaps, but a process has been established for filling those gaps, and a unified picture of the universe—from the largest to the smallest entities, and including all life-forms—is beginning to emerge. As the body of scientific knowledge has expanded, its methods have grown increasingly sophisticated and precise while the basic process has preserved a certain constancy characterized by openness of all procedures, careful attention to what has been done before (the knowledge platform), presentation of new connective theory or extension of old theory, collection of empirical data, acceptance of results of tests in regard to theory, and commitment of the total process to the inspection of others.

During the twentieth century, the scientific method became the basis for all types of problem solving, theoretical and practical. Thus the great know-how systems of practical knowledge passed down and elaborated from the

Stone Age to the Industrial Age now have a basis in the integrated knowledge system of science. The result has been an explosion of knowledge-building activities in all spheres resulting in great potential benefits for humanity. For such benefits to be fully realized, the resulting innovations from this exploding knowledge base must be spread to all the human tribes without exception. How this spread happens and can continue to happen will be discussed in the next chapter.

Chapter Nine

MODERN GLOBAL DIFFUSION
Forward Function Force #6

Knowledge is not simply another commodity. On the contrary, knowledge is never used up. It increases by diffusion and grows by dispersion.
—Daniel J. Boorstin

Our problem is to learn why, given one hundred different innovations conceived of at the same time—innovations in the form of words, in mythical ideas, in industrial processes etc.—ten will spread abroad, while ninety will be forgotten.
—Gabriel Tarde, *Les Lois de l'Imitation*

The S-shaped curve of diffusion "takes off" once interpersonal networks become activated in spreading subjective evaluations of an innovation. . . . The part of the diffusion curve from about 10 percent adoption to 20 percent adoption is the heart of the diffusion process. After that point, it is often impossible to stop the further diffusion of a new idea, even if one wished to do so.
—Everett M. Rogers[1]

The one remaining force needed to explain why progress has been accelerating nearly continuously over the last two hundred years is modern diffusion. *Diffusion* can be defined as the spread of an innovation to a larger and larger circle of potential users. The traditional modes of diffusion have been with us since the very first human tribes were formed. Direct observation of others in action and word-of-mouth transfer within and across families was how it worked. This process was described in chapter 6 as the propensity for social interactions that humans possess to a greater degree than all other animal species.

Modern humanity has invented and deployed many innovations in the process of communication itself. These new communication tools are much more powerful than the word-of-mouth of ages past, even though, in many cases, they build on the older modes of communication and would not be effective without exploiting these older modes. To understand the acceleration of *progress* within the last century, it is essential to understand the role of these new media.

The number of media that are capable of carrying important problem-solving messages has multiplied along with the knowledge base. Until the nineteenth century, the primary written medium of science was the letter. Letters are still in use in some areas but are now joined by journals, books, conferences, and meetings of all kinds. Most recently, the Internet has allowed letter writing to enjoy something of a revival since, at least in its early incarnations, the Internet has favored typed inputs in the form of "e-mail." These are all accepted media for scientific communication.

The spread of scientific findings and new products and procedures based on science now depends on a wide mix of media, including newspapers, television, Internet websites, textbooks, manuals, popular books, and magazines. The multiplication of media and their extended reach have accelerated the general diffusion of knowledge and knowledge-based artifacts to an enormous degree. Whereas it once took many years for a typical innovation to spread throughout a given community, today the same process may happen in one or two years, depending on the item, its relative advantage over existing usage, and the difficulties of adaptation to local needs.

The underlying process is much the same as it has always been because of its fundamental dependence on social networking. However, in today's information environment, professional networks extend across the globe and are facilitated by safe, rapid, and relatively inexpensive air travel, teleconferencing, and many kinds of messaging made possible by the Internet. Thus, a new discovery can be transmitted to millions in minutes. Search engines can give detailed access to the world's knowledge platforms in a single keystroke.

MASS DIFFUSION AND EQUALIZATION

Widespread diffusion equalizes knowledge possession and thus, to a degree, equalizes the opportunity to exploit knowledge for human benefit. This is especially true in any society that enjoys a high general level of education and most especially in any society that can achieve a high degree of scientific literacy.[2] The Internet thus far has been allowed to be an open system with free access worldwide, an incredible leap forward for information equality. However, some societies are clearly better equipped to take advantage of this new medium than others. As the benefits of using the Internet have become more apparent, word-of-mouth networking is already ensuring an exponential growth in its utilization as a general carrier of beneficial change.

The equalizing aspect of diffusion is more problematic with respect to new products and services as distinct from knowledge. First, this is because the economic system and the distribution of wealth are major determinants of such diffusion, and, second, because information in the form of developed products and services is very often (not always) proprietary (i.e., held privately with strictly limited diffusion to serve the exclusive economic interests of the developers). If you want it and you can't afford to buy it at the price offered, you don't get it.

Some types of knowledge with great problem-solving potential may actually be blocked from any kind of distribution, either because the business interest is protecting the market for another less-worthy product or, as in the case of governments, the R & D is deemed to be of such importance to national security that it is held in secret for many years. Such could have been the fate of the Internet, which was originally developed by the US Department of Defense to secure government and military communications in the event of a catastrophic atomic attack. Very fortunately, at an early stage of development the original "ARPANET" was deemed to be of such value in promoting scientific productivity generally that it was allowed to spread without significant government controls.[3]

Modern diffusion is also important because it connects knowledge to problems at a faster rate and on a more comprehensive scale. It multiplies the number of people who are adequately informed on a given problem and enhances the capability of all problem solvers by putting more knowledge into their frames of reference. Progress actually depends on wave after wave of diffusion, starting with the journals that publish original research, on to the synthesizing works and textbooks that then displace the outdated wisdom of previous works. The new accepted wisdom is then further diffused through teaching in schools and colleges to new generations of problem solvers. From the newly educated generation, innovation in the form of new practices and products spreads into the sectors of everyday work in business, government, and professional practice, changing the ways in which people live and work.

The merciless displacement of the old by the new is a feature of modern knowledge diffusion that curiously applies only in science and technology. In fictional literature, music, fine art, and religion, the new also emerges continuously but rarely displaces the old. Figure 9.1 suggests the vital connections between the creation of knowledge, its diffusion, and its final utilization.

The cyclic process of figure 8.3 can be assumed to be ongoing in the "Creation" circle to the left. Sensing a need, searching for information, fabricating solutions, conducting a trial, and evaluating results may all go on within an individual laboratory setting or even within an individual person's creative endeavor before there is any exposure of the innovation to the outside world. However, to have a meaningful impact, diffusion must eventually follow invention. Diffusion activity of various kinds can emanate in many directions to many possible receivers from the successful conclusion of a problem-solving effort. The arcing diffusion arrows suggest the many potential users, all interconnected through both formal and informal networks and through

FIGURE 9.1.
KNOWLEDGE CREATION, DIFFUSION, AND UTILIZATION

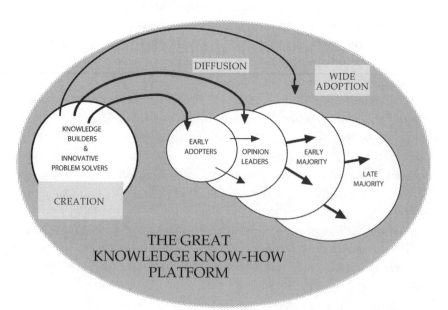

organizations. Simultaneously, the new knowledge passes on into the larger knowledge platform from which all future users may draw.

The prime social actors in the diffusion process are innovators and opinion leaders. In this context, *innovators* are defined as the first individuals to adopt an innovation. They tend to be creative risk takers and are to be found in small numbers in any large community or organization. Opinion leaders are community members who are looked upon by others as exemplars of good practice. Progressive opinion leaders always have an eye out for innovations whose time has come. Thus, they closely follow the more adventurous and risk-taking innovators. If opinion leaders are well connected to a number of innovators, an innovation will be more likely to diffuse rapidly through a system.

The early majority are the people who watch what opinion leaders do and follow their lead. The late majority are the people who follow everybody else. They adopt innovations in the later stages of diffusion because they don't want to be left behind. They are most likely to depend on outside social forces for guidance rather than their own internal needs and their own problem-solving abilities.[4]

The total process of diffusion may involve many stages, many types of media, and many types of messages that diffuse at different times and produce different effects. Modern diffusion typically combines written words with still pictures, motion pictures, tables, graphs, sounds, and images that all relate to the same innovation. Some of these messages may be designed merely to provoke awareness and interest, others to suggest how the item might work in the context of the user's life, while still others might deal with the steps involved in acquisition (such as locales, prices, guarantees, and so forth). The point is that streams of messages on many different channels are constantly converging, thus having a cumulative impact on potential users.

THE DOWN SIDES OF DIFFUSION

Diffusion, per se, is indifferent to the quality of the message. Under ideal circumstances the message sent should be something new, true, and useful. However, any message that has potential meaning and relevance to a number of receivers can be diffused, regardless of its true merit and validity. In the context of modern diffusion, any potentially beneficial innovation can be thought of as a string of information elements that arrive at the ears and eyes of the receiver in sequence. The leading edge of the message string is its reward promise, positive or negative. The substance follows, and the qualifiers and validating evidence tend to come last, if they are there at all.

Those who accept the message based only on the leading edge are unwittingly basing their belief and acceptance on faith. Since most diffused messages have no real validity and cannot stand up to the truth tests of science, such easy acceptors fall victim to all sorts of false ideas and theories. This has been the curse of the Internet up to now. All sorts of messages are easily transmitted over a network with many millions of nodal points, but when truth-value is considered this mountain of messages is almost as useless as a landfill. There are many gems in there somewhere, but it is mostly garbage. The gems are the facts of science and the know-how products of proven value. The popular search engines and services of the Internet, such as Google, sort this giant stock of messages only by word chains that do little or nothing to analyze or filter truth claims.

An explosion of media and messages aimed at every conceivable audience and interest group, large or small, characterizes advanced societies. As a result, the knowledge consumer is flooded with messages that stream down from all media. Each medium and each message competes for attention in the receiver marketplace. Winning media and winning messages (that is, those with the most appeal, the largest market share, and the ability to command the most time and attention of the largest audience) are extremely profitable. They bring great wealth and power to their lucky senders.

This media-message flood is not a progressive force, per se, unless messages with legitimate claims to reliability and scientific validity are ascendant. In a wide-open information marketplace, the most valid and reliable information will rarely come out on top unless special steps are taken to elevate its visibility and to screen out noise and trash. Within the world of science and to a large extent throughout academia such rigorous screening does take place. Thus the *New York Times* is informally but widely designated as "the newspaper of record" with the implication that its stories are reliably valid news. Within the broad and expanding field of medical knowledge, the *New England Journal of Medicine* carries the same pedigree. If an article appears there, it must have been very carefully vetted by medical researchers with impeccable credentials, and it must be *very important*!

As noted earlier, diffusion of knowledge only results in progress when the diffusion leads to utilization, either as incorporation in the receiver's individual knowledge platform or as changes in behavior and practice. Most knowledge diffusion has a sorrier fate, ending in dissipation, distortion, and degradation. Almost all messages, even the most important and useful, carry an expiration date. Yesterday's news is no longer news, and the attention span of the average receiver is woefully short. Timing is therefore crucial for effective transmission, as is redundancy. In order to take advantage of the few open moments that receivers offer in their busy lives, an important message must be delivered over and over again via many media. Only in this way can the sender mitigate the effects of message dissipation.

DIFFUSION IN THE TWENTY-FIRST CENTURY

The great scientific discoveries of the seventeenth, eighteenth, and nineteenth centuries depended on diffusion along very slender communication links in comparison to what has happened in the last century. Originally there were just a few monthly meetings in one or two places in England and on the European continent, supplemented by written messages in Latin passed around in letters. Throughout the twentieth century, with Latin long discarded, communication expanded exponentially in all areas, as did the creation of new specialties and specialties within specialties. This process now goes on at such a feverish pace that the challenge in the hottest areas is just to keep up with what everybody else is doing. Now with the Internet and its associated electronic networks, a new age of knowledge diffusion is beginning. How it is to be ultimately organized is still undetermined. From the perspective of achieving genuine human progress, knowledge quality is critical because real advances depend entirely on how good the information is. Scientists and engineers who use the Internet must be able to ascertain or to rapidly sort out both what is reliably true and what is truly new.

BRINGING ALL THE FORWARD FUNCTION FORCES TOGETHER

The six forces of the modern forward function are all of a piece. They work together more or less simultaneously and continuously. There are now many millions of people all over the world contributing in meaningful ways to this gigantic problem-solving enterprise. Great numbers are acting in coordinated ways to achieve common ends that are fundamentally progressive in character. All together, they form a grand network that sometimes operates as if it were one system. Coordination varies, depending both on leadership presence and pressure, and on the extent to which connections have been established.

The worldwide system upon which major creative problem-solving efforts now depend has been growing stronger and stronger as new media have been introduced, from writing to printing to telegraph to electronic networking. It is impossible to illustrate all these together, but figure 9.2 represents some of the key elements. It is an enormous extended system, stretching from the generation of new knowledge within the scientific community to the consumption of new products and the receipt of new benefits by ultimate consumers worldwide.

The figure illustrates some important points about the acceleration of progress and the forward function that must always be kept in mind. First of all, progress depends on a very large number of interconnecting social net-

FIGURE 9.2.
KNOWLEDGE CREATION TO
UTILIZATION AS A SYSTEM

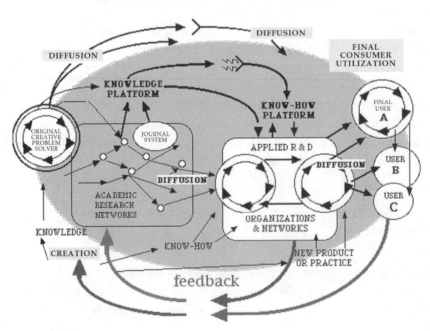

works. Some of these are very loose and open, depending on word-of-mouth and informal leadership.[5] Academic specialties and universities function in this way. Others are highly organized and formalized, as within an industrial laboratory or product-development facility. The second thing to note about figure 9.2 is that multimedia diffusion permeates the entire system, carrying diverse content via multiple channels as the knowledge-transformative process proceeds from basic to applied to product/practice formulation to manufacture to distribution to ultimate use, yet all these transfers are taking place in the service of a common set of basic human needs and desires.

Figure 9.2 also attempts to illustrate that the entire system depends on the size and quality of the underlying knowledge platform, represented by the large gray oval. To the left side, the platform is dominated by the basic knowledge derived from scientific activity, and to the right side it is dominated by more practical knowledge with direct application to human needs. The figure reminds us that the problem-solving cycle goes on both at the macrolevel of purposeful social policy and action and at the microlevel of individual learning and living. The feedback arrows add the important fact that old and new needs as well as responses from users at all levels continually reinform and reenergize the problem-solving process as a whole and each subsystem within it.

Figure 9.2 does not remotely do justice to the size and complexity of the knowledge system. Even the relationship of one academic scholar to another involves many types of interchange. Ideas and facts-in-the-making bounce back and forth many times before they really enter the knowledge platform. Research is also greatly influenced by the mechanisms of research funding, which are in turn greatly influenced by political changes in the larger society, most notably wars and economic booms and recessions. Just as one example, the G.I. Bill, enacted by the US Congress near the end of World War II, allowed hundreds of thousands of returning servicemen to attend college for the first time. This, in turn, led to a great expansion of the university system in the United States, with major increases in the numbers of people trained for and engaged in the scientific professions. The Cold War generally extended this trend, with the added spur of government demand for higher and higher levels of technology for weapons and military support. A vast new science-based knowledge–producing infrastructure came into being, involving collaborations among universities, the government, and an expanding private sector. This was the great story of the last half of the twentieth century, a great new problem-solving machine, born of war and fear yet bringing not only Americans but also much of the rest of humankind into a new era of bountiful life.

The continuing expansion of universities, including hundreds of new engineering and medical schools, ensures both the survival and the continued strengthening of the knowledge platform as it is now being passed from one generation to the next. The intergenerational transfer of scientific knowledge and technical understanding, which was tenuous for so much of human history, is now ensured through the worldwide extent of the academically embedded knowledge system, together with the journal and book publication systems; the libraries now linked electronically; the enormously expanded electronic storage and copying capacity of modern computers; and the ever more efficient, accurate, and secure hard disk and compact disc technology.

The Internet now allows the massive transmission of enormous amounts of information in many formats from any connected sender to any connected receiver. The power and potential of this system has barely begun to be realized as this is written. However, as we contemplate the gross complexities displayed in figure 9.2, we should be heartened by the fact that all the actors represented are now for the first time completely and continuously interconnected. Through this vast new web of interconnection, they will begin gradually to act more like a unified problem-solving system serving all of humanity.

SUMMARY

For the many thousands of years before there was writing, diffusion of new ideas and practices depended exclusively on word-of-mouth, person-to-person connections. Thus the extent of the social network and the nature of its structure of interconnections limited the flow of new knowledge and the extent to which it would enter into the crude but expanding knowledge platforms of human tribes. Social connections continue to be a powerful force in diffusion even today. However, social networking has now been supplemented or displaced by many other types of media. What here will be termed *modern* diffusion, which includes high-speed transport and transmission of people, goods, and all types of information, is a phenomenon so recent and so radically more powerful than traditional social connection that it should be viewed as a separate force.

PART THREE:

WHERE THE FORCES ARE TAKING US

We are just now beginning to understand the nature and direction of the human species. Yet we approach this realization with conflicting emotions bordering on both joy and trepidation. Let us hope that we overcome our apprehensions and exhibit the courage to live up to the expectations of the cosmos and the demands of our destiny.
                            —Michael G. Zey, *The Future Factor*

As Michael Zey says in the conclusion of his book on what he calls "the future factor," there is a cultural struggle going on between those who embrace growth and the extension of human capabilities and those who seek limits, fearing the consequences of human expansion. In part 3, we join Zey in embracing a positive future that builds firmly on the platform of science. The argument is presented in three forms. First, it is argued that the forward function is actually moving us onto high moral ground, well above the claims of the backward-looking knowledge platforms of the past. Second, we consider the claims of the antigrowth worriers, one by one, and provide responses that conform to what is currently known, working as much as possible from the scientific knowledge platform of today. Third, we look to the near future and consider what is likely to happen within the next fifty to one hundred years, if current trends continue to hold—especially the trend toward an acceleration of scientific knowledge and its applications. It is an exciting prospect.

Chapter 10 considers the directions in which humanity is heading from a moral perspective. It starts with the Golden Rule, which is a foundation for morality in almost all religions: do unto others as you would have them do unto you. We must accept our common humanity, which means that we should want for others what we want for ourselves, as spelled out in chapter 2. All the good things of an individual life should ideally be made possible and achievable for all lives. Short of this far-off ideal, morality should dictate that we all make efforts to move closer and closer to it. Even as we as individuals define and then aspire to greater and greater self-fulfillment, we should be opening these same doors for others to share these future delights of human experience. Indeed, what is achievable by humans as individuals cannot be fully appreciated until it is a shared experience. Thus the goal of sharing more and more widely should be integral to any individual goal we set for ourselves.

Chapter 11 anticipates and attempts some answers to the many criticisms that the forward function idea is likely to raise. What has been presented in the last six chapters leads to a generally very optimistic view of the human prospect, and though it is argued logically, it nevertheless runs sharply counter to many contemporary visions of the future. Why am I right and why are they wrong? Or is there some middle ground? Population growth, species extinctions, resource exhaustion, and global warming are the scary topics on which most futurists dwell. Science-fiction writers more often trump their gloomy scenarios with even darker hellish images of the human future. There are some real dangers ahead, but on the whole these pessimists couldn't be more wrong. Chapter 11 sums the argument.

Finally, in chapter 12 we take our own look into the near future of the next one hundred years or so. There are two scenarios for this future. In one, we just keep going as we have been, and that's pretty good. In the other, our leadership becomes more proactive and invests more in science and its applications, thus accelerating the progressive trends even further to the great benefit of those who will be alive at the time as well as to generations yet unborn.

Chapter Ten

THE EMERGENCE OF ETHICAL HUMANITY

All human beings are born free and equal in dignity and rights. They are endowed with reason and conscience and should act towards one another in a spirit of brotherhood.

Everyone is entitled to all the rights and freedoms set forth in this Declaration, without distinction of any kind, such as race, colour, sex, language, religion, political or other opinion, national or social origin, property, birth or other status. Furthermore, no distinction shall be made on the basis of the political, jurisdictional or international status of the country or territory to which a person belongs, whether it be independent, trust, non-self-governing or under any other limitation of sovereignty.

Everyone has the right to life, liberty and security of person.
—Universal Declaration of Human Rights, first three articles[1]

It's the answer that led those who've been told for so long by so many to be cynical and fearful and doubtful about what we can achieve to put their hands on the arc of history and bend it once more toward the hope of a better day.
—Barack Obama, November 4, 2008

Whoever has lived part of his or her life through the first half of the twentieth century will have firsthand memory of some of the worst calamities that have afflicted the human race in all recorded history and perhaps even in all human time on Earth. These disasters were man-made, and many were made much worse through perverse applications of the very same scientific discoveries and new technologies that are exalted in preceding chapters. How can this be? How can an "advancing" humanity countenance such mayhem, mass starvation, mass torture, and mass slaughter?

This chapter begins with an excerpt from the Universal Declaration of Human Rights, a document of moral principles, which, its authors hoped, would guide the actions of nation-states and their peoples thereafter. In some ways, the story of the United Nations since that time (at the end of the worst war in history) is a story of failure to live up to those principles. Like many such declarations, the rhetoric was way ahead of its time, and some might say its goals will be forever beyond our reach. However, that document remains important and always timely as a guide to human conduct that applies across races, religions, and cultural identities. It is also a good place to start when considering whether humanity is making progress, in these terms as well as in the other terms we have so far identified.

A PARADIGM FOR MORAL ADVANCEMENT

The Bedrock of Ethical Judgments

The idea of moral value springs from the value placed on life itself, its preservation, first of all, and then its enhancement in all ways. The dimensions of such life values are spelled out in chapter 2. The value of any human life and all human lives should be taken as a given, an a priori assumption, and the starting point for constructing a moral order. However, what we do on behalf of others, not ourselves, is what is really important from a moral standpoint. Caring for others is therefore the bedrock of ethical judgment. The common expression "no person has greater love than he (or she) who would give his (or her) own life for another" reflects this basic moral idea as a limiting ideal. Whatever else one does for another, short of giving one's life, presumably also has moral standing to whatever degree the giver sacrifices and to whatever degree the receiver benefits.

The Golden Rule, "doing unto others as you would have them do unto you," adds another dimension. It explicitly allows for the valuing of the self and implies that valuing the self has equal moral standing with valuing others. It guides the individual away from actions which would be harmful to the self and toward actions which would be life saving and life enhancing for the self. No one has stated this case more succinctly than Karl Popper:

This individualism, united with altruism, has become the basis of our Western civilization. It is the central doctrine of Christianity ("love your neighbor," say the scriptures, not "love your tribe"); and it is the core of all ethical doctrines that have grown from our civilization and stimulated it. It is also, for instance, Kant's central practical doctrine ("always recognize that human individuals are ends, and do not use them as mere means to your ends"). There has been no other thought which has been so powerful in the moral development of man.[2]

Upon reflection and considering what was covered in chapter 2, these actions and benefits, pertaining selfishly to the individual and altruistically to all others, comprise very long lists in which some items have great priority over others and hence greater moral value.

The Golden Rule requires extension in at least two directions. The first is the "doing" and the second is the "other." When we think of what constitutes the *doing*, it may be enough to include those positive or protective acts that we ourselves have experienced directly from our parents or others or from our own actions on our own behalf. However, there are many actions and benefits we can imagine receiving that we have never experienced directly but would still want for others, especially our children. Poorly educated but hardworking and ambitious people very commonly want more for their children, especially in educational terms. This might be called the "proactive golden rule," that is, doing for others as we wish would have been done for us. In a similar vein, all the life, liberty, and life-quality benefits listed in chapter 2 could be items one could help others attain, and all such efforts would have a moral status.

The other extension of the Golden Rule, which is the key to all issues of morality, is the definition of *other*. How far humans can extend their definition of that crucial *other* is a true measure of their moral progress. Different humans have different capacities in stretching their concern. For many, this concern for others applies only to other members of the tribe. As the social horizon gets larger, it might extend to one's own ethnic group, religious faith, or nation-state. In recent times, some humans have begun to extend their concern and their sense of fellowship to include peoples of different faiths and races near and far, and even to the entire human race in accordance with what is stated in the UN Declaration of Human Rights.

A general formula for considering moral progress is offered in figure 10.1. The vertical axis lists the dimensions that make life important and worth living,

FIGURE 10.1.
CALCULATING MORAL PROGRESS

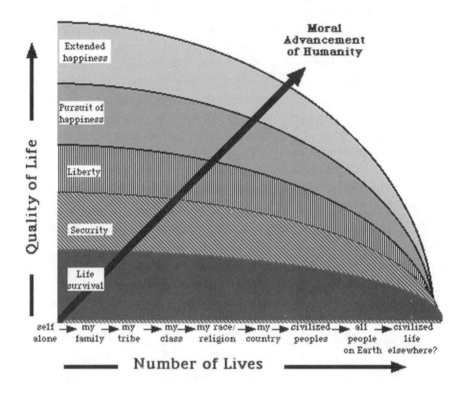

the components of the good and full life enumerated in chapter 2. The horizontal axis lists categories of humanity as they extend outward from the self, in order of relative proximity and similarity to the self, the eighth category being the sum total of humanity on Earth, and the ninth (and final) category extending even beyond our planet.

We assume that very early humans survived in small family groups similar to the way modern apes also organize themselves socially. Clusters of family groups later came together as clans or tribes, which were succeeded in the very early historical period by larger and more complex groupings. As these social clusters increased in size and territorial span, the circle of the potential "us" likewise expanded. As transportation and communication among peoples improved, the awareness of more and more remote categories of others further expanded, as did the possibilities of moral behavior toward them. Only in the latest few centuries, starting with the discovery of the Americas, did a truly worldwide perspective on morality become possible.

Likewise, the vertical axis implies a progression in time. Survival and species preservation would have been the main concern of prehistoric humans, reaching up from the dark gray zone into the zone(s) with angular stripes. With a gradual widening of possibilities and redefinitions of what constitutes a good and full life, some were able to reach into the zones with lighter shades. The emergence of civilization and its expansion over the last two centuries pushed the aspirations of individual lives further up the scale, while mass diffusion spread the scale to the right, to include larger and larger numbers of people able to achieve the higher levels of life quality.

Not included in the figure are future generations yet unborn, although these are implied. Also not included are numerous entities viewed by many as important objects of moral attention. Among these are animals other than humans, humans no longer living, Earth itself viewed as a sacred object, and the various deities toward whom many humans devote serious attention within their diverse moral frameworks. Discussion of morality in these terms is beyond the scope of this book.

THE STRANGE ROOTS OF HUMAN MORALITY

The Evolution of Moral Concern

The first and perhaps defining imperative of life is survival of the species. All living things have an imperative for replication, making copies of what they are. Preserving the self and preserving the species were two intertwined expressions of the same primitive force for survival through endless replication of cells and cell systems. In humans as in millions of other species of higher animals, this meant the protection and preservation of the self until infantile copies reached maturity and attained the ability to further reproduce, on and on through billions of replications. The root source of human morality comes from this drive to preserve the species both through children and through the protective social fabric of the tribe.

Through a process now buried in the sands of time, humans came to depend for survival on the family, then the tribe, and then larger entities of varying structure and complexity. Families and tribes always had to compete with one another for territorial dominance and access to hunting-and-gathering grounds. This process subjected them to endless rounds of feuding and fighting in which victory meant survival and defeat might mean death or perhaps slavery. The first step up the ladder of morality was therefore the recognition that personal sacrifice was required in warfare for the preservation of the greater good of the tribe. Though the self-preservative practical motive may seem obvious, the obligation was probably viewed as moral in the largest sense.

The essence of human morality grew out of this primitive necessity. It grew in fits and starts over a very long period of time and took many turns and forms that would seem very strange to the modern moralist. For example, we now think of military aggression and conquest as something quite immoral. Yet we should ask ourselves how it was that humans began to think of obligations that extended beyond the tribe? Surely the first step was via an ugly form of conquest in which the conquered were given a choice of dying or becoming slave members of the conquering tribe. From such a humble beginning may have come the first extension of the idea of "us."

A far more benign alternative would have been an alliance between tribes. In alliance, each recognizes the other as brother, typically brother-in-arms against a common foe. This was the case among the Greek city-states as they came together to defend against the invading Persians in the sixth century BCE, but long before that time we know that one after another "empire" arose merely because one particular tribe was successful in conquering neighboring tribes across the eastern Mediterranean and large land areas to the east. A similar pattern prevailed in the Far East and in the pre-Columbian Americas. These empires varied in the degree of their brutality and their willingness to accept the conquered peoples as either slaves or vassals but never partners. Alliances, in contrast to empires, are notoriously unstable and easily degenerate into bloody civil wars.

We get a small window on an ancient moral code in the old Hebrew Bible, which may date from the sixth or seventh century BCE, or earlier. This work contains a complete cosmology as well as a supposed history of Earth and of Earth's peoples. Yet the old Hebrew Bible tells its story exclusively from the perspective of one tribe, the Hebrews, and one locale, the area bordering on the eastern Mediterranean and including Egypt and Mesopotamia, but little more. Yahweh, the Hebrew god, was a tribal protector and overseer. The commandment "Ye shall have no gods before me" was clearly meant to indicate that this was the Hebrew's one god and not necessarily the god who protected or ruled over anyone else. The moral code of this god is rather confusing from a modern perspective. This god could become angry and take out his anger in monstrous and murderous ways, as is clearly illustrated in the command— only abrogated at the last moment—for Abraham to sacrifice his beloved son Isaac. The intemperate and unforgiving nature of this early Hebrew god is also well illustrated in the misfortunes bestowed upon the well-meaning, hardworking, faithful, and obedient Job. Throughout the Old Testament it is also clearly allowable for Hebrews to slay their enemies in great numbers with their god's blessing and support because these enemies, being non-Hebrews, had no significant value as fellow human beings.

The Ten Commandments of Moses may represent a step forward in morality or at least in an orderly life, but these moral decrees still applied only within the tribe. "Thou shalt not kill" refers only to other Hebrews, not (as it is later construed) as a general prohibition applying to all humans.

Killing as a Norm of Living among Prehistoric Humans

Our knowledge of human affairs before writing was invented is very limited and inferential, but it is reasonable to suppose that prehistoric men did a lot of killing. This may be the explanation for the very rapid evolution of both the brain and the ability to articulate language over the last one hundred thousand years. Those who could send and receive sounds more efficiently and develop the best strategies for winning battles were the winners. Their progeny, and only their progeny, survived to fight again and again, slaughtering their enemies in an endless sequence of intertribal and intratribal wars.

Along the way, many of these killing impulses must have become imbedded in the brain as instinctual responses. Freud, among others, observed that the minds of his presumably civilized patients were also flooded with violent imagery of killing. Such fantasies could be directed toward anyone who stood in the way of libidinal gratification. This was especially common among his male patients and especially directed toward the father or father figures. Such impulses were, of course, thoroughly inhibited, appearing only in dreams, daydream fantasy, and occasional outbursts of rage. Very rarely did the primitive instinctual impulses reveal themselves in fully destructive behavior, and even then, they usually were channeled into socially approved forms, such as police work or military service in wartime. It is noteworthy in this regard that contemporary computer games, which have become a large industry in the United States and elsewhere, are dominated by murderous violence directed by the player and by others against the player in endless combat. Much of fictional writing, starting with the perennially popular murder mystery, is preoccupied with killing in one form or another. The human need for a fantasy outlet for this underlying impulse seems apparent.

Freud speculated that the development of civilization was grounded in the inhibition of this powerful and universal killing impulse, the inhibition becoming progressively more effective over many hundreds of generations. As such repression became more successful, the underlying instinctual urge was redirected into other forms of activity that were more functional for the preservation of the tribe as a whole, and later the city, the empire, and ultimately the nation-state.[3] This truly represented a moral progression. As the killing impulse was suppressed and redirected to more distant humans outside an expanding tribal perimeter, communal living became possible for larger and larger groups.

Other inhibitions followed in the wake of the prohibition on killing as a requirement of a stable and harmonious family group. Among these, of course, were prohibitions on stealing, lying, coveting someone else's wife, and various other forms of violence to others. The rationale for such prohibitions could be viewed in purely functional terms, a tradeoff in which I agree not to harm you if you agree not to harm me, but an arrangement of multiple trade-offs doesn't really work for large numbers of people. Thus, what might be conceived as a practical matter has to be reformulated as an abiding principle of the group: the person must be taught as a child not to do these things to any member of the group, regardless of his or her age or status or direct relationship to you. The same set of prohibitions did not necessarily apply to other humans outside the group, so these basic forms of morality extended only so far as the cultural identity of the particular group extended.

Proactive Morality

Thus far we have considered only moral behavior in a prohibitive and preventive sense. However, people are obviously inclined in many circumstances to do positive good for others, to provide help, education, and gifts of money, food, shelter, and health benefits. We could call this whole range of unselfish giving "proactive morality," and certainly this type of morality is another mark of advanced civilization. The conservative view minimizes proactive morality, holding that it is up to the individual to extend the dimensions of life quality, as conveyed in the expression "God helps those who help themselves." In the liberal view, life quality is something that should be spread as widely as possible and extended to as many as possible, following Bentham's dictum of the greatest good to the greatest number. In the context of the forward function, moral progress would mean a continuing expansion of the benefits of living to a greater and greater percentage of the world's population at the same time as these benefits and the definition of total benefit are expanding with the progress of science and its applications to human well-being.

WARFARE AND THE SLOW RISE OF MORAL HUMANITY

War, Empire, and Moral Progress in Ancient Times

We know that prehistoric humans were predatory hunters, probably from their beginnings as a branch of the great ape family hundreds of thousands of years ago. It also seems probable that they fought ceaselessly with other apes and each other as well as other animals. We can only speculate on what the early prehistoric fighting was all about, but there is little dispute, first, that it was brutal and, second, that it had important evolutionary consequences. Thus, to the victors went not only the spoils but also the better chance of populating the world with their line. Somehow, it appears, the results were not all bad. We certainly got bigger and bigger brains that held more and more capacities, especially the capacity for language. Many if not most battles must have been won by those who had a better ability to organize into larger groups for self-defense as well as attack. This superior social organization was probably the key to victory in later stages of development.

The Moral Order of Imperial Rome

Rome achieved hegemony over the Mediterranean, the Middle East, and much of western Europe and Britain during the first three centuries of the Common Era by means of both superior social organization and superior technology. However, what makes the Roman Empire important in the evolution of human morality is not its victories but the way it treated its subjects. Conquered peoples were typically not slaughtered, nor were they necessarily cast into slavery. Wherever the Roman Empire extended itself, it extended Roman law, posted in a central place where all could see. If people abided by the Roman rules, they could live within the empire untroubled and protected by Rome's legions. Within each conquered land, locals were allowed to carry on as they had before, as long as what they did was compatible with the laws of the Romans.[4] We see this exemplified in the story of Jesus, where the Roman territorial overseer Pontius Pilate has first say over what the Jewish leadership can do and cannot do. Seeing no contravention of Roman law, per se, he hands jurisdiction of the case over to the locals, as must have happened time and time again throughout the empire.

The Roman system represented morality of a sort. It was a step up from what would have prevailed a thousand years earlier, and while it lasted, there was probably a sense of safety and security shared by all who were within its borders. This must have been the mystique that carried forward for two thousand years as one after another conqueror and a major religion tried on the Roman trappings and aped the Roman style as a means of asserting its authority and grandeur.

Moral Progress after the Fall of the Roman Empire in the West

In historical teaching much has been made of the decline and fall of the Roman Empire as if it were the supreme cautionary tale of civilization, a non-mythical version of the banishment from the Garden of Eden. Edward Gibbon, himself a product of the Enlightenment, attributed the fall largely to the softening and inward-turning effects of the spread of Christianity. Moralists are more likely to attribute the fall to corruption and debauchery. Careful historical analysis reveals a much more complicated process stretching out over five hundred years in the west and more than a thousand years in the east. Indeed, a closer look at the so-called Dark Ages reveals many examples of real progress during the period from 500 to 1400 CE. The social organization of feudalism, a medieval invention, could be argued to be a distinct advance on the Roman system of social organization because parliaments, universities, jury trials, and the Magna Carta (the first bill of rights) all emerged from this period—as did the modern nation-state.

Warfare changed substantially during the Middle Ages with the development first of the crossbow and then of the canon and the rifle. Gunpowder had been developed much earlier by the Chinese but was not fully exploited militarily until fairly late in the Middle Ages. The minor wars of Europe during most of the Middle Ages were fought for dominance among competing kings and princes within Christendom. The major continuing battle from the seventh century to the sixteenth was between the competing religious worldviews of Christianity and Islam, ending more or less in a draw and a division of former territories of the Roman Empire between the Christians to the north and west and the Muslims to the south and east. Christians and Muslims kept killing one another in countless wars, each side with the supreme confidence that God was always with them, even when they lost, but it was the victors who determined the moral basis for the territory won and held.

The Cruel Dialectic of War

There is a curious way in which moral behavior sometimes advances through wars and not despite them. Over time, the resources, intelligence, and perhaps moral strength of the better half of humanity carries the day. When we reflect on the American Civil War, probably the bloodiest war of the nineteenth century, we may gain some solace from the fact that a superior moral cause won out in the end against a smaller but far better-organized and better-led force that was more capable militarily and even seemingly more motivated.

The worst chapters in the history of warfare have been written nearer to our own times, especially the two world wars of the twentieth century. The enormous human cost, especially in the tens of millions of lives cut short by these catastrophic events, has to be reckoned with in explaining how we are making progress in a moral sense. We now tend to look back on World War II as the "good war," the war in which there was no moral ambiguity, in which the forces of human advancement were all on one side (fortunately the winning side) and the forces of reaction, suppression, and brutality were all on the other. With some significant exceptions,[5] this is mostly a defensible view. But what followed the war may in the long run prove to be the most significant set of events advancing the moral state of humanity. There was a short period of time between 1945 and 1950 when there was a kind of ethical awakening among most of the educated people throughout the world, including the defeated Germans and Japanese. There was none of the lingering anger and bitterness of the defeated powers that resulted from the end of the American Civil War and World War I. On the contrary, there seemed to have been a collective recognition that what had happened was truly dreadful and must never happen again. In that context and in that spirit several new world institutions were established, institutions that survive to this day and that will probably continue in gradually strengthened form through many years to come.

Evidence for Moral Progress after World War II

The political landscape of 1945, as compared to 1918, supported a more stable outcome and a greater consensus. The two remaining victorious superpowers had been allies against a common adversary, so there remained enough goodwill to continue the uneasy alliance into peacetime with a new international organization in which both would participate. Hostile intentions on both sides were soon checked by the technology of atomic weapons, ensuring that a major military confrontation would quickly result in unacceptable levels of destruction and loss of life on both sides. As a result, despite numerous peripheral conflicts often fought with surrogates, the great powers learned to live and let live as their systems jockeyed for dominance in various spheres. Ultimately, after forty years of "containment," the communist system collapsed of its own weight, unable to exploit the new technologies of the twentieth century for economic progress and unable to provide for its members benefits comparable to what were being experienced in the noncommunist developed nations.

Whether or not this long "cold war" represented any kind of advance in moral progress is open to debate. Certainly the fruits of multiple new technologies played a part in improving communication and promoting world trade. The space race, begun with aggressive motives in the foreground, became an arena for peaceful competition and unprecedented international cooperation. It greatly increased worldwide awareness of the common circumstance of all earthlings as residents of a relatively small planet hurtling through space, governed by laws of mass and motion, laws discovered only three hundred years earlier. The new knowledge platform of atomic physics also paved the way for a new know-how platform for weaponry too destructive for the achievement of practical aims.

Political discourse in the most developed countries of the world, including all of Europe, North America, Japan, South Korea, and many other pockets of prosperous modernity everywhere, has been greatly moderated in tone over the last fifty-five years of the twentieth century and the first decade of the twenty-first. Religious and ethnic slurs have been all but eliminated, even in the American South where they were once common. A major reason to hope that we are on the road to moral advancement lies in the fact that ethnic hatred has been delegitimized in all these places. In the United States, where even after World War II anti-Semitism was widespread, it has now been rendered completely unacceptable in public discourse. Other forms of antiminority actions and verbal utterances have likewise been banished within the last quarter century. In public speech and behavior, blatant exhibitions of prejudice are now thankfully out of bounds.

Deep down, human beings are both good and bad. As noted earlier, there are primitive urges in every man (and perhaps even every woman to some extent) to wreak violence on others who get in their way or in the way of their immediate families. Over time, these tendencies have been inhibited and suppressed to a greater and greater extent, thus allowing civilized life to come into being and to advance in relative safety. In the nineteenth century, the many civilized entities merged into nation-states, extending the borders of the "us" as never before to the limits of national borders and, in many cases, to the borders of colonial empires. In retrospect, considering how nation-states behaved toward one another in World War I, it is difficult to imagine that this coming together represented a moral advance, but it probably did. Only after these same nation-states had the experience, twice, of warring with each other to the death, did the ideas of a truly worldwide moral order begin to take hold.

We can now add an interesting and hopeful footnote to this discussion. Professor Andrew Mack of the University of British Columbia concluded a recent report to the United Nations, entitled "The Human Security Report," that indicates that there has been a substantial reduction in both the number and deadliness of international armed conflicts over the last fifty-five years.[6] He identifies one hundred conflicts that ended quietly between 1988 and 2005. Combat deaths have also declined sharply from an average of thirty-eight thousand in 1950 to six hundred in 2002. It is not clear that such promising trends will continue into the present century. Certainly there has been a recent rise in the deadliness of terrorist attacks, even though the number of incidents continues to fall. Nevertheless, Mack's data represent a distinct challenge to conventional wisdom and appear to be one harbinger of moral progress for humanity as a whole.

The Ambiguous Role of Technology

It is impossible to disconnect the politics from the technology of modern warfare. Political leaders have never fully grasped the significance of new technologies when they enter into new wars. They sometimes fight the new war with the technology of the last war, but they also grab what they deem to be the latest technology to gain an advantage. This advantage often eludes them as the other side quickly masters the same technology. The consequences in World War I of the wholesale adoption of the machine gun and later poison gas as major weapons on both sides led to catastrophic casualty rates as well as to a deadly stalemate on the battlefield. Other battlefield innovations that were introduced late in World War I, including tactical air support and the machine gun–defying and trench-crossing tank, became major players in World War II, tremendously increasing mobility on both sides and actually reducing the number of battlefield casualties in a war of wider dimensions.

Many people believe that modern technology deserves some if not all of the blame for the mayhem of modern wars. This charge should be taken seriously. Certainly the political leaders who foolishly and recklessly plunged themselves into World War I probably did so with confidence that their newly applied technological prowess would carry the day, not adequately reckoning that their enemies would apply the same technology with equal cunning in the shortest period of time.

The atomic bomb represents an especially interesting case of the intertwining of technology and the morality of war. The atomic bomb was perhaps the most amazing scientific and technological accomplishment of the first half of the twentieth century. Many believe that it ended the war with Japan conclusively with greatly reduced bloodshed overall. Certainly a good argument can be made for this case. Furthermore, for the sixty long years and counting since that war ended, this weapon has been refined, enlarged, mass produced, and proliferated to a terrifying extreme without ever having been used in hostilities between any two countries. Why? Many believe that this new balance of terror served as an essential deterrent between the two great powers of the post–World War II era. The subsequent proliferation of this technology has not yet resulted in a single military use. Every year that this moratorium continues to hold makes the case stronger that the invention of the atomic bomb forced the end of major war. It is far too soon to render a final judgment, but it may turn out that this terrifying science-based engineering accomplishment, by some strange and counterintuitive logic, may have marked a significant advance in human morality.

From a balance of ultimate terror we get stalemate and then peace, or so the story goes. Unfortunately, this is a story that has yet to play out. The major security concern of the great powers today is that some rogue state with fanatical and delusional leadership will employ the atomic bomb regardless of the suicidal implications of such an act. A firm international regime of surveillance and control of fissionable materials would seem to be the next necessary step to reduce this threat, followed by the progressive reduction of arsenals until there are no more.

With increasing recognition of the necessity of international agreements of all kinds, it seems possible that these steps will be taken within the next century. At the present time, there are a handful of nations who have refused to cooperate with the existing nonproliferation regime, although none of these could be classified as great powers. The advantages of peaceful coexistence and world trade were major factors in the breakup of the Soviet Union and the peaceful transformation of China over the last two decades. These same forces will probably continue to tug away at the resolve of the recalcitrant dictatorships, which now sustain themselves solely by military might. This may well be a slow process, but eventually they will not be immune from worldwide trends of such magnitude.

Another way in which science, technology, and military politics interact is through the planning and funding of research. After World War II and largely because of the mystique of the atomic bomb, political support and hence government funding for all kinds of research blossomed.[7] Physics was the chief beneficiary at first and remains so, but the new largess spread out quickly to all the sciences as the idea took hold that science education and national scientific leadership were keys to a strong national defense. The cornucopia of discoveries, inventions, and applications that flowed from this support during the full length of the Cold War, approximately 1948 to 1988, has transformed the lives of all peoples. It led to the rapid development of all types of computer technology; safe commercial aircraft; space satellites with multiple military and civilian applications; the numerous applications of radar, laser, and microwave technology; the modern mainframe computer; the modern personal computer; the modern user-friendly computer interface; the Internet; antibiotics and antivirals; fiber-optic surgery, and on and on. All these inventions, many with lifesaving and life-enhancing consequences, can be traced directly to the Cold War and to the concern of American politicians to make sure that the United States was first in all areas of new technology. Did these changes have moral implications? Profoundly so. Were these implications on the positive or negative side? Overwhelmingly, they were positive—they saved life, prolonged life, and gave people more freedom, more choices, higher living standards, and a greater quality of life on many dimensions.

Diffusion of Knowledge and Moral Behavior

Since the bedrock moral issue is the treatment of others, it follows that perception of others and valuing of others are steps along the road to caring about them and doing things to help them. The arousal of a people toward moral action should be understood as a process that develops over time. It begins with just a few people who are very concerned about some other people who are in dire need. These "other" people are perhaps far away, very different from themselves, and out of sight or even out of awareness to the vast majority in the "us" culture or country. Yet without the vocal concern expressed by these few, nothing would happen regarding the needy "others." Their voicing of a call for action, if convincing and empirically supported (eye-witness reports, photographs, film footage), spurs activity by a still small but larger group of morally attuned people among whom some will have opinion leadership within larger populations of citizens. From this early critical mass a much larger group of mainstream opinion leaders becomes involved, spreading their influence until a majority is persuaded to support direct action.

Liberty and Democracy as Issues in Moral Progress

American patriot Patrick Henry supposedly said those famous words, "Give me liberty or give me death!"; and another slogan of the American Revolution, which now adorns automobile license plates in the state of New Hampshire, reads, "Live free or die!" Such sentiments contradict the hierarchy of human need posed in chapter 2, and they are illogical on their face unless we suppose that there is some sort of liberty beyond the grave. Nevertheless, they express the high value that many in the Western world have placed on this concept of *liberty* or *freedom* in the last three centuries. Up to this point we have discussed basic morality in terms of the right to life, to live and let live. In this context, kingdoms, nation-states, and empires that ensure survival of all their members on the condition that they abide by the laws of the state represent a distinct moral advance over the anarchy of constant intertribal and intratribal warfare.

As this moral achievement spread further and became accepted public policy throughout the most developed and prosperous parts of the world in the seventeenth and eighteenth centuries, many peoples began to reach for more. This new craving inspired a series of revolutions that engulfed Europe and the Americas between, roughly, 1645 and 1870. These revolutions were largely concerned with overturning established authority in the name of liberty, and, to the degree that they were successful, they represent a significant moral advance for the affected societies.

Kant states the case as follows:

> There is, indeed, an innate equality belonging to every man which consists in his right to be independent of being bound by others to anything more than that to which he may also reciprocally bind them.[8]

A "good society" builds on its capacity to create the best conditions for such personal reciprocally acknowledged freedom. As the concept of political democracy further evolved from this idea in the nineteenth and twentieth centuries, many more wars were fought either to preserve or to extend such a condition of living, even though the many deaths that resulted from these wars tended to undermine the meaning of the concept as far as the dead victims of these wars were concerned.

There is a precedent in the American experience. One hundred and fifty years ago, the North American state established by the American Revolution came apart after seventy years of growth and increasing internal tension. The ensuing war was, as previously noted, one of the bloodiest in history up to that time, and it was fought, on both sides, in the name of liberty. For the Southern states, it was the liberty of a white man to hold his rightfully acquired property without interference by others and with the protection of the policing powers of the state. So stated, it seems to fit reasonably well within the civilized conception of freedom as articulated by Kant and other moral philosophers and as enshrined in the Declaration of Independence. And so it was thought by the Southerners of the time. Curtailment of such a right was reason enough to fight and even die.

From a moral standpoint, of course, it came down to what that "property" consisted of. Most Americans of that time and many of later times were confused about just what the African Negroes were. Were they human? If human, were they savages like the Native Americans who were slaughtered in such great numbers before and after the Civil War? Even in the North, even in the mind of Abraham Lincoln, there were doubts. Abolitionists were viewed throughout the Northern States as irrational and dangerous fanatics right up to the outbreak of the war.[9] Again with reference to figure 10.1, the extent of moral concern and the definition of who is "us" simply didn't extend that far. Yet there were enough people in the North who were sufficiently bothered by the treatment of Negroes in the South, the extensions of slavery into the new territories in the West, and the intrusion of Southern authority into the Northern states via the Fugitive Slave Acts, that they compelled a moral movement that gradually won wide endorsement after the war was started.

As often is the case, the aims and justifications for battle changed with time. By 1863, preserving the union was not quite enough of a war aim to justify the enormous battlefield sacrifice, and so the grotesque institution of slavery was finally formally abolished by proclamation and later buttressed by constitutional amendment. The story did not end with victory in the embrace of a manifestly moral cause, however. The newly "freed" Negroes were left for one hundred years more to feel the brunt of Southern resentment as a new system of separation and repression was put in place. The Northern victors, after a decade of "reconstruction," simply walked away and forgot about their Negro brethren.

In many ways, the development of modern technology paved the way for this modest moral victory. It was the mass publication and widespread distribution of Harriet Beecher Stowe's *Uncle Tom's Cabin* that lit a fire under the Northern conscience. It was the industrial might of the North that finally won the war. When segregation was finally exposed for what it was one hundred years later, it was television news, day after day, that dramatized the moral failing of the Southern system. It was also the revelation of Negroes as sports heroes and admired musicians and actors, highlighted by the new media, that allowed more and more white Americans to see blacks as fellow beings, full partners of the great "us" that makes the "US."

Our Moral Status Today: Many Competing Platforms

In previous chapters the case was made for one worldwide knowledge platform for science and another associated platform for know-how, that is, technology based on science. Within science there are competing theories and fact-generating centers, each hoping to find a niche in the larger platform and succeeding only when diffusion and empirical testing and retesting prove their solidity. In the social sciences, in contrast to the physical and biological sciences, there is no such platform, even though many social scientists would like there to be one and compete mightily through their various theory frameworks and databases to be accepted as such.

When it comes to morality, however, the platform problem is worse even than it is in the social sciences. We live in a world of multiple moral platforms with competing claims for solidity, each claim avowed by faith, by "natural law," or justified as God's command or his gift to man. None of these claims is supported by anything other than tradition or personal conviction. There is no evidentiary standard, as there has to be in science. We simply are not all of one mind regarding morality, especially when it comes to specifics. The authors of the UN Declaration of Human Rights made a valiant effort, and perhaps over time that document will become our new moral platform. Figure 10.1 offers one author's analysis, but it is recognized as only one of many possible analyses. Immanuel Kant made a heroic effort to establish a universal basis for morality in logic, and perhaps this is where we need to start again, just as science itself starts in logic, but that is outside the realm of this work.

A Chronology of Ethical Progress

Over the last few thousand years, many changes have come about in human affairs that could be counted as moral progress in one way or another. Herewith is a sampling in rough chronological order. Each change requires qualification: some changes happened for a time but were negated thereafter by other events. Most changes apply to some people in some parts of the world but not to others, and so forth. There is a ragged edge to the upward curve of moral advance. Human sacrifice did not end in the Americas until the Columbian invasion and in some parts of India until the nineteenth century. Democracy with its expansion of personal freedoms has not yet been established in many parts of the world and is negated by wars, environmental catastrophes, and plagues. Nevertheless, the list suggests not only that significant progress has been made on many fronts and among many peoples but also that it is accelerating.

Ethical Advances before 1600

- Tribes learn to not kill one another and to protect one another from threats from the physical environment, animals, and other humans outside the tribe.
- Tribes learn to trade instead of steal and plunder from other tribes.
- Conquering tribes substitute enslavement for death.
- Intratribal laws regulate relations within the tribe (e.g., the Ten Commandments).
- Human sacrifices end in most cultures.
- First written rules of law governing relations among people (within a tribe).
- Empires allow local customs and provide protection for all within conquered territories.
- Within all major religions, there is articulation of some form of the Golden Rule.

Ethical Advances from 1600 to 1700

- The principle of the divine right of kings decays.
- The first stable parliamentary government with real powers is established in the United Kingdom in 1688.
- The concept of political liberty evolves (e.g., from John Locke in 1689).

Ethical Advances from 1700 to 1800

- The concept of human rights emerges.
- Human rights are embodied in the US government (1776, 1789).
- Constitutional representative governments emerge in the United Kingdom, the United States, and France.
- The principle of free speech is established.
- The principles of religious toleration and the separation of church and state are established.

Ethical Advances from 1800 to 1900

- The first true representative democracies emerge.
- Parliamentary forms of government spread.
- Serfdom is officially ended in Russia (1867).
- State-sanctioned slavery ends in the United States (1865).
- The first worldwide humanitarian organizations appear (e.g., the International Committee of the Red Cross).
- Voting rights are extended in Western democracies to all adult males.
- It becomes widely understood that it is the obligation of the rich or of society as a whole to help the poor.

Ethical Advances from 1900 to 1945

- The first international organization to resolve disputes without war is established (League of Nations, 1919; the United States is an instigator but a nonparticipant).
- The first international treaties to limit armaments are drafted (Washington Naval Treaty, 1922).
- Voting rights in Western democracies are extended to women.
- Slavery, child labor, and forced labor are prohibited as worldwide norms.
- Statutes establish the negotiating rights of labor.

Ethical Advances from 1945 to 2000

- The first widely accepted set of standard human rights is created by the United Nations (Universal Declaration of Human Rights, 1948).
- The first nuclear test ban treaty is established.
- Treaties to limit the spread of nuclear weapons are enacted.
- The first international court to try war crimes is established (the United States is a nonparticipant).
- The international community displays substantial cooperation in space exploration and peaceful uses of space technology.
- The Cold War ends successfully without use of weapons of mass destruction.
- Equal rights for women are established as governing norm in all developed countries.

- International agencies are established to support, finance, and guide development in the third world (e.g., the World Bank, the United Nations Development Programme, the United Nations International Children's Emergency Fund, and bilateral aid agencies in all developed countries [e.g., United States Agency for International Development, Canadian International Development Agency, Swedish International Development Cooperation Agency, etc.]).
- There is great expansion of humanitarian NGOs (Doctors Without Borders, Catholic Relief Services, CARE, Amnesty International, International Red Cross and Red Crescent Movement).
- Increasing taboos are placed on discrimination against ethnic, religious, and social-sexual subgroups and minorities (mostly in developed countries).
- Communism is ended and is replaced by quasi-democratic governments in many of the states broken out of the former Soviet Union.
- Stable new democracies are established in Eastern Europe and many East Asian countries (e.g., South Korea, Japan, the Philippines, Singapore, Malaysia, and Taiwan).
- Colonialism is ended throughout the world.
- Famine is ended (except intermittently in sub-Saharan Africa, mostly caused by political unrest and anarchy among and within emerging African states).
- Major deadly diseases, such as polio and tuberculosis, are controlled.
- Malaria and other tropical diseases in most areas are partially controlled.
- Worldwide infant mortality is greatly reduced.
- The first serious attention is given to improving the environment and controlling the negative side effects of industrialization by improving air and water quality (mostly in the developed world).
- The first worldwide efforts to conserve animal species are initiated.
- Steps are taken toward enforcing the United Nations' Universal Declaration of Human Rights.
- Economic equalization is advanced through poverty and welfare programs.
- Healthcare is accepted as a right and the responsibility of the state (mostly in northern Europe, Canada, and Australia; it's slowly catching on in the United States [e.g., the provision of medical care for the aged since 1964; and the acceptance, in principle at least, of the need for a "safety net" for infants, children, and the poorest segments of society]).

COMMENT ON THE LIST OF ETHICAL ADVANCES

The above list is broadly suggestive of what has been happening on the moral front throughout the world through time. Many of the changes listed came about for a mix of reasons, moral advancement not always being uppermost in the minds of those responsible for the changes. Many are direct outgrowths of advancing science and technology (e.g., space program cooperation, ending famine [green revolution], inventing antibiotics, and improving medical and epidemiological strategies, etc.). There were probably many more genuine advances in previous centuries that could be revealed by a more comprehensive historical review. That being said, it would still appear that the trend of acceleration especially in the last sixty years is a solid fact.

Relevance of Applied Social Science

Politicians like to say that they cannot legislate morality, but, in fact, they can. It is through social rules made concrete in written law that the human race as a whole moves forward into new realms of morality, as many items on the above list attest. This book has mostly been about the growth of science and its transformation into new technologies benefiting individual humans and, ultimately, humanity as a whole. Yet science is about revealing fundamental truths about the universe, about matter and energy, about life, and about humans. Surely, therefore, there is also a branch of science that explains why we do things the way we do, why we make wars, why and how we manage to create tribes and cities and nations. By the same logic, there should also be a technology of social reconstruction that tells us how we can create and change groups and organizations to best achieve our goals and live up to our proclaimed moral standards.

There is such a science, and we call it *social science*. The trouble is, it doesn't work very well for reasons well stated by biologist Edward O. Wilson.

> It is obvious to even casual inspection that the efforts of social scientists are snarled by disunity and a failure of vision. And the reasons for the confusion are becoming increasingly clear. Social scientists by and large spurn the idea of the hierarchical ordering of knowledge that unites and drives the natural sciences. Split into independent cadres, they stress precision in words within their specialty but seldom speak the same technical language from one specialty to the next. A great many even enjoy the resulting overall atmosphere of

chaos, mistaking it for creative ferment. Some favor partisan social activism, directing theory into the service of their personal political philosophies.[10]

Wilson is saying, in effect, that there is no secure knowledge platform here, no clear way to build on what has come before, and no logical and empirical linkage to the great and ever-advancing system of fact and theory that ties all the other sciences together. Little wonder, then, that policymakers make horrendous mistakes even with the best intentions. There is no science to tell them conclusively whether one action is more likely than another to be successful.

This state of affairs has serious consequences for the predictability of moral progress in the future. We have had a very promising advance in the last half century, as the above list should demonstrate, but will it last? More than ninety years ago the president of the United States, just established as the new leader of the free world in the wake of military victory, was in a position to shape future events in a way to advance moral action, and he fully intended to do it. Woodrow Wilson was actually a scholar, a respected political scientist and former university president. The son of a minister, he was steeped in moral philosophy and earnestly desired to shape a new world order on moral principles. He composed fourteen points that he thought would be the foundation of a just peace, and the German adversaries, still powerful but losing ground, decided to accept an armistice based partly on Wilson's proposals. It was a heady moment for Wilson and the world, but, of course, it was short-lived.

Wilson's proposal for a League of Nations was implemented, but it would have been better for the world if Wilson and his colleagues had had some factual social science to build on. It would have been nice to know, for example, what the long-term consequences might be of denuding a strong and proud nation-state like Germany of all its possessions and forcing it to accept a humiliating treaty that included payment of other countries' war debts and occupation of key industrial centers. It also would have been nice if Wilson had been able to think through the consequences of a self-determination policy if carried to its logical conclusion (tribalism and intertribal warfare). But there was no such social science; and, most alarming, there *still* isn't any, as the other Wilson rightly points out.

However, there could be. Natural science follows certain principles, one of which is that all scientific knowledge is of a piece: animals, plants, and bacteria are all cell systems. Their cells function by means of large protein molecules that are composed of organic chemicals, which are composed of atoms, which are composed of tightly bundled particles, which are organized forms of energy that have been in interaction with one another for billions of years, and so on and so forth. It is time for the social sciences to follow suit and join the club. Their "findings" must become integrated with the larger knowledge system and they must relate to one another in a coherent way, discovery building on discovery, so tomorrow's knowledge base will be incrementally better than today's. That is the way of science.

The United Nations' Universal Declaration of Human Rights, unanimously adopted in 1948, suggests that humanity can collectively agree on a set of moral standards. That is not the real problem. The problem is knowing what to do to apply those principles correctly. That is what applied social science should be all about. If the basic social science is there, it is only a small step further to spell out the implications for practice at every level of society. Applied social science should be able to provide convincing answers to many questions of social policy, but it must address the most burning question of all time: How do we resolve conflicts without violence?

There is a great deal of uncertainty built into the day-to-day course of human events, and the train of moral progress has been known to run off the rails in a very bad way if circumstances conspire in the wrong direction, as they did during the 1930s. The challenge of our times is to create the kinds of safeguards against public hysteria and reflexive unthinking action that will keep the train on the tracks.

Chapter Eleven

FEARS FOR THE FUTURE

I am certain that my fellow Americans expect that on my induction into the presidency I will address them with a candor and a decision which the present situation of our nation impels. This is preeminently the time to speak the truth, the whole truth, frankly and boldly. Nor need we shrink from honestly facing conditions in our country today. This great nation will endure as it has endured, will revive and will prosper. So, first of all, let me assert my firm belief that the only thing we have to fear is fear itself—nameless, unreasoning, unjustified terror, which paralyzes needed efforts to convert retreat into advance. In every dark hour of our national life a leadership of frankness and vigor has met with that understanding and support of the people themselves, which is essential to victory. I am convinced that you will again give that support to leadership in these critical days.

—Franklin D. Roosevelt, March 4, 1933

These stirring words were uttered at a dark moment in American history. It seemed at the time that progress had come to an end. Millions were out of work and many more were desperate. Democratic governments in many countries were on the defensive, and there was a widespread belief that only a retreat into strongman tribalism would bring safety and security. With words and deeds on many fronts, Franklin D. Roosevelt managed to turn his country around. As important as any specific act was his restoration of the optimism about the future that had been a hallmark of the American national character for many previous generations.[1] Of course, there was a lot more to fear than fear itself, but Roosevelt sensed that his people's state of mind was going to be a key aspect of the recovery process, an attitude of constructive problem solving, moving forward and not back.

There are some things we should all really worry about as we reach for a positive future. The science-technology platform will continue to expand and strengthen. But things don't always get better for everybody just because the platform becomes more enlightening and useful. One might say that things ought to get better. The possibilities of living a good, long life increase year by year. Yet, somehow, a lot of things seem to get in the way of that happening. This fact seemed particularly obvious if we recall the major events from 1914 to 1945. Those years saw the worst wars in human history, and some of the worst famines and epidemics. Suffering was experienced by hundreds of millions. On top of all that was the mass enslavement in Germany, Russia, China, and many other places. After all this horror in this past century of supposed progress, one has a right to be skeptical and to ask whether we are really headed in the right direction, as many believe we are not. This chapter addresses such concerns.

The discussion is divided into three parts. Part A deals with the physical threats to human life and habitat. Part B concerns the wide inequities in life quality that exist and persist within and between human cultures. Part C concerns the differences in religion, ideology, and mind-set that continue to act as a drag on progress.

A. PHYSICAL SURVIVAL AND HABITAT

1. Thermonuclear War

When future generations look back on our times, they will think of this as the age when science and technology came to play a dominant role in human affairs. However, at first glance it would seem that they became dominant for the worst of reasons. War brought us to our present condition. It was war that pushed the most momentous applications of science in technologies of killing, first with rapid-firing guns of all sizes, then with airplanes dropping bombs, then with missiles and giant bombs. The technology and the killing reached a dramatic climax in 1945 when the Germans began to launch guided missiles with huge explosive warheads and the Americans dropped two atomic bombs on Japan. Both were technological marvels and at the same time obvious harbingers of a dark future.

Ironically, perhaps the strongest and strangest case that can be made for high tech as a benign force in modern war is the atomic bomb. As the Americans fought their way toward the Japanese mainland in early 1945, it became obvious that the Japanese were willing to fight to the death to preserve their nation, employing suicide attacks with increasing frequency and deadly effect. An invasion was planned with the expectation that there would be enormous casualties on both sides, probably going into the millions, especially when civilian casualties from bombing were counted. The two atomic bombs that were dropped in the summer of 1945 on two smaller Japanese cities with limited strategic importance served as a demonstration to the Japanese that they had no choice but to surrender or to be completely destroyed as a people and a nation. From recently uncovered archive material, it seems clear that these demonstration bombs—terrible as they were, destroying an estimated two hundred thousand lives—shortened the war by months, arguably saving a million more lives, American and Japanese.[2] Stubborn German resistance, coming before the atomic bomb was ready, required that the Allies completely overrun Germany, resulting in enormous civilian and military casualties in the last few months, even though it should have been abundantly clear who had won and who had lost.

When peace came for a brief three years after the war, the Western powers mostly disarmed and concentrated on rebuilding infrastructures and advancing their domestic economies. What resulted was a surge of growth that has continued almost unbroken into the present. The leaders of the Soviet Union did not follow suit but instead prepared for a possible resumption of war. They maintained their large and triumphant standing army with a vast supply of modern tanks and planes. It was believed by strategic analysts of the time that this force could easily overwhelm the western European states in a matter of weeks, should they ever be mobilized for that purpose. Of course, that never happened. For forty years thereafter, the two Allied winners of World War II faced each other in a military standoff that came to be called the Cold War.

Some believe that the Soviets never had such aggressive intentions, having had enough of war for five long years. There was, after all, reason for them to maintain a strong defense just in case the events of the previous decade repeated themselves and a hostile neighbor to the west would once again launch a surprise attack as the Germans had done in 1941. Whatever their real intent, the Soviet military capability was well known and their system secretive. Therefore the Western powers perceived a need for some kind of preventive shield. That counterforce was to depend heavily on a supposed Western advantage in science and technology and especially the presumed Western monopoly on atomic weapons.

That advantage seemed to disappear by 1949, as the Soviets successfully tested their own bomb. Through the next three decades, the United States and the Soviet Union engaged in a race to build bigger and better bombs. To deliver their bombs and to provide backup protection against a surprise attack, both sides also advanced the rocket technology they had each learned from the Germans. Intercontinental ballistic missiles were dug into hardened underground silos and nuclear-powered, missile-launching submarines circled the oceans. In those times there was a lot more to fear than fear itself. Each side accumulated thousands of weapons of mass destruction kept on hair trigger twenty-four hours a day. An all-out attack by either side could conceivably have killed hundreds of millions of people, leaving devastation and a poisoned environment lasting generations. It would have been a catastrophe equaling in its magnitude the crash of a large asteroid such as that which caused massive life extinctions in eons past.

Yet it didn't happen, partly or mostly because there was awareness on both sides that any such event, whatever the provocation, would have been national suicide. This mutual awareness grew stronger as the weapons became more fearsome, soon motivating both sides to consider a gradual pullback. Starting with the Partial Nuclear Test Ban Treaty of 1963, this trend has now been continuing for over forty-eight years and counting. As the years have rolled by, fear of a nuclear holocaust has receded, but an important level of danger remains, even if on a lesser scale, as smaller states with fragile and/or bellicose governments join the nuclear club. The point to stress, however, is that the real threat of thermonuclear world war disappeared in the late twentieth century and is not likely to reappear.

There is much that can be said also in defense of technological progress in the military context. First of all, it is not a given that advancing technology makes wars deadlier. Extermination of minorities and defeated enemies has a long history and probably a much longer prehistory. Even in World War II and in the rise and fall of communism, the majority of deaths resulted from starvation, an age-old tool requiring no high tech.[3] Certainly tank usage, by making front lines more mobile and by partially negating the machine gun, resulted in fewer battlefield casualties on balance. High-tech weaponry that replaces humans on the battlefield could also be argued to be lifesaving. An area of technology that has attracted serious interest in recent times has been the development of nonlethal weapons such as those that temporarily shock or immobilize a foe or disrupt an enemy's ability to communicate and coordinate hostile action.

The question of most relevance for the purposes of this book is what role science and technology played in this era. Clearly, the science-based development of frightening new weapons brought the world to the brink, but it was the very nature of these same weapons that forced the standoff and ultimately led to a prolonged period of relative world peace. It may be the supreme irony of our times that the most dreadful weapons ever made with the help of science and technology created a kind of security umbrella that brought the era of world wars to an end and allowed progress in so many spheres of human activity over a very long period thereafter.

The Nightmare of "What If"

It has been argued here that humanity makes progress both because of wars and in spite of wars. The Allied triumph over Nazi Germany was certainly a turning point that led ultimately to the present era of escalating progress. However, it must not be forgotten that the other side could have won it, if not for a few happenstances of history. For example, Hitler could have invaded England before Russia. The British had no effective defense at the time. Alternatively, the Red Army could have collapsed, failing to close the pincer at Stalingrad and failing to block German access to the Baku oil fields. President Roosevelt could have retired after two terms, leaving pacifists in control of the US government, and so on and so forth. The good guys don't always win. Well, what if? Hitler's Germany sustained the work of extremely clever, science-savvy engineers who pioneered rocket science and atomic energy. They went the right way on the rockets and the wrong way on bomb development, but there was no reluctance to forge ahead to assist the war machine in all ways possible. Nazi Germany's scientists appeared to be indifferent to the suffering of others, focused on their work and no doubt pleased by the results. This is the mad science scenario we see so often in science fiction.

Surely the forward progress of humanity would have been slowed if Hitler had triumphed. A brutal Nazi German hegemony might have lasted for some years, but it seems likely that it gradually would have come to pieces for a variety of reasons—too late, no doubt, to save millions of more Jews and Europeans—but ultimately it could not have lasted in that ugly form. History suggests that as dictators inevitably age and then die, their followers tend to splinter into competing factions. Continuous pressure from below, from the army, from the discontent of the many who are in need, and from the special interests of different economic blocks, all these forces tend to destabilize monolithic states. Meanwhile, new knowledge and new technologies continue to bubble up, challenging the status quo and giving the lie to the official state ideology, whether it comes from Stalin or Hitler or Mao. In the long run, the forward function would carry the day as it has throughout the human climb. Nevertheless, the nightmare of Hitler will continue to haunt us for generations to come, as it should.

2. Global Mean Temperature Fluctuation

In the previous chapter we identified twenty-two promising trends of the last sixty years, of which two were in the environmental arena: (1) the first serious attention to improving the environment by improving air and water quality, and (2) the first worldwide efforts to conserve animal species. There is no doubt that since it emerged as a significant force starting with the publication of Rachel Carson's *Silent Spring* in 1962, the environmental movement has been a boon to Earth and to all the people on Earth. Scientists of one type or another have played a prominent role in bringing environmental issues to public attention since that time.

The idea that we should keep track of what we are doing, measure the consequences, and then take positive remedial action is fundamental to progressive scientific problem solving.

Climate variation, storms, droughts, floods, freezes, and heat waves have been perennial human scourges. Thus, when scientists began to take measurements of weather patterns—local, regional, and worldwide—starting about one hundred fifty years ago, they attracted interest from a wide public. Predictive science, though elusive, sometimes works and has become increasingly helpful in preparing communities, particularly for the dangers of storms. It has also been observed for more than a century that human activity can sometimes affect local, regional, and even worldwide atmospheric conditions. Thus, when environmentalists, supported by data from ground-based temperature studies, began to express concern about human effects on Earth's surface temperature, a lot of people listened.

Environmentalists warned of a dangerous man-made global cooling trend throughout the 1970s. Available data supported a cooling trend over a period of thirty years, during which industrial activity had been escalating. Geological research over many years' duration had shown that giant ice sheets had overwhelmed the northern hemisphere several times in the recent geological past. A new man-made ice age would be an epic folly. There was a certain logic in connecting human activity on a large scale to climatic changes. Hence the call for drastic and immediate action. However, the cooling trend that had started in the 1940s petered out in the 1970s, and since that time surface temperatures again began rising at a modest rate up to a high point in 1998.

As the numbers turned around to warming in the 1980s, the environmentalist argument made a U-turn. Worldwide land-surface-temperature measurements began to be taken on a systematic basis beginning about 1880. Average global surface temperatures vary up and down in the range of about 0.1 to 0.2 degrees Celsius annually. Even though there is a lot of up-and-down variation, there is a discernible pattern of increase totaling about six-tenths of a degree between 1880 and 2008, or somewhat less than five one-thousandths of a degree per year. But the pattern is not consistent. It goes down for long periods and up again for long periods. Figure 11.1, taken from the official record compiled by

FIGURE 11.1.
US ENVIRONMENTAL PROTECTION AGENCY
DATA ON GLOBAL WARMING

Annual Average Global Surface Temperature Anomalies 1880–2008

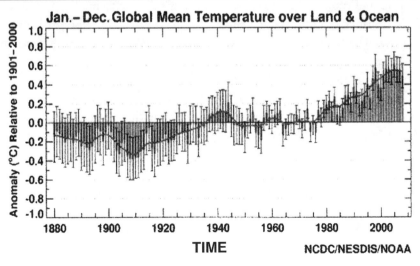

the National Oceanic and Atmospheric Administration updated to September 2009, tells the basic story of the world temperature trend.

There could be many explanations for this overall trend. The traditional favorite was the cyclical variation related to solar activity that presumably caused the sequence of past ice ages and intervening warm periods. It was known that there was a medieval warm period around the ninth century, a time seemingly much warmer than today, during which Greenland was partially settled and farmed by northern Europeans. It was also followed by the Little Ice Age, at least affecting the European continent with three minimal spikes in the fifteenth through the nineteenth centuries.[4] It was assumed by many that a gradual increase observed over the past century was more or less consonant with an overall warming trend from the most recent low point, which may have occurred on or about 1812 when the river Thames froze over in London and Napoleon made his long, disastrous retreat from Moscow, defeated by the winter.

Temperature changes are always a problem for humans and other animals, as well as plants. Through evolution, many species have been able to adapt by way of the painful process of differential survival. Mostly this adaptation has been to colder temperatures rather than warmer, as attested by the great changes and extinctions that occurred through the several ice ages of recent geological time. Humans have proven to be more adaptive to temperature variations than all other animal species by taking advantage of their expanding knowledge platform, which includes the technologies of clothing, housing, heating, and cooling. There is no sign that any of these technologies will cease their continuous improvement in the next century.[5] Therefore, some might question whether the amount of warming observed over the last one hundred thirty years, if extended into the next one hundred thirty years, represents a threat or a boon to human habitation of the planet.

The question that bothers environmentalists the most is whether observed climate change has been caused by an upsurge in human activity of a certain kind. For cooling, it was thought to be the amount of pollution from coal and other forms of burning that added particulates to the air, thus reducing sunlight. There is no doubt that there are such effects, though how widespread and how permanent these particulate effects are remains undetermined.

When the concerns shifted to global warming, the culprit was assumed to be carbon dioxide, which is a natural and inevitable by-product of burning and is essential to plant life, perhaps contributing to a warming of Earth through the greenhouse effect, the process by which sunlight bouncing off Earth's surface is trapped and reflected back by elements in the atmosphere. The principal contributor to the greenhouse effect is water vapor, but lesser amounts of methane and carbon dioxide also probably contribute. Huge amounts of CO_2 have been pumped into the atmosphere so that atmospheric concentrations are now well above levels recorded when measurements first became possible less than a century ago.

Those who were most alarmed based their concern on computer models of global circulation, which suggested that a dramatic increase in warming was about to happen. These models were accepted by the United Nations Inter-governmental Panel on Climate Change (IPCC) as manifest evidence that there was an alarming trend that had to be counteracted in some way. The principal countermeasure was proposed to be internationally enforced drastic reductions in carbon output worldwide. Environmental advocates have pushed for such actions despite the rather modest increases so far observed and the lack of evidence that the rate of change has been accelerating in recent decades. Advocates have also repeatedly asserted that the "science is settled," and political leaders, particularly in Western Europe, have generally accepted their claims. For many, climate change is the big fear of our day, replacing the fear of thermonuclear holocaust that hung over the world like a giant black cloud for so many years previous. Thus, even though there are a number of skeptics with expert credentials,[6] and though the evidence is sparse and contradictory at best, fear is widespread that the drastic predictions might come true. It is fear of what might happen that is driving public policy toward efforts to drastically reduce CO_2 emissions over the next two decades. According to some critics, such a policy would raise energy costs and severely limit economic growth everywhere, perhaps affecting the poorest countries and the poorest people in every country the most.

In any case and whatever the merits, the environmentalists have won this political battle hands down. There is a widespread consensus that national policies on energy use, a huge element in economic prosperity, must be adjusted to force substantial reductions in man-made CO_2 emissions. Actions of various sorts must now be taken by the most powerful nations of the world in response to this perceived threat. If the current trend in public opinion holds, the United States, the countries of the former British Commonwealth, Western Europe, Japan, and others will soon take steps to reduce emissions. It is a very big deal.

A "No Regrets" Approach to Global Warming Policy

James Trefil makes an interesting proposal as a guide to sensible national policies regarding climate change and other areas where scientific advice may be
open to challenge.[7] He calls it the "no regrets" approach. What he means is
that national governments and any other organizations in a position to take
some action should consider only those actions (and there are many) that
would be sensible on other grounds, even if it turns out that the global
warming threat was overstated or even that the threat is really of global
cooling (which is still a possible trend, given the uncertainty and contradiction
among current climate findings). He suggests items of both small and large
scale. Examples of the small-scale suggestions would be more efficient
engines for everything from automobiles to kitchens, and improved home
insulation. Large-scale suggested changes would be new generations of safe
nuclear power plants and alternative, nonburning energy sources. Development in all these areas would cut CO_2 emissions and would also be helpful to
the economy in many other ways. If global warming later turned out to be a
nonthreat, there would be no regrets for having pursued such policies because
they were sensible on so many other grounds. Trefil's "no regrets" approach is
very much in the spirit of the forward function.

There is every reason to continue monitoring all aspects of global climate
change and to intensify this effort in many areas to yield more reliable data,
to refine climate models and better understand the extremely complex phenomenon of climate. Accurate prediction of temperature changes and
weather patterns is a task that rivals life itself in its complexity. We are far
from reliable prediction today. That's the bad news. The good news is that the
overall pattern changes rather slowly, so there will be time to make the necessary adjustments when and if it can be shown conclusively that human activity
is either warming or cooling Earth in a way and to a degree that is persuasively
harmful to our habitat.

3. Population Stabilization

Since the time of Malthus and perhaps before him, social thinkers have intermittently feared the consequences of uncontrolled population growth. In
theory, a female human can give birth to as many as twenty-five infants in the
course of her lifetime. Again, in theory, if even a minority of females

approached this level of fertility, within just a few generations Earth would be manifestly overpopulated, with catastrophic consequences for all. But from anything we know of the historic and prehistoric record, nothing even approaching such a scenario has ever happened. We do know that from the earliest historic times until the mid-nineteenth century, infant mortality and maternal mortality were extremely high everywhere. Add to that the grim facts of high disease incidence, starvation, war, and accident, and it is understandable that the world's human population rose at a very slow rate over thousands of years and well into historic times.

Malthus was writing at a very special time in world history and in a very special place when he drew up his famous formula about food (increasing at an arithmetic rate) and population growth (increasing at a geometric rate). It was the birth of the Industrial Revolution, and England's population was growing very fast, a pattern that was to repeat itself in many other places as industrialization spread across the globe. It was an ugly sight to see: stacks belching black smoke; row upon row of dingy, grimy factory-worker residences; not to mention noise, human filth, and all the least attractive features of urbanized industrialized society in its birth pangs. Yet Malthus turned out to be wrong. The lot of these workers did not get worse; it got better and better throughout the nineteenth century and into the twentieth century. Food supplies pushed ahead of population growth even as population doubled and doubled again. The main reason conditions improved despite rapid population growth was that the Industrial Revolution was itself creating new wealth, albeit poorly distributed but distributed nevertheless. The same story held through the rest of Western Europe and the United States as nineteenth-century industrialization rolled on.

By the twentieth century, increased wealth per capita coupled with the scientific revolution in medicine and public health led to greatly reduced infant and maternal mortality. Better sanitary conditions now prevailed in the most developed urban areas, with a resulting decline in major infectious disease. With these trends another nightmare scenario emerged: overpopulation because of improved public health! This never happened either, in part because of yet another trend. After the middle of the twentieth century, when public health standards had improved substantially along with living standards, family size diminished dramatically. In the most advanced countries of the West and Far East, as increased living standards and ample food supplies became widespread, couples chose to voluntarily limit family size. This trend was unmistakable by the end of the century, with birth rates all over Western Europe below replacement level and nearing the same in Japan and North America.

Despite these well-documented trends, there has been a consistent fear of population growth in the more privileged and advanced societies in the world. Highly respected "experts" continue to follow the Malthusian logic, often using examples drawn from experiments with animals and insects and manifestly overcrowded, underdeveloped countries like Rwanda and El Salvador. Yet, contrary to the Malthusian scenario, food production worldwide has continued to expand at a rate faster than population growth. This expansion goes hand in hand with applications of science and technology in agriculture. India, a perennial favorite of the Malthusians, is now self-sufficient in food supply. This giant state, home to more than one billion people, has enjoyed gradually increasing living standards with uncoerced population stabilization within an open, democratically governed society for nearly two generations.[8]

In theory and in philosophy there certainly ought to be a long-term population problem. There must be some size limit beyond which population density becomes dysfunctional and leads to falling living standards, but it is not clear that we have reached that limit in any developed country in the world as yet. One of the most densely populated countries in the world, the Netherlands, also has one of the highest living standards. The same could be said of Singapore, a city-state. London, Paris, Madrid, New York City, Boston, San Francisco, Honolulu, and many other major cities offer attractive living for millions under manifestly crowded circumstances. All these places have pockets of poverty on a modest level, but all offer great places to live. They are also extremely crowded with people's dwellings and workplaces stacked on top of one another ten to twenty to thirty layers deep! This is a very complicated puzzle for which economists may sometime be able to provide persuasive answers. What really is the consequence of population, per se, in the optimization of human life enjoyment? Is there an optimum size or an optimum growth rate? Such riddles will remain unsolved for many years to come. For the near future, however, there should be little cause to worry. We are still a long way from running out of room, and individual prosperity depends to a large extent on there being many, many others who are also alive and able to prosper.

4. Energy Supply Stabilization

Fear of energy shortages can drive irrational policy, sometimes with devastating consequences. For example, recent United States policy in the Middle East appears to have been driven largely by fears that the supply of oil essential to the US economy could be held hostage to the whims of unfriendly dictators and religious fanatics. However, in the long term there will be no energy shortage, as was discussed extensively in chapter 3. The universe is full of energy, and the sun burns up in an instant what we humans spend in a million years. The technical problem is how to capture and store a fraction of that energy for human use. The problem for policymakers is deciding what forms of energy use should be encouraged or discouraged, based on availability, costs, and benefits, largely construed. As discussed earlier, both coal and oil appear to be in good supply at least for the next two or three generations, but they have both become increasingly problematic as sources primarily because of their environmental consequences. Other, much less polluting sources are potentially available. Each source has its own unique issues, but this evolving story is driven largely by issues of comparative costs and the state of development. The private sector, on its own, will gravitate toward the lowest-cost solutions, unless it is redirected by government action in the form of tax policy, direct subsidy, and support for research and development directed at alternative sources.

Simple economics of supply and demand tend to govern the prices of any freely traded commodity, except where governments levy heavy taxes as a matter of social policy or where cartelization controls prices. As the time approaches when petroleum will be significantly depleted to the point of a substantial and sustained price rise, the economic incentive to develop and bring on line other sources of energy will become more and more attractive. As the price rises, many of the uses of oil that we have today will also gradually fade into the background to be replaced by sources that are more attractive in one way or another (e.g., less polluting; easier to extract, store and transport; more efficient; more reliable; less dependent on international power politics, and so forth).

The petroleum producers will fight back, of course. Even as standard sources run dry, oil from tar sands, shale, and coal extend the possible supply, assuming extraction and refining technologies advance to the point that such extraction is economically competitive. There are other enormous reserves of energy waiting for the right economic climate, the right political climate, and the right sort of new technology to appear. Among these (in no particular order) are solar, wind, ocean wave, tidal, and nuclear fission. Nuclear fusion, direct atomic energy the way the sun makes it, was seen as a possibility soon after the first nuclear bombs proved to everybody that there was a lot of energy locked up inside the ubiquitous atom. Oddly, that kind of energy still eludes our grasp, despite a continuing development effort. It was said to be twenty-five years away fifty years ago. It is still said to be twenty-five years away, a very tough nut to crack. In the meantime, other sources of energy will be discovered or expanded. The point is that the problems of energy supply and consumption are problems well within the awareness and grasp of policy-makers the world over. None of these problems are insurmountable, and all have solutions that are either at hand or just over the horizon.

5. Management of All Natural Resources

Beyond the issue of oil depletion, the presumed exhaustion of "nonrenewable" resources has been a perennial source of mostly misguided fear-driven policy. The analysis of the energy supply problem given above applies also to all other natural resources. A commodity becomes scarce and expensive when new uses are found for it. The price gives incentive for exploration and exploitation of new sources. It also gives incentive for conservation, for more efficient use of existing sources, and for the invention of alternative materials that serve the same function in the same way or in a better way. This is also how the forward function works. We keep finding more of the stuff or other stuff that works better. Substitutes discovered or developed for economic reasons often turn out to be much cheaper, to work better than those they displaced, and to have multiple uses extending far beyond those of the material displaced (e.g., plastics and aluminum for wood, concrete for stone, reinforced concrete for steel, etc.). As the late distinguished professor of economics Julian L. Simon has abundantly documented in *The Ultimate Resource 2*, the prices of all natural commodities have consistently fallen over time.[9]

B. LIFE-QUALITY INEQUALITY

There are tremendous disparities among the people of the world with regard to education, wealth, access to the fruits of modern technology, and ability to live a high-quality life generally. Consider figure 11.2 as representing the population distribution of a reasonably well-developed modern state, such as the United States or Canada. Note that in the figure, the same grayscale code is used as in the opening pages of part 1, figure 0.1.

In such a country, life survival is no longer an issue. Everybody gets to eat, be clothed, and be sheltered, but there are great discrepancies nevertheless in life circumstances. This is not just a matter of wealth but also a matter of education, health, mental capacity, and ability to enjoy life, all of which are unequally distributed. As we make progress within such a country, we expect that there will be a gradual shift toward the lighter end with more and more people having full, happy lives. To reach such goals, science and technology must continuously feed the knowledge platform and more and more members must learn to take advantage of what is already there. Over the last sixty years or so, this seems to have been happening in Western Europe, Japan, South Korea, North America, Australia, and other places.

Where the same pattern is less evident is in what we call the *third world*. The situation in a typical third world country might be as depicted in figure 11.3.

If we are to accept the humanist moral creed proposed in the preceding chapter, then the most serious obligation of our time is to help all the poor countries of our world rise out of their misery, shifting the gray scale toward the lighter ends for as many as possible. The spectrum of need is broad, but the worldwide knowledge platform provides an abundance of answers in

FIGURE 11.2.
DISTRIBUTION OF LIFE SATISFACTION IN A DEVELOPED COUNTRY (SPECULATION)

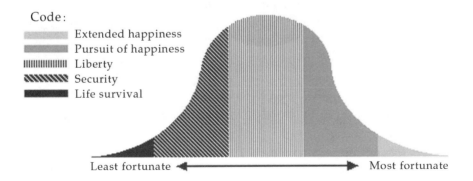

Code:
　Extended happiness
　Pursuit of happiness
　Liberty
　Security
　Life survival

Least fortunate ◀━━━━━━━━━━━━━━━━━▶ Most fortunate

FIGURE 11.3.
DISTRIBUTION OF LIFE SATISFACTION IN
A POOR COUNTRY (SPECULATION)

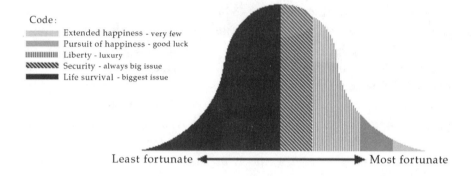

Code:

- Extended happiness - very few
- Pursuit of happiness - good luck
- Liberty - luxury
- Security - always big issue
- Life survival - biggest issue

Least fortunate ◄──────────────► Most fortunate

every sector, from food production to public health to nation building. How-ever, rational problem solving is not always evident in the way the developed world responds to the needs of the poorest countries. Raw, short-term self-interest, the dominant model of the colonial era, is still a major player.

Figure 11.4 depicts the other end of the continuum of human prosperity, what we expect to find in those few places on Earth where happy lives are possible for nearly everybody.

A few small countries can be identified as exemplars of modernity because they have virtually no poverty, very high median education and income, and very high levels of use of modern devices and technology (such as cell phones, personal computers, and Internet access). Larger countries inevitably cover a greater range. The United States is sometimes character-ized as the richest country in the world and the most advanced in nearly every sphere of modernity, but, in fact many smaller, more homogeneous countries have higher median incomes, higher mean levels of education, and higher median levels of personal life quality. This should be no surprise. The United States is very large in geography and numbers, and its population is extremely diverse. It contains a large and growing subpopulation of illegal immigrants and another subpopulation of African Americans struggling to overcome a two-hundred-year heritage of slavery and forced subservience to the white majority. Thus there remain great and troubling inequities across and within all its racial and cultural divisions.

These high-prosperity enclaves, though they may owe much of their suc-

FIGURE 11.4.
LIFE SATISFACTION IN A
VERY ADVANCED SOCIETY (SPECULATION)

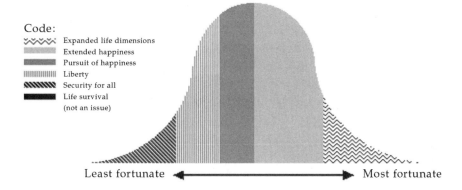

Code:
- Expanded life dimensions
- Extended happiness
- Pursuit of happiness
- Liberty
- Security for all
- Life survival
  (not an issue)

Least fortunate ⬅——————————➡ Most fortunate

cess to geography and historical accident, also serve as models for others to follow. All these states make great use of the knowledge platform to advance the welfare of all their members. Yet these societies also have a wealth of problems and they work assiduously on solutions. Thus they continue to advance, often probing new dimensions of experience that expand the idea of happiness (wavy-lined area in the figure). For example, an interesting fact about the Norwegian state is that it contributes more per capita to the assistance of the least developed countries than any other country in the world. This might suggest what was argued in the preceding chapter, that as we progress materially, we also progress in our ability to become moral beings.

The problem of inequity has to be viewed on a world stage. This is not simply a matter of different truth systems or civilizations in conflict. The fact is that some people are far richer than others, some far more powerful than others, and some far more knowledgeable about the knowledge platform than others. These discrepancies are most obvious when nation-states are compared. The poorest "nations" in the world have per capita incomes hovering just above or even just below the survival line. Almost all are in sub-Saharan Africa. Their ways are distinctly tribal, sometimes in the worst sense as discussed in chapter 10. They are living in a condition that was probably prevalent for humanity between ten thousand and six thousand years ago.

Figure 11.5 merges the three preceding figures to give a worldwide perspective on the disparity problem. As progress has been made, all the people of

FIGURE 11.5.
CULTURAL LAG AS A FUNCTION
OF LIFE-QUALITY DISCREPANCY

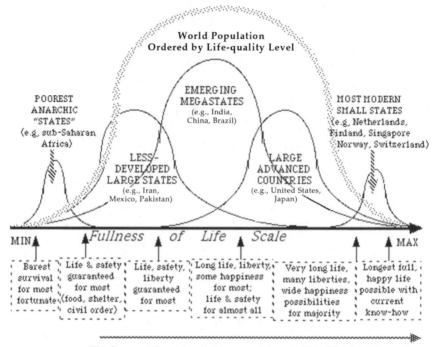

The forward function keeps stretching the "MAX" point forward,
redefining *quality of life* more expansively as it goes.

Earth have benefited to some extent, but the distribution of benefit has been grossly uneven. During the latter half of the twentieth century, the quality of life improved for nearly everyone on the planet, but it improved the most for those who were already better off, better educated, more aware of the new opportunities, more proximate to the centers of progress.

The persistence of misery at the tail end of every culture perhaps should be the greatest worry of our times. A major attraction of Marxist ideology of the past century was the notion that a society could be structured on the basis of equality, sharing all the productive wealth across all the people without distinction, leveling the top and raising the bottom. It didn't work, but the idea still continues to be a source of instability around the world, within countries and between countries. There are also continuing attempts by the rich countries to help the poor countries, even as they struggle to help their own poor. This is done with grants, loans, and various forms of advice giving via the United Nations agencies, national donor programs (such the US Agency for International Development), and numerous privately funded organizations (NGOs). These efforts have met with mixed success and are mostly modest in size and scope. In the future, the rich countries will do better if they can be induced to give more and to rigorously apply more science to the art of giving.

C. IDEOLOGY AND MIND-SET

1. Culture Wars and the Perpetuation of Tribal Thinking

As the forward function inevitably moves all societies in a progressive direction (shifting everyone in figures 11.2, 11.3, 11.4, and 11.5 more toward the right end of the continuum), it introduces new possibilities of living, new realms of choice, and new lifestyles. It continuously redefines and expands the idea of the good life. As this happens among those fortunate ones at the front end of the curve in every culture, those further back get anxious; and as their anxiety increases, they seek to impose restrictions. In the long run, such restrictions will not stop the forward function, but they may create havoc and misery in individual lives. Culture wars as an expression of cultural lag are serious business.

On the international stage this conflict between the modernists and the traditionalists can be characterized as a clash of civilizations as Huntington and others have described it. The symbolism of devout religious fanatics crashing airliners into tall buildings is dramatic and obvious, but this cultural war is far more complicated than that terrible act would suggest. The same battle between the modernists and the radical traditionalists gets played out within the United States, within India and Pakistan, within Egypt and Iran, and within many other places. It is a serious war that can become bloody.

Human beings under stress or challenge tend to forsake civilized behavior and revert to violence as a strategy of problem solving. In this regressive plunge, the moral imperatives shrink to a very restricted "us" versus "them" mind-set. This is the essence of tribalism. All those outside the tribe become redefined as fitting into one of three categories: (1) enemies who must be destroyed or brought completely under our control, (2) allies who are considered only for their instrumental value as means to assist our destructive goals, and (3) noncombatant outsiders who now have no value and who can be ridden over or even slaughtered as needs dictate on the way to destroying the enemy. Such primitive modes of thought and action probably dominated the lives of our distant ancestors. From the dawn of recorded history, warfare has been a dominant theme, and there is no reason to believe that it started just six or seven thousand years ago. Thus we have to come to terms with the fact that this dark tendency is buried in our genes, and it can always be awakened under the right circumstances.

The story of civilization is largely the story of inhibition. Over time and through painful learning experiences we have come to control and redirect our aggressive instincts, first within the family, then within the tribe, and later through extending the circle of "us" to a larger and larger group, as discussed in chapter 10. In some ways, the nation-states of the nineteenth and early twentieth centuries were an advanced manifestation of this civilizing tendency because everyone within these states came to identify themselves as part of this whole, a very large and inclusive "us." The trouble was that these nation-states could now act like individual persons in many respects, and, through their leaders, they could engage other nation-states in deadly zero-sum games. This is what happened at the outbreak of World War I, a catastrophic moment in history and the opening volley in an extended war, which lasted through 1945 with reverberations continuing past 1985.

Although major world wars, hot and cold, are thankfully unlikely in the near future, there was a large degree of chance in how we arrived at this happy moment in history, and the lessons to be learned on how we got here are both confusing and easily forgotten. The science of peacekeeping still has a long way to go. The social sciences have so far been unable to provide the kind of secure knowledge platform that could be used to guide the world leaders away from a future catastrophe of similar or greater dimensions. When great powers are confronted with aggression or terrorism, they still are often likely to respond in kind, that is, to use violence in response, in effect relying on the guidance of their tribal instincts. The result is renewed cycles of destruction and death, which can continue for decades without resolution. If these cycles cannot be broken, there is always the possibility that the weaker force will resort to suicidal terror with whatever pieces of war-making technology they can lay their hands on.

We are moving very rapidly into a new era of communication technology.

The avalanche of new devices and networks show promise for the betterment of humanity, but it is not yet clear that this promise will be fully realized. The enemies of modernism have proven capable of using all the new technologies to sustain and advance their own ancient belief systems. Such ideological movements have proved adept at using these very tools to promote tribalism and sometimes use them to attack the very foundations of science itself. There are real fears to be addressed, but in the long run there is every reason to believe that use for human benefit will prevail.

2. Competing "Truth" Systems and False "Learning"

It is a complicating fact of human civilization that "truth," even in this new age of science, is always up for grabs. George Orwell imagined the extreme of this in his gloomy futuristic novel, *1984*. Although this popular work was hardly prophetic of the last half of the twentieth century, it frightened many Western intellectuals and challenged them to rethink what kind of progress they were getting themselves into. In *1984*, Big Brother defines *truth* in absurdist fashion as the opposite of what we have been used to thinking. *Peace* is really endless war; *freedom* is really slavery, and so forth. Brainwashing consists of forcing people to deny the evidence of their own senses (e.g., "How many fingers am I holding up?") if the state demands that they see or sense something else.[10] Orwell had plenty of models for his future state construction. Adolph Hitler's nightmare police state was a recent memory. Joseph Stalin was still alive, and his model carried on in a somewhat diluted form long after his death. He was copied later by Mao Tse-tung, Pol Pot, and assorted others.

Orwell had it right in a certain sense. Every human to some extent has a different view of what truth is, and to that extent we are all at war with each other, desirous of brainwashing each other so that you will conform to my "correct" way of thinking, or I to yours. Some nation-states and many religious cults insist not only on strict observance of their rituals but actual acceptance of their dogma, their own "knowledge" platform, no matter how outlandish or logically flawed it might be. Many such "truth" systems are anchored in the fantasies of some self-proclaimed prophet, or in ancient documents of dubious authorship, perhaps in the polemical tract of some zealot (e.g., Hitler's *Mein Kampf*), or the musings of some self-proclaimed social scientist-philosopher (e.g., Karl Marx).

Each of these "truth" systems provides significant rewards to its adherents in terms of fellowship and the security of mental certainty. There is great comfort to be derived from "knowing" all the answers to life's persistent questions. In exchange, these "truth" systems require the believer to surrender both rational thought processes and an ordered view of empirical reality as perceived by the senses. The key word is *faith*, which really means accepting something as true in the absence of meaningful evidence or even in the face of evidence to the contrary, just as Orwell described.

Samuel Huntington has written of the clash of civilizations with reference to a supposed inevitable struggle between what he calls "Western" and "Islamic" civilizations.[11] The real clash may be between rationalist science with its promise of continuing progress and irrationalist religions of all stripes—Catholic, Protestant, evangelical, Muslim, Hindu, and others—some with Western origins, some with Eastern. Mainstream Christian, Muslim, Hindu, and Buddhist religions have maintained an uneasy truce with science over the last century. There is nearly universal acceptance on at least a superficial level of many of the raw facts laboriously culled from nature by science. These would include the physical laws at least of Newtonian physics; the nature of light, energy, and matter; the reality of the evidence from telescopes and microscopes; the biochemical nature of life; and the central role played by DNA in the heredity of plants, animals, and man. Where these understandings of the natural world conflict with the authority of ancient texts, religious people in general are likely to shrug off the inconsistencies as something for philosophers and theologians to worry about. This probably explains why a certain percentage of scientists the world over also adhere to one or another of the world religions. As we move from the basic sciences to their applications in engineering, agriculture, medicine, and other fields of practical endeavor, the acceptance of this dissonance is greater. For most people, if there is a logical divide between science and the religion-based civilizations, the dominant attitude toward this "clash" is to "live and let live."

3. Ignorance of Established Science: Method and Substance

We have spoken above of the dangers of adopting unvalidated or demonstrably false platforms of "knowledge." The other side of this coin is plain ignorance, the absence of or weakness in popular understanding of everything scientific. This includes the main structure of the scientific knowledge platform as a whole and its symbiotic relationship with all modern technologies.

It also includes comprehension of the methodology of science and the several ways in which scientific truth claims are validated (e.g., repeated exact observation, measurement and recording, logical reasoning, experiment, mathematical analysis, and exposure to criticism).

One reason why the principles of the forward function are not more widely accepted and appreciated is the low level of public understanding of what science is, how science relates to technology, and how technology contributes to better lives. Even though scientists are typically most impressed by what they don't know, the average citizen hardly knows anything about what scientists already know and have long known. Some political and religious groups around the world even downgrade the importance of science education and militate against the teaching of fundamental precepts in biology and geology. The Cold War provided a strong stimulus for the teaching of science as an important national goal,[12] but with the Cold War now long over, that stimulus seems to have weakened. Hopefully, some of the residual beneficial consequences of the frenzied Cold War competition and the space race (such as the mass-produced microprocessor and its communications cousin, the Internet) will provide the stimulus for continued and expanded interest in science in the future.

If people don't understand what scientists do and how they derive their facts and theories, then they have no reason to rate scientific truth any higher than any other "truth" (such as that from their own personal experience; from parents, friends, and other important people in their lives; not to mention from fiction and nonfiction writings and speeches; and from articulate or charismatic spokespersons for various cults and religions). If people lack understanding of how science establishes truth, they are more likely to select leaders who also lack this understanding. Even though, in democracies, there is a tendency for more educated people to seek and achieve political office and to be selected for leadership positions in the private sector, there is no guarantee that this means they will understand and accept science and its implications.

A related concern is an understanding of the myriad connections between science and the advanced technologies that have brought so much progress in the last half-century. The new technologies are not miracles. They do not come from God. They come from the creative ingenuity of many thousands of applied scientists and engineers who know the basic science applying to their fields and know how to use it to improve lives. If there is no appreciation of these connections, then progress can be stalled at least temporarily by thoughtless regulation, lack of funding, and other threats. Fortunately, there has been no across-the-board trend in such a negative direction, although there are specific instances where such a pattern is observable (e.g., in peaceful applications of atomic energy, use of pesticides, genetic engineering of plants, and early experimentation with stem cells).

Ignorance of science oddly also occurs among scientists themselves. In the course of their labors, scientists must move from quiet and protected environments to noisy, public, pushy environments and back again to their cloisters as they conduct their research and then expose it to the scrutiny of their colleagues and others. To be successful, they almost always have to narrow their focus, not just to a particular field but also to a particular narrowly defined set of phenomena within their chosen field. In other words, they must specialize within their specialization. This narrow focus gives more protection because a narrower subject matter can be mastered more easily, and mastery is required before findings can be exposed to the rest of the scientific community. There is a real problem with this narrowing, however, when it comes to understanding and explaining the knowledge platform as a whole. The easiest way to deal with it is to forget it or to pretend that it doesn't exist. Thus the monk Gregor Mendel could study his peas and solve important riddles of heredity without worrying that it might bring the teachings of his church into question. Likewise, Copernicus, Kepler, and even the great Newton himself could be comfortable in their firmly held Christian theology, believing that they were only revealing God's plan for the universe.

Fortunately, there are scientists who are able, often in their later years, to rise above their specialties and take on the task of teaching and publicizing the unity of science. We have had occasion to cite some of these frequently in this book. Edward O. Wilson's important synthesis under the title *Consilience* came long after he had established himself as an insect specialist. Jared Diamond wrote the very popular and insightful synthesis *Guns, Germs, and Steel* many years after he had become an expert on tropical birds. Science journalism and science-oriented documentary television also make a major contribution, countering the flood of misinformation that streams in from nonscientific sources. The continuance of public support for science depends in part on eloquent spokespersons who can rise above their specialties and make the whole fabric of science both comprehensible and interesting to the average person.

A generally neglected but vital area of public ignorance is statistics. Much of modern science and technology as well as rational decision making in private and public affairs depends on a rudimentary understanding of statistics. When people are harmed or die of war, accident, or disease, the public generally has no sense of proportionality. The spectacular accident or act of terrorism is taken as evidence for a massive breakdown in safety or a worldwide trend toward terror affecting all people. For lack of a proper statistical frame of reference, public perceptions of the true extent of a danger or a disaster can be exaggerated out of all proportion to its true meaning. The result often is hasty decision making without rational problem solving, without consideration of what the real problem is or what the best way to approach it might be. The ratio of cost to benefit from any private or public act has now been studied by economists for some years and is widely recognized as a truly rational basis for decision making, yet the general public knows almost nothing about it and major decisions by nation-states even in the most developed parts of the world pay it little heed. The consequences are often dire.

Looking backward to the eighteenth century, one might imagine that Newton's laws and his calculus would have been widely known and accepted within fifty years of his death. After all, he was famous in his own time. But such a widespread understanding or even awareness of what Newton was up to did not happen for another two centuries. His new laws were discussed and debated within only a small elite circle of men who almost all had the added advantage of being able to read and write in Latin. We might further imagine that the Victorian world was enlightened by Darwin after 1856 and came to accept his evolutionary theory, but this was also hardly the case. His revolutionary theory was avidly discussed and disputed in intellectual circles of the day, but these were still largely very privileged circles. Today, while the theory is still widely disputed in some places, scientists, including tens of thousands of biology teachers worldwide, almost universally accept it. It is most certainly the dominant theory of biology taught in most of the schools in all of the advanced countries of the West. Yet in many American high schools it is simply not taught at all because these same biology teachers fear the trouble that might be stirred up by angry religious parents.[13]

4. Pessimism

One of the enduring mysteries of modern culture is the perpetuation of a pessimistic mind-set. Despite all the advances that have come in the nineteenth century and especially the twentieth century and despite our proven capacity to find solutions to major problems as they arise, many of the most educated members of every society persist in thinking that the future will be grim. Easterbrook identifies this phenomenon as *collapse anxiety*, that is, "a hidden fear, especially among opinion makers of the United States and European Union, that people are about to exhaust the world's resources and any progress in developing nations will only hasten this outcome."[14] Easterbrook goes on to point out that these fears have no basis in empirically documented fact. A corollary view, shared by people who are more religious and less scientific in outlook, is that the past was better, going all the way back to an "original" state (e.g., the Garden of Eden) which was supposedly idyllic. In these pages, I have tried to explain why there is every reason to think otherwise. The past was miserable by today's standards, and the future promises to be better than anything we can even conceive of in today's terms.

The wonders of material human achievement through science and technology were already clear to Freud in 1930 when he, as an old man, reflected on the civilization of his time. He wrote the following:

> Man has become a god by means of artificial limbs, so to speak, quite magnificent when equipped with all his accessory organs; but they do not grow on him and they still give him trouble at times. However, he is entitled to console himself with the thought that this evolution will not come to an end in AD 1930. Future ages will produce further great advances in this realm of culture, probably inconceivable now, and will increase man's likeness to a god still more. But with the aim of our study in mind, we will not forget, all the same, that the human being of today is not happy with all his likeness to a god.[15]

Freud's metaphoric "artificial limbs" are already expanded far beyond his 1930 imaginings, yet his now eighty-year-old prediction of humankind's dismissive attitude toward its incredible achievements remains on target.

The persistence of pessimistic attitudes regarding the human future remains a great mystery, seemingly unaffected by manifest advances in knowledge and its applications in every sector of human experience. Subjective estimates of happiness are notoriously unreliable and tend to be strongly influenced by how the question is asked and how the respondent happens to feel at a particular moment.[16] It might be supposed that our primary worry, death, could be cause of a generally pessimistic mind-set by all humanity, yet research also suggests that people tend to report greater levels of happiness or well-being as they get older.

Given the prevalence of such views, is pessimism anything to worry about? The answer is *yes*, in two different ways. First of all, any phenomenon that makes large numbers of people worry unnecessarily is itself a worry because it subtracts from their enjoyment of life. There are many things people worry about a lot, even though they have no reason to do so, and their worrying can make their lives miserable. Even more important than that needless loss of potential happiness is the fact that pessimism saps energy from the forward function, slowing down the pace of progress. In 1961, had President John F. Kennedy not believed that the engineers and scientists of his time could get to the moon in ten years, he would not have considered funding such an ambitious project. If medical researchers had decided that there was no way to beat polio or AIDS, they might not have pushed so hard on these important lifesaving goals. Many more ambitious goals are in the offing as this is written. The stronger the public belief that these ambitious lifesaving goals are reachable, the sooner they will be accomplished. Baseless pessimism about the future can be a significant drag on progress.

5. Resistance to Change and the Comfort of Old Ideas

One reason why the notion of a pervasive forward function is not well appreciated lies in the fact that most people, most of the time, do not welcome change. Most people tend to regularly seek stability and routine in their lives. This is natural and as it should be. All of our life processes depend upon a steady and unbroken repetition of input, throughput, and output. It is very important not to change these processes, particularly if they appear to be working well, allowing us to survive. This stability-reliability requirement applies at all levels, within the living cell, within organs of the body, within the body as a whole, and within the more or less stable organs of society, which regulate our actions and support our living patterns.

This need for stability and a sense of permanence amid the chaos of nature is also probably a major factor in the persistent attraction of the world's religions. The messages of science are not always comforting or reassuring. Do we really want to know that our world is a tiny and impermanent speck in a vast universe, a universe filled with the deadly radiation of billions of burning stars swirling about each other? Do we really want to know that we are descended from slime molds or other semiorganic beings unknown that began to appear on this planet five billion years ago? The idea of organisms ceaselessly battling each other for survival as they crawl up the phylogenetic ladder is probably an equally disturbing image for many, however factually accurate it may be. The easier psychological path is to cling to old ideas, to take comfort in the folk myths of our cultures, ignoring the fact that dozens of other human cultures, large and small, have different norms and folk myths of their own that are partly or entirely incompatible with ours.

6. Fear Itself

Let us return finally to Franklin D. Roosevelt's famous 1933 admonition, with which this chapter began. In fact, at that time there was a great deal more to fear than fear itself. Major worries abounded. At home in America, millions of people were out of work. Farmers were broke. The economy was struggling along at less than half capacity. Abroad, the same thing was happening. Both Western democracy and free market capitalism were being seen in many quarters as abject failures. Despite the fact that there were no major wars happening, it was a really low point of the twentieth century, a seeming end of progress on all fronts. Yet the president was right to name this one element, fear, above all others as something to worry about. Luckily, the world has not faced a crisis of that kind in the eighty years since, but we are beset by irrational fears, many of which are the result of misunderstandings of what the forward function is all about and its enormous potential for future human happiness.

We can start with modern science. To the average person, science is mostly a mystery, and a mystery that they fear. The word *atom*, for example, associates first with *bomb* in many people's minds. The idea that all matter, including living things and concrete objects of all shapes and sizes, are made of atoms is difficult to grasp and (partly for this reason) is probably quite frightening to many. The failure of advanced Western countries (with the exception of France) to take advantage of clean burning atomic power plants to generate electricity has a lot to do with this fear of atoms. The same applies to chemicals, which are associated in many minds with poison. It is not widely understood that all the material things we deal with in our daily lives are chemicals. Thus, the idea that human activity continuously discharges chemicals into the environment and that we consume large quantities of chemicals daily seems like a frightening idea to many.

The same kind of fear attaches to the term *species extinction.* Most people have no clear idea that there are many millions of species and that numerous species become extinct while numerous others come into being annually. Thus, when it is reported that one or another species is nearing extinction, it is assumed, first, that this is a dreaded event (Is it a terrible thing that the smallpox virus is virtually extinct?) and, second, that human activity was the direct cause of the extinction. New species created by man are likewise sometimes viewed with horror as "unnatural" and probably therefore dangerous. Of course, some may be dangerous, and some extinctions are lamentable, but the fears are out of all proportion to the magnitude of the harm.

There is also a generalized fear of science, which has no reasonable basis. It is somewhat akin to fear of the unknown, even though science is the only way we can attack the unknown. Science-fiction literature is not helpful in regard to viewing the future without fear. The most popular themes of science-fiction writers are science run amok, mad scientists, scientists creating monsters, and scientists creating world-poisoning or world-destroying weapons. The most intellectually serious works of science fiction, such as Orwell's *1984*, are written as cautionary tales. This is what might happen if we don't change our ways or do something soon. Nevertheless, they tend to be read by many as prophesy, and the dominant prophesy, intended or not, is that doomsday is ahead. Much of religious teaching and preaching also tends in this direction.

The Ubiquity of Cycles

The cyclical nature of so many phenomena impinging on experience lends continuous reinforcement to the idea that change is nonprogressive. This starts with the life cycle, which appears to repeat over and over again with every new birth in a more or less unchanging pattern, generation after generation. The highly predictable and endless repetition of seasons of the year, which result from the axis tilt of Earth as it proceeds on its near-circular annual orbit around the sun, further confirms the idea that change is a matter of repeated cycles of spring, summer, fall, and winter. That pattern often serves as a metaphor for life. Historical analysis is also typically cast in a cyclical mold. Civilizations are seen to rise and fall, empires and epochs to come and go, and we look to the repeating patterns of this modestly understood past to find metaphors that can govern the present and the future. All these patterns and more reinforce the idea that progress is a chimera.

There is much validity to the notion that life and history occur in cyclical patterns, but it is wrong to conclude that progressive change is not taking place within these patterns. Earlier in this chapter this same idea of cyclical action was invoked to describe a key element of the forward function, but in the science-based problem-solving cycle (recall figure 8.3) the difference is that we do not end up where we started but at a state of affairs advanced over where we started. The same was true for much of the problem solving of pre-scientific times. However, progressive change before the age of science was so slow and so erratic that the progressive aspect was not always clear.

Plateaus and Regressions

The forward function is not a steady upward slope. There are times when progress seems to slow down, stop for a while, and even shift into reverse. When World War II ended with the dropping of two atomic bombs, not only was there a tremendous boost of respect for science and scientists, but it was also generally believed that significant peaceful uses of atomic energy would follow. There were some fairly significant applications of prebomb nuclear research in the form of nuclear reactor–driven electrical power generation, and a small number of nuclear-powered ships were built, notably submarines, but the realization of bomb-scale energy output from fission or fusion has yet to be realized even after many years of fairly intensive research and development. Even prototype experiments with nuclear fusion (sunpower) have failed to yield a positive ratio of energy output after all these years of trying. This is but one example of a plateau in the development of a useful technology out of past scientific discovery. Similarly, tantalizing discoveries have been made in basic research on animal and human cell structure and function, yet from this new knowledge fountain no dramatically new solutions have yet flowed. So far we have not witnessed significant inroads against the most deadly forms of cancer (the most life-destructive form of cell growth) and significant life extension (e.g., from R & D on the aging process) still seems far off.

It is very hard to predict the pace of progress in a given area, even though the path seems obvious. It is clear that we will eventually understand enough about the atom to use its energy in a controlled and beneficial way. It is also clear that we will eventually understand enough about the details of how cells function to apply that knowledge in controlling cancer completely. Unfortunately, such long delays in anticipated progress may appear to the layman as dead ends, illustrating the impossibility of further progress. Such doubters and pessimists are learning the wrong lessons from these seemingly endless slowdowns after new discoveries. These are not dead ends or stopping points but merely exposures of holes or weak spots in the knowledge platform that the scientists are still busily working to fill.

Misuse of the New Technologies of Diffusion

One of the profound ironies of advances in communicative technologies is their capacity to advance the cause of antiprogressive forces of all kinds. Starting with writing and moving on to the printing press, telegraph, radio, moving pictures, television, and now the Internet, humans have enhanced their capacities to distort truth, propagate deliberate falsehoods, exaggerate fears, promote terroristic behavior, and generally incite war and intensify tribalism. It was through the written word that the great religions of Christianity and Islam were able to spread widely and remain in place for centuries across the territories that their adherents conquered. It was also through the print reproductions of old texts that Protestantism was able to sweep across northern Europe in the sixteenth century, and it was largely through newspapers and broadside propaganda sheets that the American, French, and other revolutions of the eighteenth and nineteenth centuries found their inspiring fires. Many of these movements were progressive in one way or another, but many were also retrogressive and hurtful for the cause of human well-being.

The communications technologies of the twentieth century have brought a new threat to progress by their ability to create and propagate deliberately invented systems of pseudoreality. As motion-picture technology advanced with the ability to add sound in the 1920s and color in the late 1930s, its ability to convey a striking illusion of actual events from entirely fictional sources became firmly established. For the most part, this new creative medium conveyed harmless content under the rubric of "entertainment," but some of it was not harmless. The epic silent motion picture *Birth of a Nation*[17] mixed fiction with fact about the aftermath of the American Civil War and romanticized the Ku Klux Klan to such an extent that the Klan grew enormously during the 1920s and became a potent political force even in northern states like Indiana, despite the fact that it had nearly died out in previous decades. Adolph Hitler used radio and cinema as propaganda tools in building popular support for his regime in the 1930s, and control of the media has been a major tool of all modern despots, transforming authoritarian rule into something new and horrific for which the term *totalitarianism* was coined.

CONCLUSION

Any reader who has come this far might understandably be concerned about where the forward function is actually taking us. Over and over again the same ominous words appear: *ongoing, expanding, accelerating,* and *relentless.* Shouldn't we be worried about all this? Shouldn't someone at some point just say, "STOP! ENOUGH!"? Fortunately or unfortunately, the world just doesn't work that way. There are things to be worried about, but our human DNA dictates that we must try to control our destiny through problem solving. We should worry less about our relentless tendency to problem solve and worry more about our frequent tendency to solve problems poorly, jumping to conclusions without good evidence, failing to take the time to absorb the lessons of history and make careful observation. All the things we worry about are also things we can do something about, and as we progress, we actually become better and better problem solvers. That is the happy truth about the forward function.

Chapter Twelve

WHAT WILL
THE FUTURE BRING?
What Will Be and What Ought to Be

Let others praise ancient times,
I was glad I was born in these.

—Ovid, ca. 1–5 BCE

We live at a time when our species is making dynamic breakthroughs
that are setting the stage for a magnificent future. . . . Only when
society adopts a vision of the human species as a creative force in the
cosmos will it be able to rid itself of the pessimism permeating the
culture.

—Michael G. Zey, *The Future Factor*

Civilization has made great strides over the centuries in science,
healthcare, the arts and most, if not all, economic well-being. But it
has also given a privileged position to the development of weapons
and the threat and reality of war. Mass slaughter has become the
ultimate civilized achievement. Civilized life, as it is called, is a great
white tower celebrating human achievements, but at the top there is
permanently a large black cloud. Human progress dominated by
unimaginable cruelty and death.

—John Kenneth Galbraith, *The Economics of Innocent Fraud:*
Truth for Our Time[1]

Fasten your seat belts, the turbulence has scarcely begun. Unless evo-
lution has radically changed its ways, we are facing an explosion of
societal diversity and complexity hundreds of times greater than we
now experience or can yet imagine. If we think to perpetuate the old
ways, we should try to recall the last time evolution rang our number
and asked consent.

—Dee Hock, *Birth of the Chaordic Age*[2]

Acase has now been made for something called a *forward function*, a set of six processes embedded in the human species and in human cultures, which have evolved and grown out of the genetic material of the species. These six processes explain how we got to where we are now, for better and for worse, though we argue that it is mostly for the better. It is now that the reader might ask, "So what?" Why have we gone on this elaborate journey, recounting the basics of science, science-based cosmology, speculative anthropology, and cultural history? Here in this chapter and in other works yet to be written is the payoff, the answer to that question.

These six processes do not stop here. That is the first part of the answer. This is not "the end of history," as one writer boldly announced when the Cold War came to an end.[3] The elements of the forward function, irrevocably embedded in human culture, go on and on and will continue to operate for as long as there is human life on this planet. This seems to be a difficult concept to grasp. Just as it has been very difficult for humans to come to grips with their biological-genetic ancestry that stretches out to billions of years in the utterly remote past, so it appears to be difficult for them to realistically imagine their future, either near or far. The forward function remains in effect even as individuals die, as particular technologies become obsolete, as empires rise and fall, as particular cultures and particular religions rise and fade. It continues and builds on itself even as books are burned to block new ideas, as laws are passed to preserve the old ways and stamp out the new, even as political and military measures are taken to condemn any further progress and to slaughter the messengers. Through all these vicissitudes, the forward function relentlessly moves humanity forward toward a greater expression of human fulfillment and enjoyment of life, all the things enumerated in chapter 2 and then some, because where we are going is open-ended. The human experience is an ever-emergent phenomenon. It cannot be clearly defined by those who come before, even when they see the general direction in which it is going.

All the good things that happened to humanity after 1945 may have been partly a historical accident. This possibility can't be ruled out. It has been an unusually good time for humanity: food production has gone way up, finally outstripping hunger and population rise in most parts of the world. Some major diseases that have plagued humankind for centuries have been curtailed and a few even banished forever. Infant mortality has declined markedly even in poor countries. It has also been a time when national governments began to communicate seriously with each other on many issues of concern to all humanity, when hundreds of millions could communicate with each other in new ways across and within all continents, when all could begin to receive the same words and moving pictures concerning all subjects. The entire world has also been brought together as never before in vibrant mutual trading for mutual benefit.

There might have been special reasons why all these things happened in the particular time period between 1945 and 2010. For most of that time there was a geopolitical stalemate between two superpowers and their alliance blocs. This prolonged confrontation led to the frenzied development of new technologies. The apparent motive for most of these advances was to hold or gain a technological edge on the presumptive enemy. With the end of the Cold War, about 1990, the vigor of that competition may have ebbed somewhat, but the momentum of discovery has continued at a quickening pace.

Two major trends of the last half of the twentieth century will transform the human condition in the first half of the twenty-first. The first comes directly out of biochemistry. A new era in biology began with the unraveling of the genetic code in the early 1950s and the full integration of biology and chemistry that followed. In the next fifty years, this new knowledge platform will transform medicine, prolonging lives and eliminating some of the major threats to human health. The second comes out of physics and the applied material science to which it is wedded. Semiconductors were first discovered at Bell Telephone Laboratories at about the same time that Watson and Crick figured out the molecular structure of DNA. The Bell discovery eventually led to the electronic digital encoding, storage, and transmission of all the information contained in all the scattered knowledge platforms of science and technology. These and other discoveries in all fields of science have led to an increasingly solid knowledge platform from which future progress can be made with ever-greater certainty and speed on problems of ever-greater complexity and difficulty. This digitization promises to lead to the integration of all knowledge in the twenty-first century. With science as the foundation it will be human destiny to move forward, never backward, and to push the spectrum of human needs and aspirations ever wider, as scientific knowledge and technical capabilities accrue over time.

FUTURE EXTENSION OF THE FORWARD FUNCTION

The six elements of the forward function clearly point the way to a positive future in broad terms. Here is how they will play out in the short term of the next century.

1. The Basic (Animal) Learning Process

We always keep on learning, animal style. The more of us who are alive and healthy, the more learning there will be in absolute terms.[4] More humans means more learning in a collective sense. If humans are able to learn more from each other, pooling and integrating what they learn, there will be more collective benefit from what is learned. More people will also be able to learn things beyond survival skills as survival becomes more ensured. The stimulus environment in which people learn has also expanded enormously and will continue to expand via better microscopes; telescopes; imaging; recording; travel; Internet surfing; and exposure to more peoples, more problems, more scientific knowledge, different cultures, different animals, and other forms of life. Thanks to the forward function, more young people are being placed in secure and stimulating learning environments, in and outside the classroom.

Research and development on the learning process is also leading to more effective learning experiences, creating new social and physical environments more conducive to learning for a diversity of age groups, subject matter, or learner circumstances. To improvements in classroom and book learning, we can now add learning via television (formal and nonformal), computer-guided and programmed instruction, and Internet-mediated interactive learning. Even computer games, which worry many parents, may be inadvertently teaching problem-solving skills of a high order to a new generation of tech-oriented learners.[5] Thanks partly to the United Nations and its affiliated groups as well as to numerous education-oriented NGOs and philanthropic organizations, most of these advances are being spread to developing countries, raising literacy and numeracy rates worldwide to a substantial degree. The root of all these advances is the great body of research and development on the animal learning process, which began in the twentieth century with Pavlov, Skinner, and others.

2. Storage of Learning outside the Body of the Learner

We continue to store outside the body more and more of what we are learning, and our capacity to do so continues to expand at a remarkable rate. Every teaching-learning event, every new book written, every sound and video recording, every item added to a database, all these are examples of storage of learning outside the body. With electronic digital storage capacity doubling every eighteen months, the mountains of learning now stored and accessible in this form are already almost unimaginable.[6] As this accumulating storage continues to build and to become more integrated and more accessible, its utility in the service of human needs will become ever more obvious.

3. The Social Organization of Problem Solving

As discussed in chapter 6, two aspects of social evolution have played a major role in advancing the human condition: networking and the division of labor in the service of problem solving. Trends in both these areas will continue to expand, transforming all cultures over the next century and bringing everyone together and dividing everyone up in new, interesting, and productive ways.

Advances in networking during the last half century have been extreme and will continue at an even faster pace in the years to come. This trend includes travel by more people to more places at faster speeds as well as both one-way and two-way communication about more subjects on more channels. Every new social encounter and every visit to a new place either makes a new network or strengthens an existing one. Communication and travel will result in greatly expanded and strengthened human networks within and between countries and geographic regions.

A particularly intriguing development of the last decade has been distributed computation. The organizers of SETI (a privately funded project to search for extraterrestrial intelligence using optical and radio signals from thousands of nearby stars) have set up a program called SETI@home, which allows thousands of personal-computer owners to volunteer their unused computer time for the massive calculating task of interpreting the incoming streams electromagnetic radiation from sunlike stars in our vicinity in the expectation of eventually discovering intelligent signals.[7]

One of the important social inventions of the twentieth century was the R & D laboratory. Originally the science lab was an adjunct to a university sci-

ence department, and the development lab was an adjunct to a large manufacturing concern, but the whole idea of the laboratory and the idea that
research and development could be combined as integrated functions within
a larger R & D entity came directly out of World War II. Now even small production companies in every sector of the economy are likely to have their own
R & D labs. Each major government department has its own, and universities
have many laboratories from which private profit-making enterprises are
being continually spun off. As we start the twenty-first century, the overall
structure and size of this R & D activity is so large and diverse that it is beyond
description. There is no stopping this process. As new functions, services, and
product lines are discovered, new R & D organizations or subunits of organizations will spring up to further refine and exploit the new knowledge that
they represent.

The R & D subculture was an almost exclusively American invention, but
as the new century gets under way, every other major country is developing
its own research capacity and R & D infrastructure. European and Japanese
nonmilitary R & D is now outpacing the US investment in proportion to gross
national product.[8] The number of universities offering advanced science and
engineering degrees has also mushroomed in the twentieth century, and this
trend continues.[9]

4. The Knowledge Platform

In 1700, the existing platform of reliable scientific knowledge could probably
be contained within a single volume of one thousand pages or perhaps less
and conveyed to an eager and intelligent learner in the matter of a week or
two. By 1800, it possibly could have been contained in one hundred such volumes and learned readily by the same student in perhaps two years. By 1900,
a vastly stronger scientific knowledge base could be contained in perhaps ten
thousand such volumes and would have taken the better part of a lifetime to
be fully absorbed by this hypothetical diligent and highly intelligent student.
By the year 2000 it just couldn't happen. There would have to be more than
one million such volumes—stored now on more convenient and compact
media, of course.

However, impressive as it is, size is not all that matters in the knowledge
platform. The platform's strength derives from its logical and empirical integration. In the twentieth century there has been a great coming together of the

knowledge base across all the natural sciences.[10] As the base has increased, it has also become more coherent. This great unification through simplification began with Copernicus and reached a marvelous first climax with Newton's *Philosophiæ Naturalis Principia Mathematica.* More than a century later, Lyell showed the continuity of geologic change over time. Then Darwin built on Lyell's discoveries and explained the continuity in change of biological forms within Lyell's time scale. Fifty years after that, Einstein showed the continuity of matter and energy within time and space: and fifty more years after that, Watson and Crick showed the continuity of life within atomic chemistry. Each of these breakthroughs added to the knowledge base but also greatly simplified the overall picture of the universe and humankind's place in it.

Both the platform and the integrative principles that make the platform strong will keep expanding at an accelerated rate throughout the next century and beyond. There will never again be a shortage of teachers and students, of media for sharing, of repositories for storage. As the platform grows, it will become more integrated and more internationalized. It will be the very opposite of the legendary biblical tower of Babel, because scientists will speak the same language more, even as they invent more new terms to more accurately describe more new phenomena. Scientists are also moving inexorably closer and closer to two huge objectives: discovering the fundamental nature of life and its origins, and finding advanced forms of life elsewhere in the universe. Achieving a working knowledge of the full chemistry of even a single cell is still beyond our grasp because of the millions of complex subelements and interactions each living cell contains. However, the increased computational power already available together with improved electron microscopy will lead the way to this Holy Grail of biological science. After biologists have understood how the single living cellular organism works in all its atomic detail, they will quickly move on to understand multicellular organisms, gradually reaching up to the level of humans. This is an enormous climb, but it is becoming more and more clear where we are going and how we can get there.

There is a dialectic in science in the sense that new theories arise and become dominant, are then challenged by other theories and contradictory data, and are then discarded in place of a newer theory. However, this dialectic is not a zero-sum game as might be inferred from some writings.[11] Planks are replaced or reshaped, but the whole edifice doesn't come tumbling down just because some brilliant theorist comes up with a new twist. Sometimes one or another piece is replaced or downgraded in importance, but more typically the whole is seen in a new light that makes it more understandable. New factual information and more precise measurements also continuously stream into the platform through scientific journals, and, as the databases become stronger, new theories arise to explain and further integrate the findings. This process has no end, either on the theory side or the data side. The database gets bigger and better all the time, and the theories give us more explanatory power all the time. Such growth does not happen in a smooth upward curve but tends to come in fits and starts. A really good theory like Einstein's or a convincing model like Watson and Crick's gives an enormous push to a scientific field.

5. Processes of Problem Solving

The processes of problem solving, including both scientific discovery and the generation of useful technologies based on science, are progressively becoming more and more sophisticated. There are at least three important aspects of problem solving where this should be apparent. The first is observation and data collection. We are already in an era where units of light and atoms are routinely measurable despite their infinitesimal size on a human scale. Such measurement capability will continue to be refined, and there is no limit to such refinement. With each new step in this direction more is revealed about the fundamental nature of physical reality, and more options are opened to ways of modifying that reality in the service of human needs. At the same time, mathematics and computational science provide more elaborate and revealing ways to look at the data at hand and to interpret its meaning. The new math is further empowered by the great increase in computational power offered by modern computers. This combination of more advanced measuring tools, more complex and sophisticated mathematical algorithms for variable analysis, and faster computations will allow much further penetration into the basic nature of atoms, molecules, living cells, and whole organisms. This never-ending process will yield substantial fruits within the next two generations.

6. Diffusion

As human culture has advanced, the capacity for information sharing through diffusion has also advanced, but it has done so in distinct stages. The first great leap forward came through the invention of language perhaps fifty thousand years ago. As early civilizations arose after the invention of agriculture, they gradually developed a system of passing detailed information from one generation to the next through formulaic poetry and inscriptive pictography, starting about five thousand years ago. True alphabetic written language came along twenty-five hundred years ago, allowing for much wider dissemination within and across cultures, across long distances, and across generations—all with great fidelity to the information sources. The printed newspaper and book came along only five hundred fifty years ago, telegraphic code messaging some one hundred seventy years ago, telephone voice transmission one hundred thirty years ago, wireless radio broadcast telegraphy one hundred years ago, voice radio broadcast eighty years ago, and television voice and moving image broadcasting sixty years ago. Just twenty years ago, we began to have full digital recording and transmission with satellite broadcasting. Just ten years ago, we began to have a fully integrated digital electronic world network, user-friendly and accessible at any time for any purpose at minimal cost, connecting to millions of people from every country. From this relisting of the steps in the progression it should be fairly obvious that the trend of diffusion is toward acceleration over time.

The world has come a long way since the invention of the printing press. When print materials became widely available at modest prices, literacy quickly became a prized skill. Both literacy and numeracy expanded greatly during the nineteenth and early twentieth centuries and is approaching universality as the twenty-first century gets under way. The expansion of educational opportunities worldwide is an important aspect of modern diffusion. A more educated populace can absorb more complex messages faster and make better use of what is learned to improve individual lives in any and all of the directions suggested in chapter 2. The educational challenge for the next generation will be in the area of science. Improved science education is a distinct priority if the people of the world are to take full advantage of their new twenty-first-century knowledge platform. This means more science in the curriculum, more effective methods for teaching science, and elevating the importance and visibility of science at all levels of education.

The entire world is now connected with multiple media networking and continuous message streaming. This trend toward connectedness will continue indefinitely as more and more people enter the network and as higher-capacity media come along. These clearly foreseeable developments will allow more sharing of ever more complex data sets. As was stated above, a more educated public will be better prepared for intelligent reception and absorption of what is streamed at them. Such expanded diffusion readily crosses national and cultural boundaries in a flow that is only controllable at the margins. The trend is also toward larger signal-to-noise ratios, which means more accurate message transit and reception, allowing more true sharing of knowledge across cultures and across generations.

The Internet[12] has added a powerful new dimension to this worldwide network by offering full access to many of the most important data sources and information streams from any user-controlled entry portal. Ever-improving search engines and user interfaces already allow almost instant access by any person in any part of the globe to any type of information at the time and place of the user's choosing. No king or emperor or millionaire mogul of a century ago had such power at his or her fingertips! The Internet has already entered and affected the lives of millions in the barely thirty-five years since its invention. No one yet really knows where it is going and what its ultimate consequences for humanity will be, but it is certain to change the way the entire world functions. Almost all these changes will be favorable to the quality of life of humans individually and collectively.

Though invented for purposes of national defense, the Internet was first used extensively by computer scientists. During the middle and late 1980s, its use expanded to university research scientists in various fields, becoming an important tool for sharing data and collaborating on large scientific projects. During the 1990s it expanded out of all recognition from its origins in defense and its early uses in scientific research. As noted by Abbate,

> with the loss of a central guiding vision from ARPA, the system seemed at times to verge on anarchy, as control of the network became fragmented among diverse groups with competing interests and visions.[13]

This is an understatement. Through the 1990s and into the twenty-first century, the growth of the Internet has been explosive, extending to news, entertainment, banking, advertising, business, commerce of every kind, and— of course—knowledge and information of every kind (including all the "truth" realms discussed in the last chapter). In all these bewildering crosscurrents of use and intent, the Internet as a vehicle to further promote and further integrate the scientific knowledge platform is buried or obscured. The

Internet is definitely not the equivalent of or a substitute for the knowledge platform or even the know-how platform, yet pieces of both are scattered all over the Internet in a confusing array. Early in this new century, major efforts are likely to be made to straighten out aspects of the Internet as they impinge on the true knowledge platform and the networks specific to science. There is a need to develop search engines that are guided and screened according to the rules of science, screening out or flagging items of opinion, conjecture, and anecdote unsupported by reliable data. As this new information superhighway for science comes into being, it will usher in a new era of discovery and invention more impressive than the Industrial Revolution that preceded it.

TWENTY-FIRST-CENTURY PROGRESS IN PARTICULAR AREAS

If we begin to apply the six components of the forward function to particular areas of science and technology, a truly wondrous future begins to unfold. The purpose of this concluding section is to give only a foretaste of what this future will probably look like. Predicting the future is a perilous exercise, as the ice age forecasters of the 1970s could tell us. However, there are a few things that we know will happen within a certain time frame.

- We know that the knowledge platform will grow and strengthen.
- We know that computing power will continue to expand, doubling every five years as the cost-per-operation continues to plummet.
- We know that worldwide interconnection will continue to expand on many channels (travel, trade, telecommunications, etc.).
- We know that the world economy and world gross product will continue to grow, though at what pace in particular places is not predictable.
- And we know that the supply of scientists and engineers will continue to grow, their ranks swelled by millions from the new megastates.

We can be certain of these near-future changes for at least three reasons. First, they are already clearly established trends that have continued upward at an accelerating rate for between fifty and one hundred years with no signs of leveling. Second, they are all trends that humans view as desirable and that have had substantial tangible benefits for large numbers of people. Third, they are all firmly lodged in the forward function, building on the knowledge know-how platform, avidly employing advanced problem-solving and diffusion strategies.

There are a number of other things which, according to the forward function, are likely to happen sooner or later. Here are six qualified predictions of high importance to humanity in general:

- an end to hunger anywhere in the world,[14]
- energy abundance for all human purposes,
- climate understanding and more precise calculation of the contribution of human activity to climate change,
- control of harmful human influences on climate and environment,
- an end to prolonged pain and suffering for humans, and
- greatly extended human lifetimes.[15]

There are at least two reasons why all these things have a reasonably high probability of happening sooner or later, perhaps within the lifetimes of some who are reading this book soon after its publication. First, they are all highly desired by all peoples, and second, there are substantial research and development programs already under way in all these areas in all the wealthy countries (including the United States, which remains the world leader in virtually all forms of R & D). They are all technically feasible. They have all been realized already on a limited basis in some human environments. The realization of these important achievements is thus not a question of *if* but of *when*. *When* depends partly on the success of R & D programs, which is always somewhat unpredictable, and on the political will of the peoples of wealthier nations, which is also unpredictable.

Then, there are a number of other seemingly desirable developments that will probably happen simply because many if not most humans will continue to want them to happen and will direct their problem-solving energies to those ends:

- population stabilization (either flat at an optimal level or rising at an optimal level),
- animal and plant species stabilization or growth-extinction control to optimize within the context of evolving human values,

- a consensus-based world governance system,[16]
- an end to military solutions to human conflict,
- an end to violence in human relations, and
- indefinitely extended human lifetimes.

The uncertainty is much greater in these areas because (1) the existing knowledge base is much weaker, (2) the R & D is much less extensive and both poorly and uncertainly funded, (3) the types of R & D required include the social sciences that have yet to gain a firm footing on the scientific knowledge platform, and (4) they all require enormous quantities of political will, a notoriously uncertain ingredient.

A more extensive spelling out of the future prospects in each of these areas will be reserved for a projected *Acceleration: Book Two.* In the remainder of this chapter, five topics are singled out for special attention because they illustrate most clearly why the forward function is such an important set of guiding principles. As this discussion advances, the reader may want to keep in mind the conceptual distinction between what will be and what *ought* to be.

1. Twenty-First-Century Biology and Medicine

The areas of scientific and technical advancement that will affect life most dramatically in the twenty-first century are going to be in biology and medicine. In biology we are going to cross the threshold of understanding cellular life. This is a big step, probably much bigger than most people realize both in terms of difficulty and in terms of importance.

Let us start with the difficulty. The origins and even the constituents of life remained a nearly total mystery until Darwin was able to string a lot of observations of living and fossilized creatures into a sensible explanatory framework. There were three basic parts to the theory. The first part was that all living things, plants and animals, simple and complex, large and small (down to unicellular microbes), were related. The second part was that they all had common ancestors many millions of years ago (it turned out to be at least 3.5 billion years, but Darwin didn't realize that). The third part was that species became differentiated and new species arose as mutated variants proved more successful at survival, thereby passing on their altered genetic material to offspring. The theory was controversial from the outset but so explanatory of the fossil and living variants of life that most biologists quickly adopted it.

What remained unknown for nearly one hundred years more was what this hereditary mechanism was, how it mutated, and how the mutations managed to survive into subsequent generations. By the early twentieth century it was becoming obvious that the essence of life resided in the living cell, and that the living cell was composed of a bewildering array of complex molecules in interaction with one another. It was also obvious that each cell, even in the most complex multicellular amalgams like apes and humans, had to contain all that hereditary information. By midcentury it was clear that the genetic material in the nucleus of cells was composed of some combination of very complex protein molecules that formed in long strings of amino acids. Watson and Crick, with the help of some micrograph images and tinker-toy modeling, came up with the structure of the DNA molecule, transforming biological research forever.

Yet just knowing the structure of the molecule and how it replicates itself was only the first step in a very long series of investigations. To fully understand how this molecule could dictate all life-forms, it was necessary to break down the code, element by element. Human biology is what we all care about the most, but to get there, biologists had to start with seemingly simple biological entities. Near the bottom of this ladder is the virus, a precellular parasite that survives and multiplies by hijacking the nuclear machinery of higher-order bacterial, animal, or plant cells. In 1977, English biologist Fred Sanger was first to sequence the genome of a virus.[17] It took him thirteen years to determine the sequence of 5,386 nucleotides (later typically identified as "base pairs" or merely "bases").[18] The first actual living organism to be sequenced (by J. Craig Venter in 1995) was the "simple" unicellular bacterium *Haemophilus influenzae*. One strand of its DNA turned out to contain 1.8 million base pairs! An early favorite multicellular candidate for researchers at the National Institutes of Health, chosen for its "simplicity," was the one-millimeter-long round worm, *Caenorhabitis elegans*, which has just 959 cells when fully grown, but its genome turned out to have 97 million base pairs. The human genome has about 3 billion. These numbers are cited here to underline the enormous complexity of the problem.

Even so, by June 26, 2000, US president Bill Clinton and UK prime minister Tony Blair were able to make the joint announcement of "the completion of the first survey of the entire human genome." The historic achievement was a combined result of many developments in biological science, most occurring in the second half of the twentieth century. First of all, there was now a complete union of biology with biochemistry, with solid links, in turn, to general chemistry and atomic physics. There were now many thousands of biologists working at the molecular level to unlock the secrets of the cell. They were housed in thousands of research centers spread all across the globe, even though the greatest concentrations were in the United States. Not only is this work continuing, but the effort is also expanding with both public and private support. As the work expands, the knowledge expands. As the knowledge expands, the applications expand, applications that are incrementally saving and extending more and more lives.

Nicholas Wade divides the future of this biotechnology into three strands, which he calls "conventional, germ line, and life-extending." The first is already under way and its near-future course is highly predictable, mostly uncontroversial, and essentially unstoppable. This is the development of new drugs that act directly on the body's proteins to interfere with various disease processes. The conventional strand will then be extended to rebuilding damaged cells and organs in the body, probably using stem cells. It is harder to predict when breakthroughs will happen in this more ambitious arena, but it seems nearly certain that it will happen, probably with few ethical or politico-religious roadblocks placed in its way. The result will be the near-elimination or full containment of most if not all the ailments from which we now suffer in the course of our lives, lethal and otherwise. Thus, the average person enjoying the results of such predictable strains of research and development could expect to live out a full life of perhaps one hundred years, unless struck down in midcourse by an accident.

The "germ line" developments that will also eventually derive from bio-genetic research will be far more controversial because they involve the manipulation of heredity to produce physical and perhaps psychological characteristics in offspring deemed desirable by parents. As Wade points out, such a development would mean the end of conception via sexual intercourse as we now know it. Yet if the forward function teaches us anything, it tells us that humans will always progress in directions that make life better for themselves and their offspring. We are all eventually going to want our children to have these super genes if they do no harm and bring happier, healthier, longer lives. Thus, even though many will try to stop this trend in its tracks, such opposing forces will ultimately fail.

Microbiology is just one branch of medicine where remarkable progress was made in the last half of the twentieth century. Human organ transplant technology was invented, then refined through many experimental trials to eventually become routine for several complex organs.[19] It started with corneas (living tissues that are not served directly by blood vessels). Then came skin transplants for burn victims, then kidneys, and later heart, liver, and lung transplants. Along the way, the tremendous complexity of the immune system was revealed, understood in some detail, and brought under some degree of medical control. This knowledge became a vital platform for a rational attack on the HIV retrovirus, which became epidemic in the early 1980s. An intensive international effort was able to produce lifesaving medications within fifteen years.[20] The AIDS story underscores both the difficulties that have to be overcome to master our biology and, just as important, the vast army of biomedical researchers that is now ever more successfully filling out the knowledge platform and generating the medical know-how of tomorrow.

Serious Life Extension

With a nearly complete understanding of cellular biology, including specific knowledge of all the steps involved in generating a fully grown human being from his or her DNA, medical science will be on the threshold of the third of Wade's strands, extending life nearly indefinitely through the manipulation of the key variables that now control aging. This will not happen soon, but perhaps within twenty years at the present rate of progress we will have some strategies at hand for extending average life spans by five years. A few years after that, it will be ten years, then twenty years, until a point is reached where the rate of progress runs ahead of the longevity extension. Whether this will actually happen is certainly open to debate, and it may be even more controversial than gene manipulation in procreation, as Wade seems to think.[21]

Such possibilities are already the subject of serious debate. Life expectancy at birth in the United States in 1900 was 49.2 years. By 1940 it had jumped to 63.6 years. By 1980 it was 73.9 years, and by 2000 it had climbed to 77 years.[22] These numbers continue to trend upward, but at a somewhat decreasing rate. Nevertheless, we also keep on learning. We keep on storing what we learn and expanding the base of scientific knowledge about life, and we keep applying what we know to solve life's problems, especially in the area of biomedicine. It may seem like a slow climb as it is experienced year to year, but when the years and the achievements add up, it becomes obvious in retrospect that revolutionary changes have taken place, transporting humankind into newer realms of existence. These eventualities of medical science are not to be feared but are to be welcomed with joy.

Yet a fundamental question lingers: how far can we really extend life? We are beginning to learn from basic biological research what some have long suspected, that individual lives are self-limited although not in a precise way, so that no individual human seems to be able to live much longer than one hundred years, even with the best of luck under the best circumstances of health, diet, exercise, and safety. Nevertheless, there are very few individuals who voluntarily choose to give up their lives, and medical interventions to extend lives are always heralded. Death and dying continue to be viewed as extremely undesirable ends that medical science is dedicated to warding off as long as possible. They are "problems" to be solved incrementally—like injury and disease—one discovery, one medicine, one new procedure at a time.

Given this unmistakable trend in medicine, it becomes increasingly plausible that scientific progress in biology and its medical applications will soon allow us to leap across the ninety-to-one-hundred-year barrier after all. This momentous change in the human condition might even take place within a single generation from the time of this writing, striking down age-old verities about what it means to be human. This cumulative problem-solving process sometimes appears to be very slow, particularly for those who are suffering from any currently "incurable" condition. For those in such dire circumstances, tomorrow is just not soon enough. Nevertheless, in the larger scope of time, all these advances are happening in just an instant. As we look back over the century of medical progress that has come before now, it should become obvious that some process is relentlessly moving medicine forward. Thus today's so-called impossibilities become tomorrow's remote possibilities, and tomorrow's remote possibilities become the next day's distinct possibilities. The day inevitably arrives when the "incurable" condition falls over into the "sometimes curable" and later into the "always curable."

The vector is clear; we are moving toward extending life even as we expand the notion of "better quality of life." This limitless "better" is what we humans will always want for ourselves, and we will also want this for our loved ones, and for an extended family which, for some, reaches out to include all humanity. This quiet juggernaut *never* stops, and the day will come when the biggest prize of all in medical science, how to preserve and extend life, not just for the tribe or the species but for the individual self, will also be within our grasp. This will happen because the forward function is built into our life script. This outcome of extended life is something we all really want. We want, above all, for our lives to go on, and we want the same for all our loved ones. We dare not look too far ahead. For now it is enough to work toward near-term achievable goals, extending this or that life one day, one week, or one year at a time by intervening to kill this or that microbe, to repair and restore this or that piece of tissue, to replace this or that organ, and so forth. Yet it is clear where this trail will eventually lead, and humanity will not stop moving forward short of that goal.[23]

When philosophers and medical ethicists pronounce on the desirability of a "natural limitation" to the length of human life, they are speaking in abstractions without real meaning. When the people involved are real loved ones, our own family members or dear friends, and the time is as immediate as the ticking clock, the end point of life is always dreaded, never welcomed, unless extreme suffering is involved. Remove the suffering, and there is no desired end point. There is no age at which a person says, willingly, "enough."

2. Bio-Astronomy

The major focus of interest in exploration of the nearby planets of the solar system is the search for evidence of life, current or past, in any form. So far explorations of Earth's moon and Mars have turned up nothing. However, forms of life or protolife have now been discovered deep under Earth's surface and at the bottom of the ocean, surviving at pressures and temperatures not previously known as conducive to life. These forms do not require sunlight, nor do they require the kind of atmosphere, moderate temperature, and water environment that sustains life on the surface. We do not yet know how these forms developed and whether they have an ancestral connection to surface life, but such questions are important because they may give clues to the prevalence of life in the universe as a whole. It seems increasingly likely to the point of near certainty that life exists elsewhere in the universe. Even our own galaxy contains billions of stars. Among these there are many millions of suns very similar to our own. Within the last decade, for the first time we have observed planets revolving around a number of nearby stars. The material building blocks of life (hydrogen, oxygen, carbon, nitrogen, and all their compounds, including those that make up the all-important amino acids and other so-called organic compounds) are available in abundance even throughout our solar system.

These findings lead to one inescapable conclusion. There must be lots of life in the universe besides our own. Furthermore, if life exists elsewhere, in some places it must have coursed its way up the evolutionary ladder in the same way as it has on Earth. There are too many suns very similar in chemical composition and size to our own even within our galaxy (the Milky Way) for it to be otherwise, and the general course of evolution from simple single-cellular life to *Homo sapiens* is also reasonably well charted. It follows that there must be many, probably thousands or millions, of other planets in the galaxy supporting human civilizations at various stages of development.

Figure 12.1 illustrates this very interesting circumstance. It lays out the development of life on different planets on a scale of time. So far as we can tell from the well-established theory of stellar evolution,[24] all the stars in the galaxy have come into being at different times and follow a four-stage history of (1) consolidation, (2) stable burn, (3) supernova destabilization, and (4) blue dwarf burnout. This process takes several billion years. We also know that the sun, like many stars, is somewhere in the middle of its stable burn phase, having so far maintained roughly the same energy output for at least five billion years. Since it appears that stars come and go in this sequence while the galaxy as a whole evolves on a much larger time scale, it is reasonable to suppose that the million or so life-supporting stars are arrayed in a kind of normal distribution as in the figure. A few stars will be the very earliest in the galaxy to give life a foothold while many others will follow as their planetary systems mature.

Earth and our sun might be in this first group. We might even be the very

FIGURE 12.1.
HYPOTHETICAL NORMAL DISTRIBUTION
OF LIFE-GENERATING PLANETS

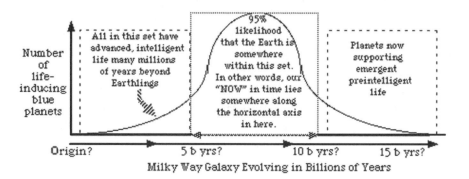

first to have reached the point of intelligent life, but that is extremely doubtful. We know that our sun is not the oldest of its size and type. In fact, it sits somewhat in the periphery of one of the great spiral arms. There are many thousands that are older, older by even as much as one billion years. It is also likely that we are not one of the last, given that our sun is of average age for its type. Most likely we are somewhere in the middle of the life pack of figure 12.1.

This likely positioning of our planet and sun has enormous significance for our future because of the way the forward function works. In all the life-supporting planets that are ahead of us, the forward function has continued to operate, advancing the condition of their humanlike cultures far beyond where we are now. If we reflect on how far we have come in just the last five hundred years, then consider how far we will go in another five thousand years! Even this five thousand years, the distance we have come since pictographic writing was invented, is just a speck of time in terms of the lead that these other civilizations have over us. So what does this mean for us?

For about thirty years, there has existed an active program to seek out messages from intelligent life elsewhere in the galaxy. It is called SETI, the Search for Extraterrestrial Intelligence (recall note 7 of this chapter).[25] It is run by respected astronomers using the most powerful radio and visible spectrum telescopes currently developed, supported by private funds. The idea is that, if there is intelligent life out there, it will be giving off wave signals somewhere within the electromagnetic spectrum. These signals might be intentional, that is, a kind of beacon to tell us who and what they are and perhaps to send us the good news of their very advanced civilization. Alternatively we might get only intercepts of messages they are sending to themselves, some of which will inevitably escape out of their space and enter ours at random intervals, just as all our own wireless messaging also goes out into space.

So far, SETI has found nothing, but its search is for the ultimate needle in the haystack. The signal it wants to detect is buried in the noise of massive streams and bursts of energy emitted continuously by every star, noise that is billions of times louder than any intentional signal is likely to be. Nevertheless, thanks to our rapidly advancing technical powers, especially our increasing ability to sort through data, we yearly double our signal-sorting and detection capabilities. It seems increasingly possible that SETI will detect a signal within the next fifty years, even at the present modest level of funding.

Where the forward function comes into play most strongly is in projecting what is likely to happen after contact. First of all, it should be clear that first contact will be receiving only. With a minimum of one hundred years needed to achieve a roundtrip message sequence, serious dialogue is out of the question for many centuries to come. We will hear from the first extraterrestrials many years before they will ever hear from us. However, the logic of figure 12.1 suggests that there will not be just one of them. Indeed, there are likely to be many thousands of cultures more advanced than our own already out there on different planets in different solar systems. If so, they will all have already gone through the contact phase with the others more advanced than themselves.

If contact, then (eventually) dialogue. Over many centuries' duration, a dialogue phase will have been achieved and a true interplanetary network established. This network has many purposes, but foremost for new arrivals will be the transmission and receipt of the treasure trove of advanced science and technology from the other planet's vastly more experienced experts and sending agents. When the people of Earth finally make this contact, it will be not with just one other intelligent world but with this entire cross-galactic network of civilizations. Once again, consider figure 12.1. Draw a vertical line on the point along the horizontal axis that represents where we are at that moment in time when contact will be realized. Then consider that all the civilizations represented to the left of that line will now be a collective source for our further enlightenment and progress if we choose to use them. Such a colossal input of new knowledge truly staggers the imagination, representing, as it will, the collective wisdom and experience of thousands of planetary civilizations dating back perhaps as much as one billion years or more.

While such projections are intriguing, they remain idle speculations until SETI is successful. They are presented here to show where the forward function is leading us. Eventually, there will almost certainly be contact. In the unlikely event that we are really the first in the galaxy or even in the universe to have achieved intelligent life, as many believe, the course will be the same, but it will be we, ourselves, who establish the first beacons in our lonely quest to find galactic companions, many centuries from now. If, on the other hand, more advanced civilizations are out there, we are, at the moment, totally unprepared to absorb what they have to tell us because very few people on Earth have given serious thought to how we might proceed.

3. Scientific Social Science and Science-based Social Technologies

In a sense, social science began with Herodotus and Thucydides in Greece during the fifth century BCE. They were the first authors to attempt an objective narration of the events of their own times and preceding times, to compare different patterns of social behavior of their own people and others, and to place all these phenomena in a coherent chronology. History through all the intervening years has wobbled between factual reporting and subjective analysis. These writings can be viewed in some ways as scientific and in other ways as a branch of literature. To this day, historians remain ambivalent about their placement in the spectrum of knowledge, but the potential of using the same truth-certifying methods as the natural sciences remains. With Machiavelli and perhaps a few other Renaissance philosophers we can see the beginnings of what came to be called *political science*, and with Adam Smith the beginnings of what came to be called *economics*. The great founders of these fields were really primarily theorists and philosophers rather than empirical scientists in anything like our contemporary meaning of that term.

Nevertheless, all these fields have grown enormously over the last century and today occupy a large sector of every academic curriculum. Social scientists have also struggled intermittently to adapt the successful methods of natural science to their own disciplines but, so far, with mixed success. Wilson characterizes their current status correctly in comparing the social science contribution to human progress to the medical contribution:

> There is also progress in the social sciences, but it is much slower, and not at all animated by the same information flow and optimistic spirit. Cooperation is sluggish at best; even genuine discoveries are often obscured by bitter ideological disputes. For the most part, anthropologists, economists, sociologists, and political scientists fail to understand and encourage one another.[26]

This is actually an understatement. There is no consensus within and among the social sciences even on the most basic issues, such as what constitutes valid measurement, what is the proper unit of study, and what constitutes either a fact or an established theory. Nevertheless, there are some signs that all this is changing and will change much more in the years to come. First of all, the applied mathematics of statistical quantification and inference is now being turned on social and economic phenomena across the board. The promise is that it will contribute to these complicated phenomena with the same happy results that were experienced in agricultural science over the last century. The promise is bolstered by our increasing capacity to study very complex data sets with ever more powerful computers and our increasing ability to quantify any kind of phenomena as "information."

Economics, as the field most obviously consumed by numbers already, may be the first to make breakthroughs. The biggest task at hand in economics is to understand to a near certainty how economic development works so that it can be applied by the World Bank and other international assistance agencies to help the poorest countries of the world and effectively put an end to world hunger.

For political science, the key task ahead is to define the parameters of political order that optimize development, minimize crime and corruption, and provide the most of life, liberty, and happiness to members of any political entity. We have for too long depended merely on tradition to carry us along. This is a prime example of the *backward function*, the tendency to honor and uphold the arrangements established in the distant past over the achieved wisdom of the present. Political science, if it is a science, should be able to compare different arrangements and constitutions to determine which are most effective and beneficial by various standards.

The big subject for sociology, social psychology, and, yes, history, is *conflict resolution*. How do we resolve disputes among people, among interest groups, among religions, and among nations without resort to violence? There are documented instances of conflicts, large and small, present and long past. Such data points run into the millions. Surely, with our powerful new tools of analysis we can come to some firm conclusions about this subject without resorting to competing ideologies (which rarely reach resolution, violent or otherwise). Can this great and worthy task be undertaken by a cooperating international team of our most respected and clever social scientists, or will a latter-day J. Craig Venter come along with his or her own ambitious plan and untie the Gordian knot for us?

Perhaps it is the role of psychology to come up with what may be the most important answers of all from the point of view of the forward function. These pertain to the question of human happiness, which we considered in chapter 2. To a great extent, the pace of future progress depends on the realization by each generation that it has made significant progress compared to the previous generation in its achievement of general well-being. This includes longer life, more liberty, and higher levels of overall happiness. The first, longer life, can be measured objectively; the second, liberty, can be subjected to a number of proxy measurements, such as the amount of leisure time available, the amount of discretionary income available to individuals and groups, and the number and range of choices available to the average person in the average marketplace.

The third, and in some ways most important, criterion, happiness, is almost entirely subjective. Those who have tried to measure happiness have found little improvement in subjective measures from one generation to the next, despite manifest improvements in all kinds of areas that should make life richer and more enjoyable: entertainment; food quantity, quality, and variety; healthier and happier children; safe and varied sexual stimulation; longer hours of sleep; more travel and recreation; more things to read, watch, listen to, and feel over a longer life; and more freedom of choice among all the alternative stimulating experiences offered.[27] With such a cornucopia, why are those most privileged members of the most privileged societies so discontent and so ready to believe that life was better in "the good old days"? Psychology needs to find an answer to that question and then make for us the metaphorical medicine to cure us of this condition. Perhaps we could call it "reality training," or maybe what is needed is just a strong dose of Dickens's ghosts of Christmas past and present.

4. New Directions in Scientific Problem Solving

The next generation is going to experience a great expansion of problem-solving capacity in every profession and every field of application. Strategies will be more science-driven and fact-based. Ever-advancing computer power coupled with increasing high-speed interconnection will lead to the more rapid evolution of all products and services in the direction of improving the quality of life. Most important, more and more of the world's population will be actively involved in productive problem-solving activity, whether it be data collection or analysis, the development of new and better instrumentation to observe and measure phenomena, or the creation of the software for new problem-solving algorithms.

The second half of the twentieth century saw an explosive growth in institutions of higher education and a greatly increasing percentage of students who have gone on to some form of advanced training or education beyond secondary school. This worldwide trend has been most pronounced within the United States, where the number of masters and doctoral degrees in virtually every field of study doubled and doubled again. While a huge national network of community colleges was springing up to provide advanced training, existing institutions upgraded their programs so that more were producing qualified doctorates where formerly they had offered only undergraduate degrees. As a result, there are many more people now qualified to do advanced research and engineering and to teach and train in these fields. This trend will continue and will probably have its greatest impact in the developing megastates of India and China, which have already demonstrated an ability to mimic the intellectual and technical infrastructures of the most developed states.

The ever-expanding Internet as well as greatly facilitated travel and communication of all kinds across the globe will facilitate more rapid problem solving in every domain. Corporations, large and small, if they want to survive in an increasingly competitive world market, will have to further develop their own capacities for research and development. This includes the capacity to efficiently retrieve, adapt, and utilize new science-derived technologies developed elsewhere.

One area that may loom very large within the next generation is network-linked and integrated basic and applied research that involves several institutions and many hundreds of individuals simultaneously closing in on important problems. The Manhattan Project to develop the first atomic bomb was an early harbinger of such cooperation, amazingly undertaken under a cloak of almost perfect secrecy. The project to land a man on the moon and bring him safely back to Earth, accomplished between 1962 and 1969, was an even more mammoth example of thousands of people in many different organizations—some governmental, some military, some private, and some academic—all cooperating to serve a common goal. Both these projects followed a hierarchical model with massive governmental financing. In the twenty-first century, some objectives of equal magnitude may be achieved by networks that are far more open and distributed.

The American Association for Artificial Intelligence has now been in business for twenty-five years, annually churning out new papers and algorithms at a quickening pace. Intelligent systems are nonhuman reasoning machines that are getting better and working faster all the time, leaving their human progenitors far behind. They are, nevertheless, just tools for our human purposes. They are problem solvers that should take us into new realms of understanding within the next two or three decades, making the science-building and invention-creating devices discussed in previous chapters a reality. There is no reason why such advanced software cannot mimic scientific problem solving with great accuracy and speed, performing intellectual feats of which human brains are incapable.

Finally, we should not forget that while the problem-solving strategies are becoming ever more sophisticated and streamlined, the data-gathering tools are also giving us depth and dimension of vision unimagined in earlier times. The electron microscope, invented by Ruska in 1937 and rapidly improved in accuracy, power, and usability in subsequent years, has opened up a whole new microworld to our eyes, demonstrating the validity of the atomic theory of matter beyond any doubt. J. D. Bernal states it well:

> The electron microscope is even a greater advance on the ordinary microscope than the microscope was on the unaided eye. It enables us to see and reproduce on photographs the whole range of structures, from those clearly visible in an ordinary microscope down to those of practically atomic dimensions. It is the most direct way of bringing the structure of small objects into the range of our ordinary senses. As such it has great philosophic importance because it gives a visible reality to unities such as molecules, which were first thought of as abstract hypotheses. Structures of such dimensions are the most interesting for the understanding of the properties of life.[28]

As if to put an exclamation point to Bernal's observation, it has recently become obvious that an unsung heroine of the DNA story was Rosalind Franklin, whose X-ray diffraction photographs of the DNA molecule clearly showed the helical shape that Watson and Crick then correctly modeled. It seems doubtful that they could have deduced this structure at that time without having seen these actual pictures.[29] That was 1951. Imaging has come a long way further since that time, and within the next few years should further expose the secrets of life, in all its dynamic chemical complexity.

5. Exploding Diffusion

The aspect of the forward function that has been most on display in the last decade is diffusion. We have entered a new era of diffusion in which virtually all the peoples of the world are finally connected to all the central sources of knowledge, scientific and otherwise. This exposure is coming over an increasingly diverse set of media. There are more and more channels available, and each channel is capable of carrying more and more message content.

For people in hitherto isolated areas or cultural islands, this increased information comes as a shock. They are ill prepared to comprehend and properly interpret what they receive so that it optimally serves their own interests. However, this is a problem that we all face, however weak or strong our educational background. To the rescue will come many kinds of new technologies and intelligent systems to help us sort through the information maze. Sorting empirical fact from opinion and fanciful imagining will be just one of the tasks that will have a priority, particularly as this applies to the Internet. Just as the Consumers Union and its magazine, *Consumer Reports*, tries to help North American consumers sort through the flood of goods and services available in the marketplace so that they can make rational choices, there is a similar need for guidance in "surfing" the Internet as a whole.

What the Internet, even in its present configuration, offers that is different from prior channels of diffusion is a high degree of user control over what comes in. Essentially, users on the Internet need attend only to what they are interested in. The new questions that now arise will be about what the users want and whether they know enough about themselves, their wants, and their true needs to make choices sensibly and rationally. Governments, vendors, and all manner of technical experts are already rushing in to clarify and/or take advantage of this huge new opportunity for, or perhaps threat to, human well-being. At the same time, the system is being shaped and reshaped continuously with new web browsers, security enhancers, and file-access-control devices and procedures which both complicate and simplify user access to the things they separately want to retrieve from this vast knowledge "system." The overall trends are hard to predict in such a dynamic environment, but a few things seem certain:

- There will be more message integration.
- There will be more and more messages.
- These messages will emanate from more and more sources.
- More and more people will be connected.
- They will be connected in more ways, in more spheres of activity.
- They will be "online" more hours of the day and week.

- There will be greater and greater message and receiver segmentation in terms of:
  * special interests,
  * political preferences, and
  * buying habits.
- Receivers/users will have more and more control over what they receive and the choice of channels on which they receive.

This massive expansion of diffusion will change humanity in dramatic ways. It will greatly increase their shared knowledge base. It will make them more alike and more aware of the differences they have. It will make them value those differences to a greater degree. It will greatly increase the realm of human experience and human enjoyment. It will, in the long run, equalize the quality of life across peoples, at least in the Jeffersonian basics of life, liberty, and the pursuit (if not the fulfillment) of happiness.

6. The Advancement of Ethical Humanity

The most important and positive outcome of the diffusion explosion will be the worldwide expansion of the concept of "us." Return once again to figure 10.1. On the horizontal axis of this figure are arrayed the various categories of what might be included as "us." This identification process starts on the left of the figure with the self and those closest to the self, the most favored and most beloved, those for whom the greatest well-being is hoped and for whom (if required) one would lay down one's own life. For early *Homo sapiens*, the circle was probably very small, first fixed on the family alone and then extended to the tribe. Gradually, through processes mostly unknown to us but probably including all manner of mayhem, suffering, conquest, enslavement, subjugation, and alliance, larger and larger tribes were formed, tribes which eventually evolved into the nation-states of our time.

The evidence of progress in the direction of widening the "us" circle is mixed, to say the least, but there are a number of hopeful signs and reasons to expect more rapid progress in the first half of the twenty-first century. There has not been a world war or a war in which major powers clashed directly for sixty years, and no such war is presently on the horizon. The Europeans are now enmeshed in a commercial, social, and military alliance, which gets stronger year by year. The Americans, the Russians, the Chinese, and the

Japanese have relatively stable and peaceful relations cemented by enormous trade exchanges. The several wars that have occurred during this period, though costly and bloody, have been localized in some of the least developed regions, even though one or another of the great powers has often been involved. The very worst examples of bloodshed have been internal to some of the least developed and isolated countries (e.g., Rwanda and the Sudan in central Africa, and Cambodia in Southeast Asia).

Increasing trade and commercial interdependency should play a major role in bringing the world together and increasing the sphere of "us." Of equal importance are the telecommunications media, especially television, which potentially brings the sights and sounds of every culture into the homes of every other culture, thus increasing mutual understanding and appreciation of similarities and differences. Increased and reduced-cost air travel, wireless telephone technology, and the Internet all add to the mix of integrative forces that drive humanity together. As these technology-driven bonds strengthen, political and legal integration will gradually follow, but how soon and in what precise form is still unclear. The major breakthroughs will come, as noted previously, with arrangements to resolve conflicts without the expenditure of physical force, essentially forbidding violence and raising the sanctions against any person or group who would resort to violence.

Applying the Forward Function to the Advancement of Human Affairs

The humanity of our time can take great comfort from just becoming aware of what has been summarized in these pages. Readers who have come this far will realize that there is a relentless forward momentum to our collective culture. This is the essential message of the forward function. Through learning, storing what we learn, building a knowledge platform from this learning, improving our problem-solving processes and capacities, and sharing what we learn with each other in an ever-widening circle, we are making life better for everybody: lives are longer, freer, happier. But is this awareness enough? Perhaps it is for the very young who need only wait for the future to unfold, but for those who are now entering adulthood and especially for those who are getting older, time is of the essence. Every new heart medication or cancer therapy means that more of us will survive a little longer. Every advance toward the control of violence in human affairs means that more people will live and live without fear for themselves and their families. If all these things will come in time, then time itself is a crucial variable. If we can somehow accelerate the process, we compress time, and in so doing we save lives by the millions. Along the way, we also allow those who are lucky enough to be alive a greater and greater measure of happiness, however that might be defined.

Accelerating the timetable of progress is not the only issue that should concern us, however. Natural forward functioning can be very erratic. Political movements and political leaders who do not understand science and who oppose science-based technical progress can take command in one place or another at one time or another. They may identify themselves with the Left, center, or Right of the political spectrum. As discussed in chapter 11, there are many things to worry about when it comes to advancing technologies and their applications, but the net effect of all worrying as applied to public policy is to slow down or even temporarily stop forward progress. The antidote for stalling and regression is knowledge coupled with reason, the same knowledge that is bound into the knowledge platform. It also helps to know what the forward function is all about and how it has already transformed the human condition in multiple beneficial ways.

If the thesis of this book, that there is a forward function driving human history, is accurate, then three broad goals stand out as implications for policymakers:

1. Strengthen and broaden science education;
2. Support all actions to make the knowledge platform stronger, more integrated, and more accessible; and
3. Invest heavily in critical areas of research and development.

1. Science Education

To secure the steady and safe advance of human society and at the same time to accelerate technical progress still further, the forward function needs to be managed wisely. This can only be done by political leaders who are scientifically literate. That means political leaders should have a good understanding of where science has brought us and where it can lead us in the future. In a democracy such leadership can only arise from an equally well-informed electorate. Therefore, a much larger percentage of the voting public should have a basic understanding of science. A sound basic education for all citizens should impart the basic facts that constitute the contemporary scientific understanding of the natural world (for example, the periodic table of elements; the nature of light; the relationship between matter and energy; the size, configuration, and age of the known universe; how atoms form molecules; the basic geology of Earth; the molecular structure and hereditary chemistry of living things; and our best current fact-supported theories concerning how life has evolved on this planet).[30]

Science education can come in many forms along many channels. It can and should be directed toward children and adults of all ages. It can and should make clear how science is done and why it has special validity, in addition to the wonderful facts and technologies it has generated. It can and should be presented in simplified and entertaining form, making special use of the television medium, exploiting animation and visualization to the maximum and accompanying it by the narration of charismatic master teachers like the late Carl Sagan and Jacques Cousteau. It should appear in diverse formats and in all the major languages of the world. Special efforts should be made to spread good science education into developing countries and all localities where the current level of understanding is low. All this is vitally important because the more the collective culture understands science, the more individuals will value it, and the more they will be able to apply it rationally to the improvement of themselves and their societies.

All the new and expanding technologies of diffusion identified earlier in this chapter can be great carriers of science education. Of particular interest are the possibilities of interactive learning that arise with the widespread diffusion of powerful personal computers and computer access to the Internet in broadband. Currently, the most sophisticated software in this arena is being developed for games of violence targeted at adolescent boys. However, with appropriately large investments from combined public-private sector initiatives, the same power of entertainment and involvement can be directed toward loftier educational goals, including a better understanding of science.

2. A Stronger Knowledge Platform

The existing knowledge platform is wonderful. It is huge and in many areas remarkably strong. Nevertheless it needs a lot more work to make it as strong as it should be, even given the limits of our existing knowledge in a collective sense. Indeed, collecting is a big part of the problem. Work to make the knowledge platform stronger, more integrated, and more accessible should have a high priority. The Internet is a great vehicle for both storing and sharing information, but it is definitely not an equivalent or a proxy for the knowledge platform as described in these pages. Elements of the knowledge platform can be found all over the Internet, mostly in unsorted pieces. The real knowledge platform is difficult to imagine in its complete form, but the closest approximation consists of a hierarchy of the most recent science textbooks from elementary general science to the most advanced graduate texts in every scientific field and subfield. All scientists and technologists working on the leading edge of any advancing field should know what has already been done and what others are currently doing. Such a systematized and integrated source would make research and development far more efficient, less duplicative, and less expensive.

Among other requirements of an online platform for science would be a jurylike certification that entries meet scientific standards as we now have in the refereed scientific journal system. We need a system that evaluates or rates any given piece of "information" in terms of its validity, reliability, and replicability. This new platform proxy would require continuous automatic renewal and upgrading. It would also have to be international and multilingual. In effect it would be a new international institution. We are already moving very fast in this direction. Internet and new electronic storage capacities make the overall concept possible, but the institutional structure would have to be worked out, responding to questions such as: Who has access? What are the standards for item entry? What should subscribers pay? and so forth.

3. Invest R & D in Critical Areas

It should be no secret by this time that scientific research and development is the goose that has been laying the golden eggs for the world economy over the last few decades. This is the forward function at work, moving us all ahead at blinding speeds in some areas and at lower speeds in others. It is possible to make the whole process work better, and the stronger knowledge platform discussed above is a good place to start. It is also possible to target certain areas for special investment either because they have great urgency or because a great opportunity for major advancement has been revealed. There are some persuasive precedents for such action from the last century and it might do well to recall them briefly.

Wars are gigantic government-spending programs involving enormous investments in R & D for particular purposes. They thus illustrate what can be done with maximum effort when the confronting problem is seen as a state-threatening emergency (the nation-state equivalent of a life-threatening emergency). Everyone thinks of the development of the atomic bomb as the major, somewhat grisly, scientific achievement of World War II, but, in fact, it was only one of many that have transformed our world. That war between 1939 and 1945, terrible and deadly as it was for so many millions, stimulated a great leap forward in many areas of technology. The Germans made substantial advances in jet-propelled aircraft and rocketry even as their murderous empire was collapsing. The British and Americans made even more important advances in microwave radar and associated technologies that led directly to the transistor and the full gamut of semiconductor technology; core memories in digital computers, masers, and lasers; and a host of other advances that have transformed our world.[31] If there had been no war and no massive governmental investment, it is probable that many of these earth-shaking advances would have been delayed by decades.

There was a realization by many of the wartime scientific leaders, such as Vannevar Bush, that governmental support for research and development should continue into peace time at equivalent or greater levels, both for peaceful and defense purposes. Thus were born the National Science Foundation, the Office of Naval Research, and the Air Force Office of Scientific Research, all in the first decade after the war. The Cold War, which soon followed, gave an additional spur to all types of scientific research under both military and civilian leadership. Notable in this category were the R & D projects supported by the National Aeronautics and Space Administration (NASA), which rapidly developed satellite technologies and numerous spin-off applications from the space race (with the Soviets, of course). Another great contributor to technical advances in the 1960s, 1970s, and 1980s was the Defense Department's Advanced Research Projects Agency,[32] from which came modern computer chips; the window interface found on all modern computers, large and small; and the Internet.

The idea that government could provide support to accelerate discoveries was not limited to hardware technology. The National Institutes of Health, founded in 1944 as part of the war effort, was rapidly expanded in the postwar years. In 1947, its total budget was about $8 million. By 1957, it had climbed to $178 million; by 1967, $1.1 billion; by 1977, $2.2 billion; by 1987, $4.8 billion; and by 1997, $9.1 billion. In 2004, after four years of the first combined "conservative" leadership in the White House and both houses of Congress, it had jumped to about $20 billion![33] These sums are far beyond what could be done with private initiatives or indeed what was being supported by the rest of the world.

Not all progress comes from government activity. It is far more complex than that. Those who have traced the influence of governmental direction and support find that the private sector, business as well as academia, also plays a major role—sometimes generating the original ideas from which governments then proceed, and sometimes taking the spin-off from government-supported R & D and finding new profit-making applications in the private sector.[34] It appears that mixed economies do vastly better than planned economies in this regard.

Although the deliberate intent was lacking, both World War II and the Cold War resulted in a massive technological push that led in turn to our current US and world prosperity and to a transformation of human life undreamed of by our ancestors. We know what we can do. Can we now arouse the political will to follow through on these great advances in the twenty-first century? Projecting out into the near-term future of about two hundred years, and starting from the end of the first decade of the twenty-first century, the possibilities are enormous. There are two scenarios: one is merely a projection of our present post–Cold War trends. The other is a projection based on a new drive to apply forward function thinking and planning to human problems on an even larger scale, something equivalent to the moon-landing project of the 1960s.

SPECIFIC TARGETS

There are many directions in which to proceed. Which deserve the highest priority, whether initiated by governments or other sources?

(1) Biomedical R & D

A good argument can be made that medical advances are the top priority because they are lifesaving. Therefore medical research and development, which already gets substantial support, deserves to be granted much more support and funding, perhaps doubling every five years or so. There are at least four critical areas where breakthroughs seem possible within one or two decades if there is a strong push. These are:

- understanding our genetic structure;
- understanding the full chemistry of the living cell;
- understanding the chemical codes and sequencing for the growth of complex organisms (currently being investigated under the terms *stem-cell research* and *cloning research*); and
- spelling out the biological applications of nanotechnology, the use of molecular robotic devices to repair and reconstruct tissue at the sub-cellular level.[35]

All these areas are somewhat controversial. There is a fear by many that such advanced technologies tamper with our basic biology in ways that will harm humanity irreparably.[36] It is indeed the case that this new biotech world will transform us in many ways, but the potential for enormous good overwhelms any conceivable harm, and the way ahead is guarded by a biomedical establishment that puts a very high value on making wise and balanced choices, abiding faithfully by the dictum in the Hippocratic oath, *primum non nocere*, "first, do no harm."

The worldwide biomedical establishment has the duty to move forward because lives are at stake. People all over the world are suffering and dying just because their doctors don't yet know what to do for them or because the medical system can't deliver what they already know and can do. What has been done to resolve polio and AIDS is a model for what can be done if there is a sense of extreme emergency stimulating maximum effort backed up by widespread political support and funding. By midcentury, significant life extension will emerge as a new priority, emerging from the success of conventional medical R & D.

(2) Bio-astronomy

The space programs of the United States and other countries have already yielded a great deal of new biomedical information. We now know all the requirements to support humans in space. We can create habitats in space that are able to sustain small groups of humans for months at a time. From ever more sophisticated robotic space probes we have also learned enough about the planets and moons of the solar system to know that among them Earth alone is able to sustain advanced forms of life. Being able to operate in space and to use space for more and more human purposes has already had some positive benefits for life on Earth, but the real prize is finding *intelligent* life elsewhere in the galaxy. Contact with just one other world would constitute a great leap into the future, for reasons stated previously.

The US government, through NASA, made a contribution to SETI in its early stages, advancing the sophistication and power of the search by a factor of thousands. It is now many years since the US government played a direct role in SETI's funding, but the work still goes on, and the search is now many hundreds of times more potent in number of wavelengths searched and parts of the sky sampled. It remains a huge task to sort out any intelligent signal from the billions of energy pulses that strike Earth daily from these far-away places. A new government-sized effort in this century might be enough to get us there. Already, Microsoft partner Paul Allen has made a very large private donation for a new, more powerful radio-telescope array. If governments get back into the act in the next few years, we can proceed at a much faster rate and on a much grander scale.

(3) Making the Social Sciences Scientific and Useful

There is a real possibility that the social sciences will become much more scientific in the next century and thereby come into a position to provide great benefits to humankind as a whole. All this may come about thanks largely to the ways in which the forward function is now playing itself out. An expanding knowledge platform and new tools for problem solving that may allow the social sciences to become much more like the natural sciences are just now becoming available. We are getting better and better at collecting the raw facts of human experience. We can now make sound photographic records of virtually all human activities as they happen, and we can record all transactions down to the smallest details. These mountains of data can also be digitally merged, sorted, summarized, and correlated in ways undreamed of by earlier researchers. Potentially every sequence of actions can be analyzed in terms of its antecedents, its course, and its outcomes. When similar sequences are grouped for comparison and their outcomes rated in terms of positive and negative consequences, we will gradually realize which are pathological and which are beneficial. Based on this more certain knowledge, we will also be in a position to then fashion certain remedies or countermeasures to offset social pathologies, just as medical science is now able to intervene to counter the pathologies of the human body.

A revitalized and solidly empirical social science could be able to advance the human experience in at least the following three vital areas:

[i] Science-based Social Technologies to Curb Violence

The number one problem in the world today, as it has been throughout history, is how to minimize violence as a strategy for resolving human conflicts. This includes violent crime, wars of aggression, murder, genocide, ethnic cleansing, enslavement, torture, dispossession, vandalism, and all acts of cruelty—whether one-on-one, tribe-on-tribe, state-on-state, religion-on-religion, or ideology-on-ideology. Every such happening can be analyzed as a sequence of events engaged in by people exhibiting certain characteristics. Why do some events lead to violence while others do not? What are the critical differences? What specific actions can then be taken in such situations to turn down the temperature of hostility and disarm the aggressor? These are things we urgently need to know, and there is a good chance that the social scientists of the twenty-first century will begin to have some answers.[37]

[ii] Facilitating Reality-based Optimism:

Over and over again in this book it has been proposed that there are two ways to conceive our world. One is to look backward and emulate our ancestors, and the other is to look forward, building on the wisdom of the past but discovering a much more profound wisdom and new levels of human happiness in a future based on science and its offspring technologies. Collective humanity knows more today than it has ever known in the past and can do many more things to make lives better by using that knowledge. However, if the vast majority of humans cling to the idea that the human past was somehow better, thereby denigrating the great achievements of the last few centuries, their mind-set will remain a self-fulfilling prophesy, which is a huge drag on progress. It is therefore a matter of great importance to persuade more and more people that things are better. It is important to make them realize that their lives have become much longer, much safer, much more comfortable, and, on balance, far more enjoyable in total than the lives of their ancestors. Perhaps this kind of monumental shift in attitude is something social scientists can work on. What is needed first is to understand the roots of these backward-looking beliefs, and second, to propose ways in which a shift toward forward-looking beliefs can be made, a new mind-set that is both more healthful in a psychological sense and more reality-based.

[iii] Moving toward a Global Civil Society

There has been a strong trend toward internationalism throughout the last century. It started with a world war; followed by a League of Nations and various treaties of world scope; followed by a worldwide depression; then a second world war; followed by the United Nations, a World Trade Organization, a World Health Organization, an International Monetary Fund to stabilize currencies, a World Bank for Reconstruction and Development, a world court, and numerous worldwide NGOs that have gotten larger and stronger through the years. Thus there is a de facto world government that exists on many levels and through a diverse network of institutions. The governance structure for this world "system" is chaotic and unreliable. It institutionalizes arrangements that are often grossly unequal, unfair, undemocratic, and unjust. Clearly there is a need to gradually right the wrongs of this world order, and we should be able to enlist a newly empowered and more solidly scientific social science in this cause.

Producing such great outcomes will not be easy because of the current disarray of social science as a science. Many who think of themselves as social scientists are dismissive of quantification. Some may fear that a new empiricism will undermine their long-held favorite theories. Some others fear that massive data collections threaten civil liberties. Political leaders will be understandably skeptical, especially where popular opinion and conventional wisdom run counter to what the scientific data seem to show. Nevertheless, the stakes are high and the potential long-term benefits are enormous. What may help is the dawning realization of what science has already done for us in so many other areas affecting our lives.

CONCLUSION

Humans are advancing and changing in fundamental ways as a result of their own recently developed science and technology. These changes are taking the human race in directions that Darwinian survival evolution could never have gone, and all this is happening at a speed many hundreds of times faster than would be possible with naturally occurring genetic mutation. The ability of humans to broadcast messages to millions of others in an instant, to move about continually on the ground at speeds approaching one hundred miles per hour and through the air at hundreds of miles per hour, to store knowledge in print or electronic form in ways that can also be retrieved in an instant, to make millions of computations in seconds, and to have the results of such computations available to anyone wherever they are, these are all changes that now belong to the whole of humanity. Having tasted of these strange new fruits, there is no turning back. These new creations will not go away. We will not change back; we are becoming something entirely different from what we were even three or four hundred years ago, and our changed nature is not the consequence of any changes in our genetic material.

NOTES

PART 1 INTRODUCTION

1. Aeschylus, *Prometheus Bound*, 7, 441–71, probably written about 460 BCE. This translation is by Eric A. Havelock, *The Crucifixion of Intellectual Man* (Boston: Beacon, 1951).

2. The abbreviations *CE* and *BCE* refer throughout to *Common Era* and *Before the Common Era* which, by convention in Western writing, starts at a time either when Jesus was born or roughly when the Roman Republic became the Roman Empire with Augustus proclaimed first emperor—in either case, approximately 2010 years ago.

3. This myth had particular resonance for Aeschylus because he had been plagued throughout his career as a playwright with accusations that he had revealed the secret "mysteries" associated with the town of Eleusis, where he was born.

4. Sir Charles Lyell, *Principles of Geology* (London: John Murray, 1838; London: Penguin, 1997).

5. There is a likely connection between this insight and the Industrial Revolution that began in England. First of all, the coal on which so much of the new industrial vigor depended contained many fossils of plant life. Second, the new railways that now traced across the countryside required numerous cuts through hillsides, which revealed the layering of the sedimentary rock as well as its fossil content.

6. Lyell's importance for geology and for grasping the significance of extended time in the evolution of Earth and life on Earth is well reflected in the quote from Charles Darwin: "The very first place which I examined...showed me clearly the wonderful superiority of Lyell's manner of treating geology, compared with that of any other author, whose work I had with me or ever afterwards read." *Encyclopædia Britannica*, CD-ROM, 2002, http://www.britannica.com/EBchecked/topic/352672 Sir -Charles-Lyell-Baronet (accessed July 9, 2007).

7. By current estimates Earth appears to be about 4.6 billion years old, and the oldest rocks discovered are about 3.9 billion years old. Life probably originated not too long thereafter. "The discovery of stromatolites (layered or conical sedimentary structures formed by sediment-binding marine algae) in 3.5-billion-year-old limestone in several parts of the world indicates that blue-green algae existed by that time." US Geological Survey, *Age of the Earth*, http://pubs.usgs.gov/gip/geotime/age.html (accessed July 9, 2007).

8. The discovery of the structure of the DNA molecule by Watson and Crick in 1953 established definitively the chemical basis of heredity and laid the groundwork

for connecting all currently living organisms, including all plants and animals, to a common ancestry.

CHAPTER 1: THE IDEA OF PROGRESS

1. This estimate of one hundred thirty thousand years is given by Michael Cook, *A Brief History of the Human Race* (New York: W. W. Norton, 2003), but the essential DNA that defines *Homo sapiens* as a distinct species is probably much older, perhaps one million years.

2. Hugh G. Evelyn-White, *Hesiod, The Homeric Hymns and Homerica* (Cambridge, MA: Harvard University Press, 1964), vol. 57 of the Loeb Classical Library, p. xiv.

3. St. Augustine of Hippo, *The City of God* (Latin: De Civitate Dei), trans. Henry Bettenson (Harmondsworth, UK: Penguin Books, 1972).

4. "Muhammad and the Religion of Islam," *Encyclopædia Britannica*, http://www.uv.es/EBRIT/macro/macro_5003_29_22.htm (accessed November 11, 2009).

5. In our own times, this type of thinking has returned in an intellectual guise, thanks to the teachings of Leo Strauss, an ardent Platonist at the University of Chicago. His student Alan Bloom published a popular polemic in 1987, *The Closing of the American Mind* (New York: Touchstone, 1987), in which he attacked liberal thought and the kind of science-based progressivism advocated here as relativist, deviating from what he imagined was the "canon" of the great books and wise men of our historic past, particularly Plato and Aristotle. Bloom and others of the Strauss school gave an intellectual caste to contemporary conservative thought that had been lacking in previous years or at least since the earlier writings of William F. Buckley Jr. (e.g., *God and Man at Yale* [Chicago: Regnery Gateway, 1951]).

6. For example, biologist Edward O. Wilson in his otherwise excellent synthesis of modern science, *Consilience* (New York: Knopf, 1998).

7. The most influential and widely read of these doomsday books was the so-called Club of Rome report, by Donella H. Meadows, Dennis L. Meadows, Jørgen Randers, and William W. Behrens, *Limits of Growth* (London: Potomac Associates Books, 1972), that reportedly sold nine million copies worldwide, having been translated into twenty-nine different languages. Among the many howlers in this book, based on presumably scientific projections, gold was supposed to be exhausted by 1981, silver and mercury by 1985, and zinc by 1990. Needless to say, none of this happened nor are there any empirically based trend lines heading in such a direction. A notable recent doomsday book reasoning along the same lines was US presidential candidate Albert Gore Jr.'s *Earth in the Balance: Ecology and the Human Spirit* (Boston: Houghton Mifflin, 1992).

8. Gregg Easterbrook, *The Progress Paradox* (New York: Random House, 2003).

9. Sociologist Pitirim Sorokin devoted his career to studying and conducting empirical research on this important topic. P. A. Sorokin, *Altruistic Love: A Study of American "Good Neighbors" and Christian Saints* (Boston: Beacon, 1950).

10. The moral necessity of a benign world order was first argued by the great eighteenth-century philosopher Immanuel Kant in his treatise "Science of Right," *Great Books of the Western World* (Chicago: Encyclopædia Britannica, 1952), 42:438–39.

CHAPTER 2: MEASURING PROGRESS IN HUMAN TERMS

1. Free English translation by Stephen Mitchell, *Gilgamesh: A New English Version* (New York: Free Press, 2004).

2. For example, Lee M. Silver, *Remaking Eden* (New York: Avon Books, 1997) welcomes a future of genetic manipulation; in contrast, Francis Fukuyama, *Our Posthuman Future: Consequences of the Biotechnology Revolution* (New York: Farrar, Straus and Giroux, 2002) is full of dread.

3. No one has captured this social aspect of childhood development better than Erik H. Erikson, *Childhood and Society* (New York: W. W. Norton, 1950), particularly in the first four of his eight stages, pp. 219–27.

4. Jared Diamond, *Guns, Germs, and Steel* (New York: W. W. Norton, 1997), p. 36. Estimates range from 1 million to 7 million, depending on the criterion (e.g., ability to stand erect, brain size, tool-making ability, etc.). A specific gene related to language ability dates from approximately five hundred thousand years ago, according to a comment on *Science Friday*, National Public Radio, March 19, 2004.

5. J. Bronowski, *The Ascent of Man* (Boston: Little, Brown, 1973), pp. 45–46.

6. Noted in the Public Broadcasting Service series, also issued in book form as Geoffrey C. Ward, Richard Burns, and Kenneth Burns, *The Civil War* (New York: Alfred A. Knopf, 1990).

7. Freud also postulated in some of his writings that aggression is the other basic self-preservative instinct that likewise undergoes transformations and sublimations in multiple ways, some relatively harmless, others not so harmless. My preference is to view libido as basic and aggression as a response to frustrated libido, in other words, a cycle of problem solving that fails at critical junctures, triggering a renewed cycle with added energy that spills out on the surface as anger.

8. In starkest theoretical form: "Act only according to that maxim by which you can at the same time will that it should become a universal law." A more earth-bound version is "So act as to treat humanity, whether in your own person or in another, always as an end, and never as only a means." Quoted in *Encyclopædia Britannica*, CD-ROM, 2002.

9. See Julian Simon, *The Ultimate Resource 2* (Princeton, NJ: Princeton University Press, 1996) for an extended analysis of values in this arena. See also Lee M. Silver, *Remaking Eden* (New York: Avon Books, 1997) for a positive view of cloning experimentation; Francis Fukuyama, *Our Posthuman Future* (New York: Farrar, Strauss, and Giroux, 2002) for an opposing and sharply negative view; and Nicholas Wade, *Lifescript* (New York: Simon and Schuster, 2001) for a good summary of the contemporary science emerging from DNA discoveries. The debate is also carried on by Gregory Stock in *Redesigning Humans: Our Inevitable Genetic Future* (Boston: Houghton Mifflin, 2002) and by Leon Kass in "Preventing a Brave New World: Why We Should Ban Cloning Now," *New Republic*, May 21, 2001, 30–39.

10. The "species" named are, of course, along with many others, human creations that were selectively bred over hundreds of generations to acquire the attributes for which they are now prized.

11. For example, Martin Seligman, author of *Authentic Happiness* (New York: Free Press, 2002), directs the "Positive Psychology Center" at the University of Pennsylvania; Ed Diener studies "subjective well-being" at the University of Illinois; and Daniel Gilbert, author of *Stumbling on Happiness* (New York: Alfred A. Knopf, 2006), is a professor of psychology at Harvard.

12. For example, Simon Chapple (lead author), report by the Organisation for Economic Cooperation and Development (OECD). Thirty developed countries were rated, and the key metric was "subjective well-being," defined as life satisfaction. Here are some sample questions offered in the report: Did you enjoy something you did yesterday? Were you proud of something you did yesterday? Did you learn something yesterday? Were you treated with respect yesterday? In each country, a representative sample of up to one thousand people, aged fifteen or older, were surveyed. Denmark, Finland, and the Netherlands rated as the top three. Reported by Lauren Sherman at Forbes.com, May 15, 2009.

CHAPTER 3: THE CASE FOR PROGRESS

1. United Nations, Population Division, *The World at Six Billion*, http://www.un.org/esa/population/publications/popnews/News73.pdf.

2. Most notably Paul R. Ehrlich, *The Population Bomb* (New York: Ballantine, 1968).

3. Actually, the fact that Malthus was such a popular intellectual figure in the early to mid-nineteenth century had many consequences, some positive for the future of science. In Charles Darwin's *The Autobiography of Charles Darwin and Selected Letters*, edited by his son Francis Darwin (New York: D. Appleton, 1892; Dover Publications, 1958), on page 42 we find this interesting quote from the great man himself: "In October 1838, that is fifteen months after I had begun my systematic enquiry, I hap-

pened to read for amusement Malthus on *Population*, and being well prepared to appreciate the struggle for existence which everywhere goes on from long-continued observation of the habits of animals and plants, it at once struck me that under these circumstances favourable variations would tend to be preserved and unfavourable ones be destroyed. The result of this would be the formation of new species. Here, then, I had at last got a theory by which to work; but I was so anxious to avoid prejudice, that I determined not for some time to write even the briefest sketch of it." By 1842, he composed his first draft of the theory in writing, elaborated in 1844, but so timid was he that the full work was not published until November 1859, and then only at the urging of Lyell and because he knew that A. R. Wallace was hot on the trail of the same concept. Wallace later noted in a letter to a colleague (in 1887): "The most interesting coincidence in the matter, I think, is, that I, *as well as Darwin*, was led to the theory itself through Malthus—in my case it was his elaborate account of the action of 'preventive checks' in keeping down the population of savage races to a totally fixed but scanty number. This had strongly impressed me, and it suddenly flashed upon me that all animals are necessarily thus kept down—'the struggle for existence'—while *variations*, on which I was always thinking, must necessarily often be *beneficial*, and would then cause those varieties to increase while the injurious variations diminished" (pp. 200–201, original italics).

4. Ehrlich, *Population Bomb*.

5. Ehrlich appeared on national television in the United States several times and over a number of years after *The Population Bomb* was published in 1968, and he was a frequent guest on the very popular late-evening talk show hosted by Johnny Carson. Thus his views were disseminated to many millions.

6. For example, Paul R. Ehrlich and Anne H. Ehrlich, *Betrayal of Science and Reason: How Anti-Environmental Rhetoric Threatens Our Future* (Washington, DC: Island Press, 1996).

7. Julian Simon, *The Ultimate Resource 2* (Princeton, NJ: Princeton University Press, 1996).

8. Ibid., pp. 87–91, fig 5.1; this shows per capita worldwide food production increasing steadily from 1948 to 1990, based on data compiled for UNFAO's *Production Yearbook* and the US Department of Agriculture's *Statistical Abstract of the United States*. Figure 5.2 shows wheat price divided by wages steadily decreasing from 1800 to 1980. Many other sources are cited.

9. Ample evidence for this worldwide trend is provided in a recent monograph by Nicholas Eberstadt, "Four Surprises in Global Demography," *Watch on the West: Newsletter of the Foreign Policy Research Institute* 5, no. 5 (July 2004), which also appeared in *Orbis* (Fall 2004): "To maintain long-term population stability, a society's women must bear an average of about 2.1 children per lifetime. According to projections of the US Census Bureau, Europe's total fertility rate (or births per woman per lifetime) is about 1.4. Indeed, nearly all the world's developed regions, Australia and New Zealand, North

America, Japan, and the highly industrialized East Asian outposts of Singapore, Hong Kong, Taiwan, and South Korea, are reporting subreplacement fertility."

10. Gerard Piel, *The Age of Science: What Scientists Learned in the Twentieth Century* (New York: Basic Books, 2001), pp. 433–36. Piel notes that near zero population growth has now been achieved in all industrialized countries, combining low death rates and low birth rates, very low infant mortality, and life expectancy exceeding seventy years. In contrast, life expectancy in the least developed countries, almost all in sub-Saharan Africa, is less than thirty years, with very high infant and child mortality, a condition that characterized most of humanity until the industrial era.

11. Edward O. Wilson, *Consilience: The Unity of Knowledge* (New York: Alfred A. Knopf, 1998).

12. By some measures, the Netherlands may be the most successful country on Earth. In a recent issue of the *Economist* (February 11–17, 2006), it was suggested that indices of Gross Domestic Product per capita be adjusted for the hours worked and amount of leisure time afforded on average in a given country. Adjusted in that way, the Netherlands had the highest standard of living of the developed countries listed, including the United States, far exceeding such prosperous states as Canada, Sweden, Australia, and Japan.

13. From United Nations, *World at Six Billion*, table 4, p. 11.

14. Among possible reasons were sharply reduced infant mortality caused by the worldwide introduction of improved public-health procedures and the reduction of many devastating infant-killing diseases worldwide. These changes came along simultaneously with the withdrawal of Europeans and the end of their colonial systems of governance. Left to their own devices, many African countries reverted to the tribal systems they had lived under for thousands of years before colonialism swept over them.

15. This term was coined by social forecaster John Naisbitt, *Megatrends: Ten New Directions Transforming Our Lives* (New York: Warner Books, 1982). Naisbitt's ten trends of 1982 were on the money in 2009, mostly in line with what is said here. He adds that the future belongs to those who can handle ambiguity. Of the vast majority he says: "We have done the human thing: We are clinging to the known past in fear of the unknown future."

16. Derived from Angus Madison, *The World Economy: A Millennial Perspective* (Paris: OECD, 2001), table B-18, "World GDP, Twenty Countries and Regional Totals, 0–1998 AD."

17. United Nations, *Human Development Report* (New York: United Nations, 2002), as cited in Gregg Easterbrook, *The Progress Paradox* (New York: Random House, 2003), p. 69.

18. Jeffrey D. Sachs, *The End of Poverty* (New York: Penguin, 2005), p. 3.

19. Piel, in *Age of Science*, notes that a man-year, meaning the net output of mechanical energy from a typical manual laborer in a year, has been calculated to be

the equivalent of one hundred fifty kilowatt hours. The gross power output of central electrical generating stations in the United States comes to about thirty thousand kilowatt hours per capita. By division, this comes out to two hundred person hours. It should be conceded, of course, that "per capita" does not mean it is equally distributed. Even so, the average worker even at the lower end of the scale is likely to get some multiple of what the common laborer once earned in a year.

20. One example among many from the 1970s is Reid Bryson's "Environmental Roulette" in John P. Holdren and Paul R. Ehrlich, eds., *Global Ecology: Readings Toward a Rational Strategy for Man* (New York: Harcourt Brace Jovanovich, 1971). Simon, *Ultimate Resource 2*, page 267, quotes Bryson as follows: "I believe that increasing global air pollution, through its effect on the reflectivity of the earth, is currently dominant and is responsible for the temperature decline of the past decade or two." Simon also cites Lowell Ponte's 1976 book, *The Cooling* (Upper Saddle River, NJ: Prentice-Hall, 1976), which provides this scary scenario: "the cooling will cause world famine, world chaos, and probably world war, and this could all come by the year 2000."

21. Historically, gasoline prices, a significant index of the supply/demand ratio, have been on a gradual but consistent downward slope since 1920. Thus, in constant-dollar terms, the price of gasoline in 1994 was lower than it was in 1920, 1930, 1940, 1950, 1960, and 1970, from the Bureau of Labor Statistics, Energy Information Administration, "The Real Cost of Gas," *Washington Post*, July 6, 2005, D3.

22. Donella H. Meadows, Dennis L. Meadows, Jørgen Randers, and William W. Behrens III, *The Limits of Growth* (London: Potomac Associates Books, 1972).

23. Simon, *Ultimate Resource 2*, pp. 35–36. Evidently Simon was inspired by reading Ehrlich's 1970 off-the-wall prediction: "If I were a gambler, I would take even money that England will not exist in the year 2000." This quote was taken from Bernard Dixon, *What Is Science For?* (New York: Harper, 1973). According to Simon, neither Ehrlich nor any other environmental scientist had any interest in taking him up again on the same terms after they lost in 1990, still on offer when Simon died.

24. The invention of a reliable sea-going clock was a necessary aid to navigation across oceans, allowing the accurate measure of longitude. The story of the invention of the ship's clock through a prize competition is well told by Dava Sobel, *Longitude* (New York: Walker, 1995).

25. As this is being written, the issue of outsourcing has invaded the US political scene. This is a world-trade phenomenon in which less-skilled manufacturing jobs move to countries where labor costs are lowest, assuming the output can be returned to the consumer in the more prosperous high-wage country with a net gain to the manufacturer. As transportation and telecommunication costs come down and advanced computers make just-in-time inventory planning easy for retailers, outsourcing becomes more and more attractive. The net effect is to increase worldwide distribution of goods at a lower cost while equalizing wages worldwide in those types

of jobs. The new twist is that some types of routine white-collar jobs are now being exported to countries, like India, that have a large, highly educated, and English-speaking middle class surviving on a very low salary base by US standards. Whether this trend is specifically beneficial to the most advanced countries remains somewhat controversial, an issue explored by John Cassidy in the *New Yorker* (August 2, 2004).

26. There are several methodological problems related to conveying accurate figures for literacy, including two main issues. The first is that increments get smaller as literacy in a given population reaches saturation at 100 percent. This applies to all developed countries today. In the developing world, absolute numbers of increase have been impressive over recent decades, but actual rates are falling because of population increases. Thus while many more people in the third world are literate, more are also illiterate. This is not true for China, which has seen a jump in literacy by nearly 100 million. See UNESCO Institute for Statistics, *International Literacy Statistics: A Review of Concepts, Methodology and Current Data* (updated April 24, 2009).

27. International Telecommunication Union, *Measuring the Information Society: The ICT Development Index* (Geneva, Switzerland: International Telecommunication Union, 2009), p. 108.

28. Note the somewhat curious and difficult-to-translate line from our introductory quote from Aeshylus:

> For them in triumph intellectual!
> Did I devise the count numerical.

When the Greeks invented mathematics, they really thought they had something, and, of course, they were right! Indeed, the Pythagoreans, followers of the great mathematical theorist, became a kind of mystic cult of high prestige.

29. Easterbrook, *Progress Paradox*, p. 49.

30. Cassidy, *New Yorker* (see n. 25), cites World Bank figures indicating that between 1981 and 2001, the number of people in East Asia living on less than one dollar a day in constant-dollar terms was reduced from 800 million to under 300 million, an enormous advance at the lowest end of the economic scale. Cassidy is making the case for increased world trade as a boon to less-developed countries, but the improvements he notes are more significantly attributable to advances in technology, particularly computer-enhanced telecommunication that allows work to be performed anywhere in the world to supply consumers anywhere else in the world.

31. Jean-Jacques Rousseau, *The Social Contract and Discourses*, trans. G. D. H. Cole (London: J. M. Dent and Sons, 1913).

32. See, for example, J. E. Lovelock and L. Margulis, "Atmospheric Homeostasis by and for the Biosphere—The Gaia Hypothesis," *Tellus* 26, no. 1 (1974): 2–10; or J. E. Lovelock, "Hands up for the Gaia Hypothesis," *Nature* 344, no. 6262 (1990): 100–102.

33. See, for example, James E. Lovelock, *The Revenge of Gaia: Earth's Climate Crisis and the Fate of Humanity* (New York: Basic Books, 2007).

34. A major instance of this trend was the donation by the heirs of John D. Rockefeller of large tracts of beautiful land in the eastern and western United States for the establishment of national parks.

35. A number of recent books have made the same general point with similar listings of those things that have gotten better. Easterbrook's *Progress Paradox* has already been cited. A much longer and fully persuasive list is contained in Stephen Moore and Julian L. Simon, *It's Getting Better All the Time; 100 Greatest Trends of the Last 100 Years* (Washington, DC: Cato Institute, 2000).

PART 2 INTRODUCTION

1. For an analysis of the latest findings and theories concerning the earliest life forms, see Robert M. Hazen, *Genesis* (Washington, DC: Joseph Henry, 2005).

2. Estimate derived from Jared Diamond, *Guns, Germs, and Steel* (New York: W. W. Norton, 1997), p. 36. Very crude stone tools became common about this time, and they improved very slowly.

CHAPTER 4: ANIMAL LEARNING

1. The word *replicate* is scientific jargon for "being repeated under the same conditions with the same type of subject or materials." No finding can be considered as reliably valid in science if it cannot be replicated to produce the same outcomes as were originally reported.

2. The website emTech (for "emerging technologies," http://www.emtech.net/learning_theories.htm) contains an excellent summary listing of prominent learning theories, including those discussed here.

3. A very recent find in Africa, a nearly complete skeleton dubbed *Ardipithecus ramidus*, dated to 4.4 millions years, suggests that the common ancestor to the other great apes was very much earlier than previously thought. "Ardi" had a brain about the size of a chimpanzee but clearly walked on two legs like later homonids. John N. Wilford, *New York Times*, October 1, 2009.

4. These numbers are taken from James Trefil, *Human Nature: A Blueprint for Managing the Earth—By People, for People* (New York: Times Books, Henry Holt, 2004).

5. There are long strings that appear to be totally redundant, signifying very little, if anything, of a directive nature for the organism.

6. Richard Dawkins, *The Ancestors' Tale* (New York: Houghton Mifflin, 2004)

explains in some detail how this tracing of mistakes in DNA works and how much it can tell us about the distant human past. Humans have a common ancestor with chimpanzees at 6 million years. He keeps going back, via common ancestors at critical life divides, to bacteria at three billion years.

7. Sigmund Freud, *Totem and Taboo: Resemblances between the Mental Lives of Savages and Neurotics* (1913; London: Penguin Edition, 1985) and *Moses and Monotheism* (New York: Vintage, Alfred A. Knopf, 1939).

8. Humans, of course, are not the only animals to make and use tools for the purposes of completing certain tasks; in fact, simple tool use has been observed in other primates, birds, and even some sea-dwelling creatures (e.g., dolphins and otters). The level or sophistication of tool use is perhaps the distinguishing attribute of humans, and is no doubt connected to brain development. Neanderthals developed and persisted in using primitive stone tools to sustain their hunting culture, but their craft advanced very slowly over tens of thousands of years. In contrast, early modern humans developed more and more refined tools (axes, spears, arrows, and so forth), making distinct traceable progress across many generations. Donald Johanson, "Origins of Modern Humans: Multiregional or Out of Africa?" *ActionBioscience* (May 2001), http://www.actionbioscience.org/evolution/johanson.html.

CHAPTER 5: EXTERNALIZING LEARNING

1. Excerpted from *2001: A Space Odyssey*, by Stanley Kubrick and Arthur C. Clarke (Borehamwood, Hertfordshire, UK: Hawk Films, MGM Studios, 1965–68), http://www.palantir.net/2001/script.html (accessed December 5, 2009).

2. The earliest finds of stone tools, evidently hand-shaped by presumably humanlike animals, date from 2 million years but show very modest improvements for at least 1 million years thereafter. Davidson and McGrew have done a thorough review of the literature on the development of stone tools, perhaps the first phase in the development of human culture as distinct from the groupings and behavioral accomplishments of other primate species. The common ancestor probably had a primitive tool-making capacity as we observe today in the ability of chimpanzees to use rocks to crack coconuts and stripped sapling sticks to extract ants from a nest. Since the large apes, like *Homo sapiens*, have large brains and are prodigious learners, just how and why humans broke away has been a long-running puzzle among anthropologists and primatologists. One factor may have been the physical human ability to aim powerful blows of rock-on-rock with great accuracy. Iain Davidson and William C. McGrew, "Stone Tools and the Uniqueness of Human Culture," *Journal of the Royal Anthropological Institute* 11, no. 4 (2005).

3. Donald Ryan, "Ancient Languages and Scripts: The History of Writing," Cul-

tural Heritage News Agency, http://www.plu.edu/~ryandp/texts.html (accessed December 5, 2009).

4. Studies on this topic are nicely summarized by Matt Ridley as follows: "There's no question that human beings, unless they're unlucky and have a genetic mutation, inherit a capacity for learning language. That capacity is simply not inherited in anything like the same degree by a chimpanzee or a dolphin or any other creature. But you don't inherit the language; you inherit the capacity for learning the language from the environment." Matt Ridley, interview by John Brockman, ed., and Russell Weinberger, "The Genome Changes Everything: A Talk with Matt Ridley," *Edge* (2003), http://www.edge.org/3rd_culture/ridley03/ridley_print.html.

5. David Whitehouse, "Cave Paintings May Be 'Oldest Yet,'" *BBC News Online*, November 1, 2000, http://news.bbc.co.uk/2/hi/science/nature/1000653.stm (accessed December 5, 2009).

6. Jonathan Yardley, review of *Lincoln: The Biography of a Writer*, by Fred Kaplan, *Washington Post Book World*, November 2, 2008.

7. Ryan, "Ancient Languages and Scripts."

8. This point is clearly argued and elaborated by E. A. Havelock in his last work, *The Muse Learns to Write* (New Haven, CT: Yale University Press, 1986).

CHAPTER 6: SOCIAL CONNECTIONS

1. Eric H. Erikson, "Growth and Crises of the 'Healthy Personality,'" in Clyde Kluckhohn and Henry A. Murray, *Personality in Nature, Society, and Culture*, 185–225 (New York: Alfred A. Knopf, 1954).

2. No one has done more to explain the crucial importance of these early connections than the psychoanalyst Eric H. Erikson. He adds to the quotation that leads this chapter: "It is as true to say that babies control and bring up their families as it is to say the converse. A family can bring up a baby only by being brought up by him. His growth consists of a series of challenges to them to serve his newly developing potentialities for social interaction." Kluckhohn and Murray, *Personality in Nature, Society, and Culture*, p. 189.

CHAPTER 7: KNOWLEDGE PLATFORMS

1. It is not known whether language development advanced before or after elaborate tool making. It may be that they had a reciprocal effect, each innovation in tool making leading to an advance in language, and vice versa. The fact that innovation in stone tools proceeded slowly for nearly two million years and then advanced rapidly

in sophistication within the most recent one hundred thousand years suggests the possibility that the invention of language came later and then had a greatly accelerating effect on other types of innovation, including tool making. The issue is explored in Iain Davidson and William C. McGrew, "Stone Tools and the Uniqueness of Human Culture," *Journal of the Royal Anthropological Institute* 11, no. 4 (2005).

2. In the 1930s, J. M. Hutchins advocated a general curriculum for undergraduate education built around what he viewed as the "canon" of his time. He assembled a group of distinguished scholars to come up with a list. They couldn't agree, but Hutchins went ahead anyway, creating the list. In accordance with Hutchins's belief, the university for a time awarded a BA degree to anyone who could demonstrate mastery of this list, regardless of age or number of years of schooling. In the 1950s, he also organized the publication of the *Great Books* series as a kind of canon for our times. He felt that an educated person could be defined as someone who had read the bulk of this collection with understanding.

3. Samuel P. Huntington, *The Clash of Civilizations and the Remaking of World Order* (New York: Simon and Schuster, 1996), p. 310.

CHAPTER 8: SCIENTIFIC PROBLEM SOLVING

1. John Gribben, *The Scientists: A History of Science Told through the Lives of Its Greatest Inventors* (New York: Random House, 2002), pp. 68–72.

2. This interpretation of life as problem solving was most extensively spelled out by the twentieth-century philosopher Karl Popper in a number of books, the last of which was a collection of essays under the title *All Life Is Problem Solving* (London: Routledge, 1999). The author was not familiar with Popper's work when most of this book was being written, but his ideas run along similar lines, including the view that human progress is continuous and open-ended.

3. Morris R. Cohen and Ernest Nagel, *An Introduction to Logic and Scientific Method* (New York: Harcourt, Brace, 1936), p. 291.

4. It has always been an irritant to mathematicians that Alfred Nobel did not include their field as deserving of this high award for intellectual achievement.

5. Cohen and Nagel's *Introduction to Logic and Scientific Method* conclusively demonstrates that "logical" and "mathematical" are essentially the same thing.

6. Calculus was perhaps invented independently by each, but both built on prior work by Descartes and others. J. D. Bernal, *Science in History*, vol. 3, *The Natural Sciences in Our Time* (Cambridge, MA: MIT Press, 1971), p. 484.

7. Ibid.

8. David Hume, "Inquiry concerning Human Understanding," sec. 7, pt. 2 cited in Philip Frank, *Philosophy of Science* (Englewood Cliffs, NJ: Prentice-Hall, 1957), p. 280.

9. Frank, *Philosophy of Science*, p. 281.

10. Thomas S. Kuhn, *The Structure of Scientific Revolutions*, 2nd ed. (Chicago: University of Chicago Press, 1970).

11. This program has been ongoing from 1977 to the present. See the *NIH Office of Medical Applications of Research*, http://prevention.nih.gov/omar/default.htm. The home page reads as follows: "The Office of Medical Applications of Research (OMAR) is the focal point for evidence-based medicine at the National Institutes of Health (NIH). Located in the Office of the Director, OMAR works closely with NIH institutes, centers, and offices to assess, translate, and disseminate research findings to the biomedical community and to the public. OMAR is home of the NIH Consensus Development Program and [the] NIH Medicine in the Media Program, as well as the Medicine: Mind the Gap seminar series." Evaluations of the program have been sporadic. See, for example, Institute of Medicine, *Consensus Development at the NIH: Improving the Program* (Washington, DC: National Academy Press, 1990).

12. American Association for the Advancement of Science, *Science for All Americans*, ed. F. James Rutherford (1989; rev. repr., New York: Oxford University Press, 1994). This volume was issued as the centerpiece of Project 2061, "a long-term initiative of the AAAS to reform K-12 education in natural and social science, mathematics, and technology."

13. Edward O. Wilson, *Consilience* (New York: Knopf, 1998).

14. Ibid., p. 10.

15. Robert Buderi, *The Invention That Changed the World* (New York: Simon and Schuster, 1996); this history of the evolution of antisubmarine microwave radar describes the early evolution of R & D as a distinct set of coordinated actions. One of Franklin D. Roosevelt's principal science advisors, Vannevar Bush, is sometimes credited with inventing the term *R & D* to describe all the different activities that went into the creation of new weaponry and other devices during World War II. At the suggestion of Bush, FDR created a new federal agency, the Office of Scientific Research and Development, in June 1941 (p. 115). There followed an explosion of such activity, all of it conducted at government expense and usually under the auspices of major universities. Harvard, MIT, Princeton, the University of Michigan, the University of California, and California Technical Institute were among the many distinguished institutions that participated extensively. Many private firms were also involved, notably the Bell Telephone Laboratories, and many new upstart companies. RAND Corporation, founded as a defense-contracting research and development firm, took its name directly from the phrase *R & D*.

16. National Science Foundation, "Methodology of Statistics on Research and Development," NSF-59-36 (Washington, DC: Government Printing Office, 1959), as cited by Fritz Machlup, *The Production and Distribution of Knowledge in the United States* (Princeton, NJ: Princeton University Press, 1962), p. 149.

17. AAAS, *Science for All Americans*.

18. It was recently made clear that Watson and Crick's discovery of the structure of the DNA molecule depended in significant degree on electron microscopic evidence of X-ray diffraction patterns, suggesting what looked like a seeming double helical structure in the atomic arrangement of this huge protein molecule. This crucial photographic evidence resulted from the work of Rosalind Franklin, who some believe deserved equal recognition for her contribution to the discovery. Likewise, it was only after the placement of the one-hundred-inch Wilson Observatory telescope that astronomers were able to observe that certain "nebular" starlike objects actually were not a part of the Milky Way galactic system but gigantic and distant circulating spirals of billions of stars at very remote distances, thus enormously expanding the known size of the universe.

19. The necessity of having a unified cosmology was also accepted by the great Isaac Newton who firmly believed that his laws were merely a revelation of how God put the universe together. During the last years of his life he blissfully occupied his time writing religious tracts in support of the Church of England.

20. It was more or less possible for a highly educated person at the end of the nineteenth century to be nearly encyclopedic in understanding the knowledge platform up to that time. William James (1842–1910) may have been one such example; he was a Harvard-trained medical doctor fully conversant with the biology, physiology, and basic science of his time, and a founding father of psychology. He is also remembered as the first great American philosopher. "William James," *Stanford Encyclopedia of Philosophy* (first published September 7, 2000; substantively revised September 28, 2009), http://plato.stanford.edu/entries/james/#1.

21. Story detailed by J. Bronowski, *The Ascent of Man* (Boston: Little, Brown, 1973), pp. 200–206.

22. Thomas S. Kuhn, *The Structure of Scientific Revolutions*, 2nd ed. (Chicago: University of Chicago Press, 1970).

23. The "Nobel Prize" in Economics was established by the Bank of Sweden to stand beside the other prestigious awards for science, literature, and peace established by the wealthy inventor and munitions manufacturer Alfred Nobel. A review of the history of these awards over the last few decades gives ample testimony to the rise and fall of various paradigms in the field of economics, still struggling to make its case as a "science." Award recipients have espoused many theories that oppose each other diametrically, as the supposed wise men of one generation become dunces to the next. No Nobel awards are given in the many important scientific specialties that have come to the fore in the last century, including computer science, information science, psychology, sociology, anthropology, geology, not to mention the grandfather of them all: mathematics. Apparently Nobel didn't think much of mathematicians, and one has to wonder if he would have thought much better of economists.

24. A prime example of how this process works is offered by the recent award of a Nobel Prize in Chemistry to three scientists who had made detailed mappings of how ribosomes, key cell elements, are able to manufacture proteins, building blocks in the intricately complex and continuous process of cell renewal. *Washington Post*, October 8, 2009, A8.

CHAPTER 9: MODERN GLOBAL DIFFUSION

1. Everett M. Rogers was the first and most important synthesizer of modern diffusion research. Much of this chapter rests on the knowledge platform of his immense scholarship. This particular quote is from *Diffusion of Innovations*, 4th ed. (New York: Free Press, 1995), p. 259.

2. Note again the program to infuse US schools with a new curriculum designed to achieve a minimal level of scientific literacy. American Association for the Advancement of Science, *Science for All Americans*, ed. F. James Rutherford (1989; rev. repr., New York: Oxford University Press, 1994).

3. See R. G. Havelock and David S. Bushnell, *Technology Transfer at the Defense Advanced Research Projects Agency* (Arlington, VA: George Mason University Technology Transfer Study Center, 1985) for an account of the crucial and central role of DARPA in the creation of the Internet (originally called "ARPANET") as well as the rapid development of microprocessor technology and the modern computer-user interface.

4. This is a very condensed summary of the social interaction effects that have been shown to drive the diffusion process. The best integrated summary of this research is to be found in Rogers, *Diffusion of Innovations*.

5. One of the most consistent findings of diffusion research, discussed in the previous note, is the critical importance of what have been called "opinion leaders," persons who hold central positions in influence networks and to whom others look when considering the adoption of new practices and products.

CHAPTER 10: THE EMERGENCE OF ETHICAL HUMANITY

1. The Universal Declaration of Human Rights was adopted by the General Assembly of the United Nations on December 10, 1948. The full text has a preamble and thirty articles that give more explicit operational meaning to the first three quoted here. All member countries were urged "to cause it to be disseminated, dis-

played, read and expounded principally in schools and other educational institutions, without distinction based on the political status of countries or territories."

2. Karl R. Popper, *The Open Society and Its Enemies* (Princeton, NJ: Princeton University Press, 1971), p. 102.

3. See Sigmund Freud's *Thoughts for the Times on War and Death* (London: Hogarth, 1915) and *Civilization and Its Discontents* (London: Hogarth, 1929), both of which were reprinted in Robert Maynard Hutchins, ed., *Great Books of the Western World*, 54 vols. (Chicago: Encyclopædia Britannica, 1952), vol. 54.

4. Charles Van Doren, *A History of Knowledge: Past, Present, and Future* (New York: Ballantine Books, 1991), pp. 67–69.

5. There are two issues regarding the Allies' conduct of the war that are troubling from a moral progress perspective. We now know that the British Bomber Command and, to a lesser extent, the United States Army Air Force targeted German civilians and killed and maimed them in large numbers for questionable effect on the war outcome. For the British there might have been a revenge motive, but the action overall would seem to be indefensible on moral grounds. The same could be said of American targeting of Japanese cities, including, of course, the two atomic bomb drops. As the war recedes from memory, these terrible actions linger, casting a cloud over the Allied victory and the claim of the victors to moral superiority. The other morally indefensible Allied action was the call for unconditional surrender, a policy that fails the test of reason and may have unnecessarily prolonged the war in both theaters.

6. Colum Lynch, *Washington Post*, October 18, 2005.

7. Richard R. Nelson, ed., *Government and Technical Progress: A Cross-industry Analysis* (New York: Pergamon, 1982). Ten economists took on seven different areas, including semiconductors, computers, commercial aircraft, automobiles, agriculture, pharmaceuticals, and construction. They revealed strong government influence in all sectors over the roughly one hundred years previous, through either support of basic and applied research in universities and elsewhere, military procurement, direct subsidy of private R & D, standard setting, and regulation. In all but a few cases, the government role pushed the technology forward rather than holding it back.

8. Immanuel Kant, *Introduction to the Science of Right*, trans. W. Hastie (Edinburgh: T. and T. Clark, 1785), reprinted in Robert Maynard Hutchins, ed., *Great Books of the Western World*, 54 vols. (Chicago: Encyclopædia Britannica, 1952), 42:401.

9. The marginality of the antislavery movement in the intellectual landscape of the 1840s and 1850s is well documented by Louis Menand in *The Metaphysical Club: A Story of Ideas in America* (New York: Farrar, Straus, and Giroux, 2001). Most educated people in America in those times, including those in the Northern states and apparently Abraham Lincoln, essentially believed that Negroes from Africa were an inferior race.

10. Edward O. Wilson, *Consilience* (New York: Knopf, 1998), p. 182.

CHAPTER 11: FEARS FOR THE FUTURE

1. That renewed optimism, which included a strong faith in progress in science and technology, was very much on display at the enormously successful New York World's Fair of 1939, which trumpeted a future of electric kitchens, superhighways, and robots—not too far off the mark for fifty years down the road, but a gruesome six years was to come first.

2. A summary of the use of the first atomic bomb is offered by Atom Central:

> On July 26, Truman issued the Potsdam Declaration, which called for Japan's unconditional surrender and listed peace terms. He had already been informed of the successful detonation of the first atomic bomb at Alamogordo, New Mexico, ten days earlier. The Japanese were warned of the consequences of continued resistance by the terms of the Potsdam Declaration, which was signed by President Truman and Prime Minister Attlee of the United Kingdom, with the concurrence of Chiang Kai-shek, president of the National Government of China.
>
> When Japan rejected the ultimatum, Truman authorized use of the bomb. Secretary of War Henry L. Stimson felt the choice of using the atomic bomb against Japan would be the "least abhorrent choice." This would be weighed against sacrificing the lives of thousands of soldiers. Military advisers had told Truman that a potential loss of about 500,000 American soldiers was at stake. . . .
>
> On September 2, the Japanese government, which had seemed ready to fight to the death, surrendered unconditionally. Winston Churchill estimated that the lives of a million Americans and two hundred and fifty thousand British soldiers and sailors had been saved by this sudden shortening of the war.

AtomCentral, "The Bombing of Hiroshima and Nagasaki," AtomCentral.com, 2006, http://www.atomcentral.com/hironaga.html (accessed November 10, 2010).

Controversy persists, however, and many argue that use of the bombs was a war crime.

3. It is estimated that Stalin, Mao, and Pol Pot in different periods of the twentieth century allowed tens of millions of people to starve to death in the course of carrying out misguided collectivization and social simplification schemes in the name of some sort of theory. Hitler starved and worked to death millions of Jews before resorting to his "final solution" with gas chambers. Poles, considered another inferior breed, fared little better. Both Russian and German prisoners of war on the Eastern

front were simply herded into barbed wire enclosures and allowed to starve to death. The Red Army probably lost over a million soldiers in this manner and the German army lost a proportionate number.

4. Brian M. Fagan, *The Little Ice Age: How Climate Made History, 1300–1850* (New York: Basic Books, 2002).

5. "Two countries at different ends of the earth, both of which are generally considered to be economic success stories, are Finland and Singapore. The average annual temperature in Helsinki is less than 5°C/41°F. That in Singapore is in excess of 27°C/81°F. If a man can successfully cope with that, it is not immediately apparent why he should not be able to adapt to a change of 3°C/5.4°F, when he is given a hundred years in which to do so." So observes Nigel Lawson in commenting on the UN Intergovermental Panel on Climate Change (IPCC) report of 2007 that had come forth with that projection. Nigel Lawson, *An Appeal to Reason: A Cool Look at Global Warming* (Woodstock, NY: Overlook, 2008), pp. 27–28.

6. Bjørn Lomborg, in *The Skeptical Environmentalist* (Cambridge, UK: Cambridge University Press, 2001), does not deny that there may be a human effect on global warming but questions its severity as a crisis and the countermeasures so far proposed to combat it. Counteradvocates include Lawrence Solomon, *The Deniers: The World-renowned Scientists Who Stood up against Global Warming Hysteria, Political Persecution, and Fraud—and Those Who Are Too Fearful to Do So* (Minneapolis, MN: Richard Vigilante Books, 2008), which reviews the work of several distinguished scientists who doubt the significance of any human effect; and Lawson, *Appeal to Reason.*

7. James Trefil, *Human Nature: A Blueprint for Managing the Earth—By People, for People* (New York: Times Books, 2004), pp. 144–46.

8. India's fertility rate declined by 42 percent from the mid-1960s to the mid-1990s. Contraceptive prevalence rose from 13 percent in 1970 to 41 percent in 1993. US Department of Commerce, Economics, and Statistics Administration and Arjun Adlakha, "Population Trends: India," *Bureau of the Census International Brief* 97, no. 1 (April 1997).

9. Julian L. Simon, *The Ultimate Resource 2* (Princeton, NJ: Princeton University Press, 1996).

10. George Orwell, *1984* (New York: Harcourt Brace Jovanovich, 1949).

11. Samuel P. Huntington, *The Clash of Civilizations: Remaking of World Order* (New York: Simon and Schuster, 1996).

12. The National Defense Education Act of 1958 was the first significant attempt by the federal government to provide funds for improving education nationwide. Improving science education was an important goal of the legislation. As the wording of the law implies, it was prompted by the launch of *Sputnik*-I in 1957 and the fear that the Soviets had somehow gained a technological advantage in the Cold War. In the 1960s the National Science Foundation established a separate directorate for science

education under congressional mandate. The Defense Advanced Research Projects Agency (DARPA) was responsible for much of the development of microcomputer technology and its all-important user interface components, such as the mouse and window file display as well as the Internet in its entirety. For documentation on the historical importance of DARPA for advancing the creation and widespread use of technology, see R. G. Havelock and David S. Bushnell, *Technology Transfer at the Defense Advanced Research Projects Agency* (Arlington, VA: George Mason University Technology Transfer Study Center, 1985). In these and many other ways, the Cold War gave a tremendous impetus to technological advancement, accelerating the application of the forward function in every sector. Further documentation on DARPA's central role in the creation of the Internet and the democratization of computer technology can be found in Janet Abate, *Inventing the Internet* (Cambridge, MA: MIT Press, 1999).

13. See Cornelia Dean, "Evolution Takes a Back Seat in US Classes," *New York Times, Science Times*, February 1, 2005.

14. Gregg Easterbrook, *The Progress Paradox* (New York: Random House, 2003), p. 34.

15. Sigmund Freud, *Civilization and Its Discontents* (London: Hogarth, 1929), reprinted in Robert Maynard Hutchins, ed., *Great Books of the Western World*, 54 vols. (Chicago: Encyclopædia Britannica, 1952), 54:778–79.

16. Easterbrook, *Progress Paradox*, pp. 167–68, citing research by Princeton University psychologists Daniel Kahneman and Amos Tversky.

17. Directed by D. W. Griffiths and released in 1915, this was the first full-length epic movie and is admired by cinematic historians for its innovative advances in filmmaking. It was also the first film to be seen by millions of people in theaters, many of whom must have taken it simply as the telling of a true story from the historical past. President Woodrow Wilson, a noted progressive of his time but also a native Virginian, viewed the film in the White House. There is controversy over his reaction. One source, the promoter of the film, claimed that Wilson enjoyed the film and approved of its content as basically accurate. However, Wilson aide Joseph Tumulty denied that he gave any such reaction. It has been acknowledged in more recent times as an outrageous piece of racist propaganda. See, for example, Melvyn Stokes, *D. W. Griffith's* The Birth of a Nation: *A History of the Most Controversial Motion Picture of All Time* (New York: Oxford, 2007).

CHAPTER 12: WHAT WILL THE FUTURE BRING?

1. John Kenneth Galbraith, edited extract from *The Economics of Innocent Fraud: Truth for Our Time* (Boston: Houghton Mifflin, 2004) appearing in the *Guardian*, July 15, 2005.

2. Hock had a special perch from which to view change in our times, being founder and first CEO of the trillion-dollar financial exchange system known as VISA.

3. Francis Fukuyama, *The End of History and the Last Man* (New York: Free Press, 1992).

4. Julian Simon argues in his two major works, *The Ultimate Resource* and *The Ultimate Resource 2*, that progress actually depends on an ever-increasing population. The larger population not only generates a vastly greater stockpile of wealth, expanded markets for goods, and so on, but also adds to the collective knowledge base from which prosperity for everybody ultimately flows. Such views are anathema to those who view population control as a major issue facing humanity, for example, Paul Ehrlich, the Stanford University entomologist and author of *The Population Bomb*.

5. So argued by Steven Johnson in his *Everything Bad Is Good for You* (New York: Riverhead, 2005). Each new generation of computer games requires more and more advanced skills in memory, perception, and problem solving for mastery. Herein may reside the important clues to progress in learning that educators have been looking for since the time of John Dewey.

6. The entry for *Moore's Law* in the Webopedia, an online encyclopedia dedicated to computer technology, reads as follows: "The observation made in 1965 by Gordon Moore, cofounder of Intel, that the number of transistors per square inch on integrated circuits had doubled every year since the integrated circuit was invented. Moore predicted that this trend would continue for the foreseeable future. In subsequent years, the pace slowed down a bit, but data density has doubled approximately every eighteen months, and this is the current definition of Moore's Law, which Moore himself has blessed. Most experts, including Moore, expect Moore's Law to hold for at least another two decades." "Moore's Law," Webopedia, http://www.webopedia.com/TERM/M/Moores_Law.html (accessed November 11, 2010).

7. Michelangelo d'Agostino, "BOINC! Do Try This at Home," *Berkeley Science Review*, May 31, 2005. *BOINC* stands for Berkeley Open Infrastructure for Network Computing. This program "has been downloaded by over 5 million users in 226 countries, some 600,000 of whom still remain active. Together, they've contributed over 2 million years of computing time. Its message boards form an online community where people can socialize (several couples have met through SETI@home and married) and keep track of how much work their computer accounts have completed."

8. US House of Representatives Subcommittee on US Competitiveness, "Focus: R & D—Innovation, Technology, Process, and Advancement of Knowledge," *Subcommittee Report 2004*, http://www.manufacturing.gov/pdf/competitiveness_rd_051105.pdf (accessed December 4, 2009).

9. National Science Board (National Science Foundation, Division of Science Resources Statistics), *Science and Engineering Indicators—2002*, April 2002, http://www.nsf.gov/statistics/seind02/ (accessed December 4, 2009). See especially chap. 2, p. 5.

10. For evidence of this elegant integration, see the finely written paean to today's knowledge platform by biologist Edward O. Wilson, *Consilience: The Unity of Knowledge* (New York: Alfred A. Knopf, 1998). Unfortunately, Wilson couples his insights with an illogically derived dark view of the future, a view widely held in academic circles but inconsistent with the forward function.

11. Thomas S. Kuhn, *The Structure of Scientific Revolutions*, 2nd ed. (Chicago: University of Chicago Press, 1970) suggests that fields of science tend to be dominated by a particular paradigm that is accepted as the basic structure for understanding observed phenomena until displaced by some new paradigm that better explains the same phenomena. There would be a struggle of the minds between the two paradigms for some years until the new one becomes dominant, somewhat on the lines of Hegel's dialectic theory of history. Kuhn's hypothesis has been used and misused especially in the social sciences as theorists battle for dominance. Such a pattern may be descriptive of the rise and fall of Marxism, from 1848 to about 1988.

12. The origin of the Internet as a mechanism for US national defense in the Cold War context is a fascinating story, well told by Janet Abbate, *Inventing the Internet* (Cambridge, MA: MIT Press, 1999).

13. Ibid., p. 182.

14. See, for example, Robert W. Fogel, *The Escape from Hunger and Premature Death, 1700–2100* (Cambridge, UK: Cambridge University Press, 2004).

15. Ibid., p. 40: "Indeed, there was more than twice as much increase in life expectancies during the past century as there was during the previous 200,000 years." Clearly there is an accelerating trend here, but how far it will go and whether it will eventually level off remain insoluble uncertainties.

16. This is an idea that is still discussed primarily among intellectual elites in advanced countries and is generally feared by the nationally and tribally oriented majority, so it may be a long time in coming. Nevertheless, the idea is compelling and the number of internationalized sectors of human activity continues to grow (e.g., banking, Internet, trade, science, medicine, and most areas of technology). See John Keane, *Global Civil Society?* (Cambridge, UK: Cambridge University Press, 2003), for an interesting speculative take on this idea.

17. Nicholas Wade, *Life Script: How the Human Genome Discoveries Will Transform Medicine and Enhance Your Health* (New York: Simon and Schuster, 2001), p. 40. Quantitative details in this section are drawn mostly from Wade.

18. Nucleotides are also known as "base pairs," strings of amino acids linked by sugar molecules. Protein molecules are composed of long chains of nucleotides, also a Sanger discovery. His work garnered him two well-deserved Nobel Prizes.

19. For a good summary of the remarkable progress in transplant medical technology from 1954 to the present, see Lawrence K. Altman's story in the *New York Times*, December 21, 2004. He quotes Dr. Thomas E. Starzl, who led the team that

performed the first successful kidney transplant in 1954, as follows: "The truth is that none of us in the 1950s remotely envisioned the height to which transplantation would rise and the way it has changed the face of medicine. Transplants have had trickle-down effects on all aspects of society, like acceptance of criteria for brain death, passage of anatomical gift acts, and the growth of biomedical ethics."

20. See, for example, Mark Cichocki, "The History of HIV/AIDS: The Birth of the Protease Inhibitor," About.com, August 23, 2009, http://www.aids.about.com/od/newlydiagnosed/a/hivtimeline_2.htm (accessed December 4, 2009).

21. Wade, *Life Script*, pp. 174–75.

22. Centers for Disease Control and Prevention and the National Center for Health Statistics, "Life Expectancy," FastStats, June 28, 2010, http://www.cdc.gov/nchs/fastats/lifexpec.htm (accessed November 11, 2010).

23. There are a few scientists with good credentials who believe that serious life extension is fairly close at hand. They are led by Cambridge University biomedical gerontologist Aubrey de Grey. His book with Michael Rae, *Ending Aging: The Rejuvenation Breakthroughs that Could Reverse Human Aging in Our Lifetime* (London: St. Martin's, 2007), states the case. De Grey leads a group called SENS for "Strategies for Engineered Negligible Senescence," which holds periodic meetings and has attracted the attention of many optimistic futurists.

24. See, for example, Dina Prialnik, *An Introduction to the Theory of Stellar Structure and Evolution* (Cambridge, UK: Cambridge University Press, 2000).

25. See Amir Alexander, "The Search for Extraterrestrial Intelligence: A Short History," Planetary Society Online Series, 2004, http://www.planetary.org/explore/topics/seti/seti_history_00.html (accessed November 11, 2010).

26. Wilson, *Consilience*, p. 182.

27. See Gregg Easterbrook, *The Progress Paradox* (New York: Random House, 2003), especially his discussion of current "happiness" research by Kahneman and others.

28. J. D. Bernal, *Science in History*, vol. 3, *The Natural Sciences in Our Time* (Cambridge, MA: MIT Press, 1971), p. 787.

29. John Gribben, *The Scientists: A History of Science Told through the Lives of Its Greatest Inventors* (New York: Random House, 2002), p. 563.

30. The American Association for the Advancement of Science, through its Project 2061, has been developing such an integrated curriculum for some years. In 1990, an outline of the content was first published as *Science for All Americans*.

31. Detailed in Robert Buderi, *The Invention That Changed the World* (New York: Simon and Schuster, 1996).

32. R. G. Havelock and David S. Bushnell, *Technology Transfer at the Defense Advanced Research Projects Agency* (Arlington, VA: George Mason University Technology Transfer Study Center, 1985).

33. Estimates derived from the National Institutes of Health's website, "NIH Almanac: *Appropriations*," http://www.nih.gov/about/index.html (accessed November 11, 2010).

34. Richard R. Nelson, ed., *Government and Technical Progress: A Cross-industry Analysis* (New York: Pergamon, 1982) shows how government and the private sector interact to promote progress in various fields (e.g., semiconductors, aircraft production, computers, agriculture, pharmaceuticals, motor vehicles, and residential construction).

35. For example, see K. Eric Drexler, *Engines of Creation: The Coming Era of Nanotechnology* (New York: Anchor, 1986); or Ed Regis, *Nano: The Emerging Science of Nanotechnology* (Boston: Little, Brown, 1993).

36. Typified by Francis Fukuyama in *Our Posthuman Future: Consequences of the Biotechnology Revolution* (New York: Farrar, Strauss, and Giroux, 2002). Again, see also Easterbrook, *Progress Paradox*, regarding "happiness" research.

37. It should be noted that there are already databases, journals, and institutes around the world that are dedicated to such tasks. A few among the latter deserve special mention: the International Peace Research Institute, Oslo (PRIO); the Stockholm International Peace Research Institute (SIPRI); the Peace Research Foundation; the Copenhagen Peace Research Institute (COPRI); the International Peace Institute, adjacent to the United Nations building in New York, formerly called the International Peace Academy; and the recently created and congressionally funded United States Institute of Peace (USIP). All these organizations generate databases of regional conflicts, defensive and offensive strategies, peace negotiations, consequences of conflict, settlements, and so on. They also generate a number of journals and other publications based on empirical analysis of such databases.

ANNOTATED
BIBLIOGRAPHY

E ach of the following books informed the writing of *Acceleration: The Forces Driving Human Progress* in one way or another. Each source is marked with a code indicating how it was used or why it has special relevance. For example, several were synthesis books (Syn), useful in getting the facts straight about history and science, past, present, and future. Then there are the argument books, some advancing the idea that progress is happening and that it is altogether a good thing (Pro), and several others that were cautionary or alarmist about what humans have been doing or will be doing in the name of progress (Con). Still others are ambivalent (Amb), seeing the potential for good and the potential for bad in the evolution of modern science and its technological offspring. A few are about the phenomenon of acceleration itself, instances or recorded moments in time when humanity made a great leap forward (Acc). A few explain what science is all about (Sci). Of these forty-eight sources, fifteen provide a grand synthesis (Syn), seventeen take a strongly positive view of the future with or without a synthesis (Pro), seven take a negative or alarmist view of the future (Con), six are ambivalent or mixed in their view of the future (Amb), six highlight specific achievements or turning points on the way to progress (Acc), and four are concerned with what science is and what it does (Sci).

Abbate, Janet. *Inventing the Internet.* Cambridge, MA: MIT Press, 1999. Perhaps the most profound and life-changing invention of our time is the Internet. Many people in the general public who now use this information superhighway in all manner of ways as a big part of their daily lives have no idea about where it came from and how it emerged. They should be told. In fact, it was a child of the Cold War, fully conceived and developed by officials of the US federal government (Advanced Research Projects Agency of the Department of Defense) working with professors at a handful of prestigious universities. (Acc)

American Association for the Advancement of Science. *Science for All Americans.* Edited by F. James Rutherford. New York: Oxford University Press, 1989, 1990, rev. 1994.

This volume was issued as the centerpiece of Project 2061, "a long-term initiative of the AAAS to reform K–12 education in natural and social science, mathematics, and technology." It outlines a very broad range of subject matter that should go into the modern science curriculum, including many of the topics of social science that have traditionally been ignored at the high school level. The author was a consultant to the project for several years. (Syn, Sci)

Bernal, John Desmond. *Science in History.* 4 Vols. Cambridge, MA: MIT Press, 1971. Publisher's summary: "The first full-scale attempt to analyze the relationship between science and society throughout history, from the perfection of the first flint hand ax to the construction of the hydrogen bomb" (p. 787). This monumental four-volume work was a useful, if somewhat dated, reference source for the present work. (Syn)

Bloom, Allan. *The Closing of the American Mind: How Higher Education Has Failed Democracy and Impoverished the Souls of Today's Students.* New York: Simon and Schuster, 1987. This popular conservative polemic attacked liberal thought and the kind of science-based progressivism advocated here as relativist, deviating from what he argued was the canon of the great books and wise men of our historic past, particularly Plato and Aristotle. Leo Strauss was an ardent Platonist at the University of Chicago. His student, Bloom, and others of the Strauss school gave an intellectual cast to contemporary conservative thought that had been lacking in previous years or at least since the earlier writings of William F. Buckley Jr. (e.g., *God and Man at Yale: The Superstitions of "Academic Freedom."* Chicago: Regnery, 1951). (Con)

Bronowski, Jacob. *The Ascent of Man.* Boston: Little, Brown, 1973. This was originally a BBC television series commissioned by David Attenborough. Bronowski was a mathematician and physicist with a very broad range and an optimistic view of human destiny. His title is derived from Darwin's *The Descent of Man and Selection in Relation to Sex,* and he covers the full scope of human development from the Stone Age to modern times in an engaging style. Bronowski was a great synthesizer and teacher, one of the giants on whose shoulders I stand. In his own words, "We are all afraid—for our confidence, for the future, for the world. That is the nature of the human imagination. Yet every man, every civilization has gone forward because of its engagement with what it has set itself to do. The personal commitment of man to his skill, the intellectual commitment and the emotional commitment working together as one, has made the Ascent of Man." (Syn, Pro)

Buderi, Robert. *The Invention That Changed the World.* New York: Simon and Schuster, 1996. This interesting book details evolution of antisubmarine microwave radar within the bigger story of how the R & D process emerged as a distinct set of coordinated actions. One of Franklin D. Roosevelt's principal science advisors, Vannevar Bush, is sometimes credited with inventing the term *R & D* to describe all the different activities that went into the creation of new weaponry and other devices during World War II. At the suggestion of Bush, FDR created a new federal agency, the Office of Scientific Research and Development, in June 1941 (p. 115). There followed an explosion of such activity, all of it conducted at government expense and usually under the auspices of major universities. Harvard, MIT, Princeton, the University of Michigan, the University of California, and California Technical Institute were among the many distinguished institutions that participated extensively. Many private firms were also involved, notably Bell Telephone Laboratories, and many new upstart companies. RAND Corporation, founded as a defense contracting research and development firm, took its name directly from the phrase *R & D*. (Acc)

Burke, James. *Connections*. New York: Little, Brown, 1995. Burke's view, that the development of civilization depended in large part on the sometimes chance circumstances and connections from one human to the next and one event to the next, is generally in line with the analysis of how knowledge platforms are built, proposed in the chapters 4 through 6 of *Acceleration*. His presentation, based on his arresting and continuously fascinating television series, plays down the role of individual genius and creativity that dominates too much of history in general and the history of science in particular. What Burke lacks is a comprehensive theory of why we have turned out the way we have, and he slights the importance of the scientific revolution and the evolution of the R & D process in the mid-twentieth century, when deliberate planned effort on both small-scale and large-scale work began to produce a cornucopia of useful inventions at a rate with no historical parallel. However, Burke's piecing together of the evolution of knowledge as a series of interrelated cause-and-effect relationships is brilliant. In his own words: "My purpose is to acquaint the reader with some of the forces that have caused change in the past, looking in particular at eight innovations—the computer, the production line, telecommunications, the airplane, the atomic bomb, plastics, the guided rocket, and television—which may be most influential in structuring our own futures. Each one of these is part of a family of similar devices, and is the result of a sequence of closely connected events extending from the ancient world until the present day. Each has enormous potential for humankind's benefit—or destruction." (Syn, Pro)

Cohen, Morris R., and Ernest Nagel. *An Introduction to Logic and Scientific Method*. New York: Harcourt, Brace, 1936. Cohen and Nagel conclusively demonstrate that *logical* and *mathematical* are essentially the same thing and are at the core of what we now call *science*. It is unfortunate that most scientists have little education in and perhaps little concern for the philosophical foundations of science. Such courses are thus relegated to the history of science or the field of psychology, which has the most concern of all the disciplines about proving itself to be a true science.

Cohen and Nagel remains a definitive source to explain what science really is. (Sci)

Cook, Michael. *A Brief History of the Human Race.* New York: W. W. Norton, 2003. Cook, Princeton University professor of Middle Eastern studies, displays wide knowledge of different cultures in this book. He looks for telling anecdotes or curious features to explain key differences among cultures, ancient and modern. He tries to figure out if we are all the same and whether civilization as we know it would have evolved, for example, in China or pre-Columbian America without the evolution of thought and invention in medieval and modern Europe. He argues that most of the features and progressive steps that we attribute to the uniqueness of particular cultures or personalities would probably have happened sooner or later in other places and other times. The relatively warm and stable climate of the most recent ten thousand years may have also played an important role in the emergence of our present civilization. (Syn)

Diamond, Jared. *Guns, Germs, and Steel: The Fates of Human Societies.* New York: W. W. Norton, 1997. In his own words, the author's main thesis is as follows: "History followed different courses for different peoples because of differences among peoples' environments, not because of biological differences among peoples themselves." Told through interesting historical notes, *Guns, Germs, and Steel* reveals a broad understanding of all the elements that conspire to make a culture, including its technology, geography, climate, and resources. Diamond is one of the great synthesizers of our day. (Syn)

———. *Collapse: How Societies Choose to Fail or Succeed.* Viking Books, 2005. Diamond, a geographer with an enormous range of scholarship tied to great writing skills, has a complex five-factor theory of what makes societies succeed or fail. These include climate change, hostile neighbors, trading partnerships, geographical challenges (like being an island), and the choices made in response to these problems (i.e., the adequacy of the problem solving within each culture). His case studies, which take up the bulk of the book, are intrinsically interesting and well-written, even when they don't quite fit his complex theoretical model. They each trace the rise and often the fall of disparate cultures, Greenland Vikings, Hispaniolans, Easter Islanders, Pitcairn Islanders, Montanans, and many others. The book has huge scope. The tone is reasoned and nonapocalyptic despite the promise of the title. Diamond wants us all to act reasonably in a measured way, bringing together people with differing politics and economic concerns to serve their common interests in maintaining their environment and culture. (Amb)

Easterbrook, Gregg. *The Progress Paradox: How Life Gets Better while People Feel Worse.* New York: Random House, 2003. Easterbrook summons a lot of statistics to prove the point, also argued and presented in *Acceleration*, that the worldwide quality of life has been steadily improving, particularly in the recent half century. These advances include improved nutrition, declining crime, increasing longevity, and reduced environmental pollution. His "paradox" is that majorities of the people in the modern Western world do not report subjectively that they are "happier," and many say they think things are getting worse all the time. He then tries to parcel out the reasons for this, citing in particular the way mass media cover events. However, some of the "paradox" might be explained by the ways in which "happiness" is measured. See, for example, Gilbert's *Stumbling on Happiness*, cited below. Easterbrook is a prolific writer and editor as well as a policy analyst. Thus, he spends a good deal of time noting all the world conditions that are NOT what they should be and exhorting his fellow humans to do something about them (hunger, AIDS, etc.). He does not provide a comprehensive theory to explain either why things are getting better or why there should be so much resistance to the idea that things are better. (Amb)

Ehrlich, Paul R. *The Population Bomb.* New York: Ballantine, 1968. Ehrlich took Malthus as gospel and turned up the rhetoric several decibels to make a bestselling horror book, but his predictions of doom have been laughably off the mark. Despite this, he remains popular in many quarters and is viewed as one of the great prophets of the environmental movement. The basic problem with his theorizing and his supposedly scientific formulas, as noted by Julian Simon, among others, is his notion that resources are fixed, not amenable to either expansion or substitution as human needs increase. It can be argued in his favor that his polemical writing influenced many millions of people to think more seriously about their human and physical environment and to engage in activity to deal constructively with some of the problems Ehrlich got us to worry about. Thus, despite the falsity of his own doomsday predictions, he may have helped push human problem solving forward in some critical areas. (Con)

Ehrlich, Paul R., and Anne H. Ehrlich. *Betrayal of Science and Reason: How Anti-environmental Rhetoric Threatens Our Future.* Washington, DC: Island Press, 1996. Ehrlich is nothing if not a combat soldier in the environmental wars. The "betrayal" he speaks of could be equally applied to his own approach to intellectual discourse. This is a war. They, people who argue with or without scientific evidence against our position, are the enemy. Attack! (Con)

Fogel, Robert W. *The Escape from Hunger and Premature Death, 1700–2100.* Cambridge, UK: Cambridge University Press, 2004. Chicago economics professor and Nobelist Fogel cites improvements in the technology of food production as a prime cause of increased longevity, larger body size, fewer hours of work, and more leisure. He points to many of the same variables cited by Julian Simon to demonstrate that the lot of humanity has been improving consistently for at least the last three hundred years, roughly the time since science was born and the Industrial Revolution began. On page 40 he notes: "*Indeed, there was more than twice as much increase in life expectancies during the past century as there was during the previous 200,000 years.*" Clearly there is an accelerating trend here, but how far it will go and whether it will eventually level off remain insoluble uncertainties. (Pro)

Freud, Sigmund. *Civilization and Its Discontents*. Original publishers, London: Hogarth Press, 1930; printed as vol. 54 in Robert M. Hutchins, ed., *The Great Books of the Western World*. Chicago: Encyclopædia Britannica, 1952. This is one of several books in which Freud argued that civilized life depended heavily on the suppression and redirection of basic human instincts, particularly sex and aggression. Although his writings have been out of fashion for many years, he is an excellent writer and an extremely cogent thinker who still deserves our full attention. Contrary to popular belief, most of his theories about basic drives and their relation to manifest behavior still stand up to scrutiny, even though his psychiatric therapies proved to be impractical or ineffective as solutions to mental health problems. Chapter 2 of *Acceleration* was significantly influenced by my longtime respect for his work. (Amb)

Fukuyama, Francis. *The End of History and the Last Man*. New York: Free Press, 1992. In his own words, "What we may be witnessing is not just the end of the Cold War, or the passing of a particular period of postwar history, but the end of history as such. . . . That is, the end point of humankind's ideological evolution and the universalization of Western liberal democracy as the final form of human government." The end of the Cold War was indeed a great achievement for the people of Earth, no matter how it came about. However, the simplistic Hegelian-Marxian theory on which Fukuyama riffs never was anything like true science, and the idea that liberal democracy is the end point of human destiny is not a very progressive idea. (Amb)

———. *Our Posthuman Future: Consequences of the Biotechnology Revolution*. New York: Farrar, Straus and Giroux, 2002. In this work, Fukuyama expresses his profound ambivalence about recent progress in biotechnology, fearing that the drive toward applications in life extension and human transformation will undermine the liberal democratic polity which he, like other neo-Platonists, views as the human ideal. (Con)

Gilbert, Daniel. *Stumbling on Happiness*. New York: Alfred A. Knopf, 2006. A professor of psychology at Harvard, Gilbert goes all over the word *happiness* and the various subjective meanings of *happiness*, happiness seeking, and its psychological consequences. If you are looking for happiness, this is probably not the place to find it. Chapter 2 of *Acceleration* tries to come to terms with happiness as a necessary concomitant of progress. If there is no net happiness in what humans strive for and achieve, then, almost by definition, there is no progress. This is not the way Gilbert deals with the topic. He does not tell us what happiness really is, but he stumbles around the topic, citing numerous studies, noting all the contradictions and vagaries with which humans surround this idea. Nevertheless, the book has been hugely popular. (Pro)

Gribben, John. *The Scientists: A History of Science Told through the Lives of Its Greatest Inventors.* New York: Random House, 2002. This is the way we like to read history, through the lives of individual people. These stories are enlightening and fascinating, but they tend to miss the main point of this book, which is that the advance of progress depends on the problem-solving ability of the human race as a whole, building on all our past achievements. (Syn, Sci)

Havelock, Eric A. *The Crucifixion of Intellectual Man.* Boston: Beacon, 1951. This is an English translation of the Aeschylus play *Prometheus Bound*, with extensive commentary regarding its relevance to our times. It was the first of a series of books by E. A. Havelock, which argued for a renewed consideration of the pre-Platonic Greek thinkers, of whom Aeschylus was representative. The Prometheus myth as presented by the poet describes the ongoing struggle between tradition, which calls us back, and human invention, which propels us forward. (Pro)

————. *The Liberal Temper in Greek Politics.* New Haven, CT: Yale University Press, 1964. First printed in 1957. Havelock continues and expands on the theme of progress versus regress as it plays out in Periclean Athens. Democritus in particular argued for an open-ended, broadly democratic, and hopeful view of human nature and what humans can do by their own creativity to improve their condition. Havelock believed that Plato and his followers, when they established their school, sought to suppress the views of previous philosophers that contradicted their teachings regarding authority and the fixed nature of truth. Havelock also believed that the transition from orality to writing represented a profound shift in both patterns of thought and education, with consequences that were progressive in many ways as argued here but also potentially stultifying, as the written word became sacred, and deviation from the written word of the ancient wise men came to be considered apostasy. See also, Havelock's *A History of the Greek Mind*, vol. 1, *Preface to Plato.* Cambridge, MA: Belknap, 1963. Eric A. Havelock, 1903–1988, was my father. (Pro)

Havelock, Ronald G., in collaboration with Alan Guskin et al. *Planning for Innovation through the Dissemination and Utilization of Scientific Knowledge.* Ann Arbor, MI: University of Michigan, Institute for Social Research Publications, 1969. This was the first major monograph to review the literature pertaining to the creation and diffusion of scientific knowledge, illustrating the patterns by which information flows through social systems and how it gets transferred and translated into useful applications in all fields. This publication was the foundation for a series of projects by the author and others at the University of Michigan's Institute for Social Research and later at the Knowledge Transfer Institute of the American University in Washington, DC. It went through seven reprints as an ISR bestseller and was widely cited. In many ways it was the foundation and inspiration for *Acceleration*. (Syn)

Havelock, Ronald G., and David S. Bushnell. *Technology Transfer at the Defense Advanced Research Projects Agency*. Arlington, VA: George Mason University Technology Transfer Study Center, November 1985. This was one of the many projects inspired by *Planning for Innovation*. The unpublished monograph provides an account of the central role of DARPA in the creation of the Internet (originally called *ARPA-NET*), as well as the rapid development of microprocessor technology and the modern computer-user interface. In these and many other ways, the Cold War gave a tremendous impetus to technological advancement, accelerating the application of the forward function in every sector. Further documentation on DARPA's central role in the creation of the Internet and the democratization of computer technology can be found in Janet Abbate, *Inventing the Internet*, cited above. (Acc)

Keane, John. *Global Civil Society?* Cambridge, UK: Cambridge University Press, 2003. This is a speculation on this idea, which is still just an evolving concept (note the question mark in title) discussed primarily among intellectual elites in advanced countries and generally feared by the nationally and tribally oriented majority, so it may be a long time in coming. Nevertheless, the idea is compelling and the number of internationalized sectors of human activity continues to grow (e.g., banking, telecommunications, Internet, trade, science, medicine, and most areas of technology). A global civil society would surely adopt the United Nations' Universal Declaration of Human Rights as a guiding document; see discussion in *Acceleration*, chapter 10, "The Emergence of Ethical Humanity." (Pro)

Kuhn, Thomas S. *The Structure of Scientific Revolutions*, 2nd ed. Chicago: University of Chicago Press, 1970. Kuhn suggested that fields of science tend to be dominated by a particular paradigm that is accepted as the basic structure for understanding observed phenomena until displaced by some new paradigm that better explains the same phenomena. There would be a struggle of the minds between the two paradigms for some years until the new one becomes dominant, somewhat on the lines of Hegel's dialectic theory of history. Kuhn's hypothesis has been used and misused especially in the social sciences, as competing theories battle for dominance. Such a pattern may be descriptive of the rise and fall of Marxism, from 1848 to about 1988. It is somewhat at odds with *Acceleration*'s emphasis on civilization as a cumulative process. (Sci, Amb)

Lovelock, James E. *The Revenge of Gaia: Earth's Climate Crisis & the Fate of Humanity*. New York: Basic Books, 2007. There is a branch of environmentalism that imagines Earth as a whole with all its life as one system. This system is seen to have a natural balance or homeostasis that is threatened by humans, especially the civilized and civilizing humans who cut down the forests, fish out the waters, dig and drill the landscape, and otherwise despoil Earth and the habitat for all the other creatures. Lovelock, an Oxford professor, is one of the leading advocates of this view. Gaia was the mythical Greek goddess of the earth. "Gaiaism" is so fervently followed by Lovelock and his followers that it takes on aspects of religious belief. Like Ehrlich, Lovelock uses apocalyptic rhetoric to drive home his ideas, which are similar. (Con)

Maddison, Angus. *The World Economy: A Millennial Perspective.* Paris: OECD, 2001. Maddison has been one of the great quantitative macroeconomists of our time, and his data, collected over a period of fifty years, largely confirms the claims made throughout *Acceleration* that the circumstances of humanity have been improving steadily over time and at an accelerating rate during the past half century. The following is a quote from his OECD report: "Over the past millennium, world population rose 22-fold. Per capita income increased 13-fold, world GDP nearly 300-fold. ... From the year 1000 to 1820 the advance in per capita income was a slow crawl—the world average rose about 50 percent. Most of the growth went to accommodate a 4-fold increase in population. Since 1820, world development has been much more dynamic. Per capita income rose more than 8-fold, population more than 5-fold." He goes on to identify other indicators of advance in human welfare that accompanied GDP, such as life expectancy and relief from hunger and disease. (Pro)

Meadows, Donella H., Dennis L. Meadows, Jørgen Randers, and William W. Behrens. *Limits of Growth.* London: Potomac Associates, 1972. This is the famous "Club of Rome" report, which reportedly sold 9 million copies worldwide and was translated into twenty-nine different languages. Among the many howlers in this book, based on presumably scientific projections, gold was supposed to be exhausted by 1981, silver and mercury by 1985, and zinc by 1990. Needless to say, none of this happened nor are there any empirically based trend lines heading in such a direction. Nevertheless, the Malthusian notion that growth of everything but human population has hard-edged limits persists and is generally perceived as common sense despite all quantitative indicators to the contrary. The Club of Rome group used predictive models but made no effort to track the historical and economic record to see if their models were a good fit with the past. This is what Maddison, Simon, and other quantitative economists tried to do, and their results sharply contradict the alarmist prophesies of Meadows, et al., the Ehrlichs, Lovelock, and their followers. (Con)

Naisbitt, John. *Megatrends: Ten New Directions Transforming Our Lives.* New York: Warner Books, 1982. Naisbitt's ten trends of 1982 are on the money in 2010, mostly in line with what is said here. He foresees the industrial economy being overtaken and subsumed by the information economy, and national economies increasingly merged in a globalization process. He also correctly forecasts the increasing linkage of high tech to the human interface, a trend most obvious in what has been done by Apple, Inc. and the telecom industry, bringing people closer together and facilitating all types of interpersonal connection, from business to entertainment. He adds that the future belongs to those who can handle ambiguity. Of the vast majority he says: "We have done the human thing: We are clinging to the known past in fear of the unknown future." (Pro)

Nelson, Richard R., ed. *Government and Technical Progress: A Cross-industry Analysis.* New York: Pergamon, 1982. Free-market enthusiasts tend to ignore the vital role of governments in inspiring, initiating, and subsidizing almost all the great innovations that drive modern economies. This book goes a long way to clear up this misapprehension. Ten economists took on seven different areas, including semiconductors, computers, commercial aircraft, automobiles, agriculture, pharmaceuticals, and construction. Their careful analysis documented the strong government influence in all sectors over the roughly one hundred years previous, either through support of basic and applied research in universities and elsewhere, military procurement, direct subsidy of private R & D, standard setting, or regulation. In all but a few cases, the government role pushed the technology forward rather than holding it back. This important monograph clearly documents how government and the private sector interact to promote progress. (Acc)

Paepke, C. Owen. *The Evolution of Progress: The End of Economic Growth and the Beginning of Human Transformation.* New York: Random House, 1983. This impressive work of scholarship is a rumination on progress by a polymath attorney. He first documents the case for progress in material terms, which can also be found in Simon, Maddison, and other works, as well as *Acceleration.* Yet he argues that material progress is reaching a level of saturation from which it can proceed no farther. This does not mean that it will stop, nor does it mean that we are about to go into the tailspin predicted by Ehrlich and the Club of Rome. He explicitly rejects the "limits of growth" thesis. Rather, it means that progress will assume new, less materialist forms, what I would prefer to characterize as quality-of-life improvements. The second part of his book delineates his ideas of what these advances might look like, including artificial intelligence, life extension, genetic engineering, and so forth. While not recommending the book, economist and columnist Paul Krugman made the following cogent comment: ". . . after another thirty years or so progress will start to mean something very different from what it has meant in the past—if only because everything will start to become strange. We are on the edge of technologies that will change the human condition as never before, that will change even our definition of what it means to be human." (Syn, Amb)

Piel, Gerard. *The Age of Science: What Scientists Learned in the Twentieth Century.* New York: Basic Books, 2001. Piel notes that a man-year, meaning the net output of mechanical energy from a typical manual laborer in a year has been calculated to be the equivalent of one hundred fifty kilowatt hours. The gross power output of central electrical generating stations in the United States comes to about thirty thousand kilowatt hours per capita. By division, this comes out to two hundred person hours. It should be conceded, of course, that "per capita" does not mean it is equally distributed. Even so, the average worker even at the low end of the scale is likely to get some multiple of what the common laborer once earned in a year. Piel also notes that near-zero population growth has now been achieved in all industrialized countries, combining low death rates and low birth rates, very low infant mortality, and life expectancy exceeding seventy years. In contrast, life expectancy in the least developed countries, almost all in sub-Saharan Africa, is less than thirty years, with very high infant and child mortality, a condition that characterized most of humanity until the industrial era. (Pro)

Popper, Karl. *All Life Is Problem Solving* (Alles Leben ist Problemlosen). English translation by Patrick Camiller. London: Routledge, 1999. This collection of papers serves to summarize the work of the great German philosopher and refugee from Nazi Germany, Sir Karl Popper (1902–1994). Popper's work informs *Acceleration* in a number of ways. He was a prominent philosopher of science and an advocate for an open-ended and expansive view of "truth" and how it is to be determined. He was also a strong advocate for the open society and a critic, along with Eric A. Havelock, of the authoritarian concept of knowledge as the "canon" passed down through the ages from Plato and Aristotle. The title of this collection could have stood as an alternative title for this book, as it expresses one of the major themes of *Acceleration*. (Pro)

Rogers, Everett M. *Diffusion of Innovations*, 4th ed. New York: Free Press, 1995. Rogers (1931–2004), the son of an Iowa farmer, began studying innovation diffusion among farmers and later branched out into similar studies in many other fields, becoming the chief synthesizer of empirical diffusion research. His book is a landmark of empirical quantitative sociology and a major contribution to science generally. Starting with the first edition, published in 1962, he was able to incorporate thousands of studies in a coherent framework, covering such widely dispersed fields as medicine, education, business, legislative actions, community development, social programs, and the marketing of commercial products. Rogers pointed out consistent common patterns among findings from all these studies, one of the very few areas in which social science has been able to establish a secure knowledge platform. Rogers was one of the giants on whose shoulders I stood in all my past research and in the writing of *Acceleration*. Chapter 9, "Modern Global Diffusion," owes a lot to Rogers. (Syn, Acc)

Sachs, Jeffrey D. *The End of Poverty*. New York: Penguin, 2005. The *New York Times* has called him "the most important economist in the world." Sachs has long realized that advancing technology in agriculture as well as other areas is now making it possible to raise the living standards of all the peoples of the world, and he puts forward the practical steps that will allow this to happen on a vastly accelerated basis. He has turned the heads of many of the world's movers and shakers, including billionaire philanthropist George Soros and entertainment media star Bono. Little has been made of the contradiction between the practical and proven progressive steps advocated by Sachs and the popular neo-Malthusian rhetoric of the leading environmentalists. Sachs exemplifies the forward function in action in our own time. (Pro)

Seligman, Martin. *Authentic Happiness.* New York: Free Press, 2002. Professor Seligman directs the Positive Psychology Center at the University of Pennsylvania, and is one of a relatively new group of "happiness" researchers, along with Gilbert. This book provides a fairly exhaustive taxonomy and reviews a number of studies that suggest the same paradox discussed by Easterbrook: that reported "happiness" does not correlate well with objective measures of well-being and life quality. Not satisfied with leaving the matter here, Seligman goes on to formulate what he thinks real happiness consists of, as distinct from what the word *happiness* conveys to an unreflective questionnaire respondent. This is a useful source for expanding on the analysis of what makes for a good life and life quality, as presented in chapter 2 of *Acceleration.* Another important source on this general subject is Ed Diener, who studies "subjective well-being" at the University of Illinois. See, for example, Diener et al., "Subjective Well-Being: Three Decades of Progress," *Psychological Bulletin* 125, no. 2 (1999): 276–302. (Syn, Pro)

Silver, Lee M. *Remaking Eden: How Genetic Engineering and Cloning Will Transform the American Family.* New York: Avon Books, 1997; and Silver, Lee M. *Challenging Nature: The Clash of Science and Spirituality at the New Frontiers of Life.* New York: Ecco, 2006. Silver welcomes a future of genetic manipulation, in contrast to Fukuyama's *Post Human Future* (see above). Genetically modified foods (GMs), widely feared in many parts of the world including modern Europe, are celebrated by Silver, as are genetically modified animals and humans, present and future. Silver fearlessly takes on the religious and the spiritual, the fearmongers as well as the merely hesitant and worried, like Fukuyama. Silver's writings influenced both the discussion of fears in chapter 11 and future trends in chapter 12 of *Acceleration.* (Pro)

Simon, Julian. *The Ultimate Resource 2.* Princeton, NJ: Princeton University Press, 1996. Julian Simon argues in his two major works that progress actually depends on an ever-increasing population. The larger population not only generates a vastly greater stockpile of wealth, expanded markets for goods, and so on, but also adds to the collective knowledge base from which prosperity for everybody ultimately flows. Such views are anathema to those who view population control as a major issue facing humanity (e.g., Paul Ehrlich, cited above). Yet no other academic has ever gone to such great lengths to document a thesis with hard data drawn from diverse sources. The book is also a convincing refutation of the "limits of growth" thesis of the Club of Rome and other doomsayers who deplore the changes that have been wrought in the world by the spread of industrialization and science-based technology. If you doubt the picture of the human progress painted in *Acceleration*, read Simon! (Syn, Pro)

Sklair, Leslie. *The Sociology of Progress.* London: Routledge, 1970. Professor emeritus at the London School of Economics, Sklair prepared this thorough analysis of the concept of progress as his doctoral thesis. He argues that progress and sociology grew up together and are intertwined historically and conceptually, being "mutually reinforcing aspects of the movement in thought." The treatment of morality as a critical dimension of progress in chapter 10 of *Acceleration* is very much in line with Sklair's views as presented in part 2 of his treatise: "Progress is nothing if it is not a moral concept, and to decide whether or not a particular social phenomenon represents progress is a moral decision." (Pro)

Stock, Gregory. *Redesigning Humans: Choosing Our Genes, Changing Our Future.* Boston: Houghton Mifflin, 2003. Stock agrees with Silver that genetic engineering of humans is on the way, and he welcomes it, marshaling arguments in favor and rebutting arguments against a forward push in this direction. He also poses the interesting idea that the bioengineers of the near future may find themselves in a kind of competition with the artificial-intelligence engineers of the silicon cyber world. Amazon.com reviewer Dr. Lee D. Carson summarizes Stock neatly: "Genetic engineering of humans: we can do it; we should do it; and we will do it." (Pro)

Trefil, James. *Human Nature: A Blueprint for Managing the Earth—By People, for People.* New York: Times Books, 2004. Trefil is a physicist with a broad conceptual reach. In this book he is not telling us about human nature as such but about how human concerns fit in the natural scheme of things. His views are broadly in accord with those offered in *Acceleration* regarding the extraordinary advancements made in the quality of human lives as a result of continuing advances in science and its applications. Where these advances come into seeming conflict with a habitable planet, we humans are fully capable of finding solutions through the very same science and technology. In a rather gentle way, he takes on environmental extremists regarding the issues of global warming and animal extinctions, noting that there are already at hand many solutions that belong in the "no regrets" category. In other words, even if the extremist projections are ultimately proven to be either wrong or grossly overstated (as he implies they are), these solutions will have positive benefits for our culture in any case. Most obvious in this category would be clean energy to rid us, once and for all, of stinky, gooey, dangerous petroleum. There is also long-term benefit for humans in creating forest and wilderness preserves that restrict various kinds of human activity. This book was an especially useful resource for chapter 11 of *Acceleration*, "Fears for the Future." Trefil is unafraid. (Syn, Pro)

Van Doren, Charles. *A History of Knowledge: Past, Present, and Future*. New York: Ballantine Books, 1991. Van Doren boldly goes where few scholars would even attempt to go, summarizing the major events in the evolution of the (mostly Western and Arab) knowledge platforms of the past, starting with the Greeks and the Romans. Medieval Christian and Islamic scholars are given their due, and the rise of science through key figures like Galileo and Newton are well presented. Van Doren also is aware of the drag on forward progress that can derive from a canonical view of the great classics, a topic covered also in *Acceleration*. The book, though an amazing tour de force, is marred by lack of footnotes and bibliography. (Syn)

Wade, Nicholas. *Life Script: How the Human Genome Discoveries Will Transform Medicine and Enhance Your Health*. New York: Simon and Schuster, 2001. Wade, a science writer for the *New York Times*, provides a good summary of the contemporary science emerging from DNA discoveries. It seems fairly clear that in future years the breaking of the genetic code will lead to a transformation of humanity, changing the way medicine is practiced and the way medical research is conducted, conquering diseases, and extending lives by who knows how many years. Some of the conclusions about our future course, laid out in *Acceleration*'s chapter 12, derive from Wade. (Acc)

Wilson, Edward O. *Consilience: The Unity of Knowledge*. New York: Knopf, 1998. This work is an excellent synthesis of modern science, with a discussion of how the social sciences could contribute to a larger view of humanity, if only they could find an empirical base to stand on. Wilson couples his insights with an inexplicably dark view of the future. His view, for example, that the small and troubled central African state of Rwanda is a harbinger of the human future is difficult to reason on any grounds, but his gloomy view is widely shared in academic circles. Needless to say, such a view is opposite that argued in *Acceleration*. Nevertheless, *Consilience* is a great book and is perhaps the best synthesis of all of modern science accessible to the general reader. It could be read as a companion to the AAAS curriculum outline, *Science for All Americans*, cited at the beginning of this bibliography. (Syn)

————. *The Future of Life*. New York: Vintage Books, 2003. This book starts out as a polemic in the Club of Rome tradition. Wilson flatly asserts, "The constraints of the biosphere are fixed" (p. 33). He seems to assume that this case is closed since he does not bother to provide specific footnotes to back up any of his apocalyptic assertions about the dreadful human footprint. Humanity has been driving unaccountable numbers of species to extinction and destroying natural habitats with unthinking abandon. Yet this is not an entirely pessimistic book. He notes the many cases where environmentalists and scientists have teamed together to preserve nature and protect endangered species. He also notes that population is leveling out in the developed world, and may do so eventually in poorer countries as they develop. Thus he sees us at what he calls a "bottleneck," a period when things will get worse before they get better. "Adequate resources exist," he says, to end worldwide poverty, perhaps contradicting his earlier bemoaning of resource "limits" (p. 189). After that, perhaps we will all come to our senses, harmonize our interests, and enjoy the natural balance that nature can supposedly provide. (Con)

Zey, Michael G. *The Future Factor: The Five Forces Transforming Our Lives and Shaping Human Destiny.* New York: McGraw-Hill, 2000. Dr. Zey has a strong, positive vision of the human future not too different from what is put forward in *Acceleration.* Dr. Zey is less interested in explaining how we got where we are today and more interested in telling us where we are going in the future, near and far. It is pretty exciting! He sees humanity as driven forward by what he calls *vitalization.* Within this overall concept he posits four forces: dominionization, species coalescence, biogenesis, and cybergenesis. *Dominionization,* the force that E. O. Wilson worries about the most, is the human mastery of the natural world and the transformation of the natural environment to suit human needs, a process that describes our ascent to where we are today. In *Acceleration,* this force is subsumed under chapters 5, 7, and 8. *Species coalescence* is the coming together of humanity into one cultural and functional whole, a process that started long ago but that has recently been accelerating, thanks to the invention and diffusion of new forms of communication, transportation, and world trade. In *Acceleration* this trend is described in chapters 6 and 9. *Biogenesis* and *cybergenesis,* the transformation of humanity by applying biological and computer science, are covered in the final chapter of *Acceleration* as two of the many promising trends that will probably lead to improved quality of life for all. (Pro)

INDEX

AAAS. *See* American Association for the Advancement of Science

Abbate, Janet, 266

acceleration, 256

accelerating change in the wrong direction, 29. *See also* backward function; regression

accelerator of progress, 8–9, 12, 89, 187, 188, 194, 218, 267–68, 286. *See also* forces that drive progress; forward function; progress

diffusion as an accelerator, 10, 265. *See also* diffusion

of knowledge growth, 75–76, 95, 188, 197

problem-solving accelerators, 179. *See also* problem solving

world population growth, 68–74

Acceleration: Book Two (Havelock), 269

"acquire" as an element in advanced problem solving, 167, 168, 169, 172, 173, 178

"act" as an element in advanced problem solving, 167, 168, 169, 172, 173, 178

acute learners, 111–12

advanced problem solving, 143, 144–45, 167, 168–70

See also problem solving

advancement of human affairs, 30–31, 65, 80, 105, 129, 179, 209

educational advancement, 58

examples of, 74–88, 269–84

forward function applied to, 285–90

moral and ethical advancement, 32, 200–203, 211, 221, 284–85

population growth as a factor, 70–71

Aeschylus, 15–16

aggression, civilization as a control of, 244

AIDS epidemic, 89, 251, 272, 291

air pollution, 79, 89

alarmists, population, 69–70

Alexander the Great, 127

Alexandria Library, burning of, 35, 127, 153, 185

Allen, Paul, 292

altruism

as a component of human morality, 32

and individualism, 201

American Association for Artificial Intelligence, 281–82

American Association for the Advancement of Science, 176, 178, 182

American "culture," 47

American Revolution, 87, 214, 215

Amnesty International, 220

"analyze" as an element in advanced problem solving, 167, 168, 169, 172, 173, 178

animal learning, 12, 97–113, 156

causal analysis, 161–62

future extension of, 260

stimulus-response in the animal learning process, 100

channel building and networking, 130

See also forces that drive progress; learn, capacity to

antigrowth worriers, 197

anti-Semitism, decline in, 211

Aristotle, 127, 129, 149, 150, 181

ARPANET. *See* Internet

use of in science, 152, 156, 173, 180,
   230, 231, 233, 247, 264
medicine, 42, 53, 126, 138, 152, 181
   advances in, 51, 62, 63, 235, 259, 269–
      72, 273
   and life extension, 269, 272–74
   medical research, 177, 290–91
   See also science
mediums for storage of external knowledge, 153
   ancient language, 121–22
   another human as an external
      resource, 131
   diffusion involving many types, 10, 13,
      190, 195–96
      explosion of media and messages,
         192–93
   electronic storage and transmission,
      13–14
   future extension of, 265–66
   and the learning process, 260
   new technologies for storing, 127
   pictures, 123–24
   poetry, 123
   science journalism countering misin-
      formation, 248
   written language as ultimate storage
      solution, 124–25, 255–56. *See also*
      writing, importance of for progress
   See also Internet; printing
megatrends, positive, 74–88
Mein Kampf (Hitler), 245
memories, 12
Mendel, Gregor, 248
mental attitude putting past before the
   present. *See* backward function
Messiah (Handel), 153
microbiology, 271–72
microprocessor, invention of. *See*
   computers

Microsoft Corporation, 292
Middle Ages, 138, 209, 1800
   craft guilds protecting their know-
      how platforms, 152
   moral progress after the fall of the
      Roman Empire, 208–209
   religion during, 28, 147, 148, 149, 150
   warm period during ninth century,
      230–34
mind-set, 243–53
   pessimistic mind-set, 29, 171, 226,
      249–51, 293–94
modernists vs. traditionalists, 243–45
Mohammed the Prophet, 28–29, 44
moon, first landing on, 32, 35, 251, 281, 290
moral progress, 13, 31–34
   based on value placed on life, 200–203
   calculating moral progress, diagram
      of, 202
   democracy and liberty as issues,
      214–16
   diffusion of knowledge and moral
      behavior, 214
   and an ethical humanity, 199–223,
      284–85
   evolution of moral concern, 203–207
   forward function moving toward,
      197–98
   human morality
      multiplicity of moral platforms,
         221–23
      questions framing concept of, 31–34
      relevance of applied social science
         to morality, 221–23
      roots of, 203–207
      warfare and rise of moral humanity,
         207–11
   measure of, 201
   proactive morality, 206–207
   See also ethics